THE
INTERACTIVE STRATEGY
WORKOUT

FT Prentice Hall
FINANCIAL TIMES

In an increasingly competitive world, we believe it's quality of
thinking that will give you the edge – an idea that opens new
doors, a technique that solves a problem, or an insight that
simply makes sense of it all. The more you know, the smarter
and faster you can go.

That's why we work with the best minds in business and finance
to bring cutting-edge thinking and best learning practice to a
global market.

Under a range of leading imprints, including Financial Times
Prentice Hall, we create world-class print publications and
electronic products bringing our readers knowledge, skills and
understanding which can be applied whether studying or
at work.

To find out more about our business publications, or tell us
about the books you'd like to find, you can visit us at
www.business-minds.com

For other Pearson Education publications, visit
www.pearsoned-ema.com

Pearson
Education

THE
INTERACTIVE STRATEGY WORKOUT

THIRD EDITION

**Analyze and develop
the fitness of your
business**
DR CYRIL LEVICKI

FT Prentice Hall
FINANCIAL TIMES

An imprint of **Pearson Education**

London • New York • Toronto • Sydney • Tokyo • Singapore
Hong Kong • Cape Town • Madrid • Paris • Amsterdam • Munich • Milan

Pearson Education Limited

Head Office:
Edinburgh Gate, Harlow
Essex CM20 2JE
Tel: +44 (0)1279 623623
Fax: +44 (0)1279 431059

London Office:
128 Long Acre, London WC2E 9AN
Tel: +44 (0)20 7447 2000
Fax: +44 (0)20 7447 2170
Website: www.business-minds.com

First edition 1996
Second edition 1999
Third edition published in Great Britain in 2003

ISBN 0 273 65912 X

British Library Cataloguing in Publication Data
A CIP catalogue record for this book can be obtained from the British Library.

10 9 8 7 6 5 4 3 2 1

Typeset by Pantek Arts Ltd, Maidstone, Kent
Printed and bound in Great Britain by Bell & Bain Ltd, Glasgow

The Publishers' policy is to use paper manufactured from sustainable forests.

About the Author

Dr Cyril Levicki started life in the tough streets of inner urban London. After leaving school he worked as a labourer. Later he ran his own, wholesale and retail businesses.

After a successful business career he attended London University, aged 32, and studied economics and politics. After graduating he was awarded a scholarship to study for his PhD at the London Business School. He completed three years later and was invited to turn his research into an advanced strategy and policy elective for the LBS MBA programme, which he also taught.

Cyril was appointed a Visiting Professor at Queen Mary College soon after. He also served as Visiting Professor at Baruch College in New York. He is now teaching at Reading University.

Since 1983 he has acted as a consultant for many international organizations, usually helping chairpersons and chief executives to formulate or revise the long-term strategy of their businesses. He is usually retained for long periods thereafter to help these organizations change the behaviour of their top teams to ensure successful implementation of the strategies they have devised.

Cyril lives in the countryside in Oxfordshire.

In loving memory of my mother and father

Contents

Foreword   ix

Acknowledgments   xiii

Preface to the Third Edition   xiv

Part One: Methodology for strategic analysis

1 Introduction to the workout method   3

2 Mission and vision statements   11

3 Examining the non-controllable environment   29

4 Studying the competitors   48

5 Market and business analysis   61

6 Organizational self-analysis: strengths, neutrals
and weaknesses   84

7 Organizational culture   120

8 Value chains and how to analyze them   136

9 Numerical evaluation   157

10 Being creative about the long-term strategy   175

11 Organizational structure   206

12 Short-term tactics to build the long-term strategy   229

13 International considerations   243

Part Two: Implementation through leadership and management

14 Leadership   263

15 Strategic management   286

Epilogue   296

Part Three: Measure your final strategy workout fitness

Workout audits   301
Further reading   325
Index   329
How you can get the most from your strategy
workout: a note from the author   343

CD of all the workouts   Inside back cover

Foreword

Welcome to strategy and its supposed mysteries. There are fewer secrets to strategy than some would have you think – but enough to fill this book.

Why a strategy workout? Because learning to write a strategic plan is a basic skill required at every level of management. If you cannot do it you will not survive as a manager or a leader.

This book is designed to be user friendly. There is a minimum of jargon and pseudo science. I try to specialize in common sense, aided by the good fortune of having spent 20 years formulating and implementing strategy with many leaders of usually large corporations and their teams. I do this through my consulting practice which specializes in helping leaders formulate or change the mission and strategy of their business. The leader often contacts me when he or she has some particular problem in their business or corporation which is preventing them from moving forward. I go in to help him or her remove the immediate problem from the table. I often then help them work with their team to understand and overcome the problems of implementation of the new mission and strategy which they have devised with me as their catalyst. That pattern of behaviour has forced me to design highly practical strategies that work easily with the set of people and resources at the leader's disposal – including their personal aptitude. I stay around long enough to be found out if the ideas don't work!

Methodology and layout

The book is divided into three parts. The first part gives you to the methodology for strategic analysis. It enables you to judge how much more you need to study aspects of the organization to sharpen your understanding and capacity to analyze each specific area of strategy. Each chapter ends with a page or two of 'workout' which is there to enable the reader to test whether he or she has understood the content by asking brief questions about their own business. If they can answer them without reading the chapter I advise them not to bother. The last two chapters describe how you apply the strategic analysis to an organization and what thinking needs to go into the implementation of the strategy.

Readers can do the total workout on their own or, even better, with their team. The book has a complete version of the workout at the end. Try it out over a weekend to practise the skills. To arrive at an agreed strategy with your team get all of them to complete the in-depth exercises in the chapters during an afternoon or a day away from the office. Then get together for a day and check where you agree or disagree with each other. Then reach consensus. Use the book to discover what you do or do not know. If you do not fill it in as you go you are more likely to miss an important subject you have not really understood properly.

All the workouts are also included on the CD accompanying this book and can be completed, circulated and compared in electronic format with colleagues.

Strategy can be fun, so enjoy yourself. You cannot use your imagination too often at work. Creating strategy is one of the few times when you should be as imaginative as possible.

The objectives of the book

Most leaders and managers just don't have time to think about their business and its future. They are too busy running the business. To help them find the time to think about strategy at all I have had to reduce the creation of new strategy to its barest essentials, to help leaders focus fast on the key factors they need to consider when deciding the strategic thrust of their organization. The system has been tested in all sizes of organization and is intended to be learned and used in a minimum amount of time. Time, for senior managers, is always in short supply.

This book shows you how to achieve the same speedy strategy analysis used by successful executives. It also tells you how to develop leadership and managerial qualities to implement your strategy successfully. Because all my clients are always short of time, this workout is designed to give shorthand methods to assemble the information you need to take decisions about the strategy of the organization as quickly as possible. The 'strategy workout' system was evolved for that process. Going fast also has another value. My experience tells me that when it comes to strategy and competitive advantage, being a first and fast mover is always better than arriving in a second or third best position long after the exciting morsels have been removed from the market. Also, moving fast enables you to use your instincts and intuition, which tend to get buried and lost the longer you hesitate and worry about the problems surrounding all your opportunities. Hesitation creates the 'Hamlet syndrome' where you think so long about the revenge you must take for the murder of your father, you fail to take revenge at all.

The 'workout system' has been continuously honed to be suitable for use in any industry and most circumstances. I noticed that my clients continued to use it long after they were taught the system. They usually took it with them when they changed employers or industries. I realized then that I had a general strategy analysis tool that would be useful to a wider public.

Implementation is much harder

As I became more proficient at helping clients devise new strategies, I also realized that the really difficult problems were not related to devising new strategies. That is relatively simple, once you get the knack. The killer problem is always strategy implementation. That takes a special chemistry of leadership, management, luck with the economy, skill and care in the development of your employees and the controlled evolution of unique competencies in your organization. The only other key ingredient, in my experience, is **corporate integrity**. Everybody in the business, at every level, has to believe that his company is providing great and valuable services or products, that it treats its people and its customers properly and keeps to the rules of business and society in general. Organizations that do all those things succeed. Those which lack that necessary moral fibre eventually fail. That has become an essential part of my credo.

The final chapters of the book are intended to give some brief guidelines on how implementation can go wrong and how to get it right. Essentially it is people, working within the organizational culture of their business (the atmosphere in which people do their work), who are difficult to change. The very hardest people of all to change are leaders, usually because by the time they get to the top, their capacity to see the organization, its people or its strategic future with fresh eyes has diminished.

Great leaders know that it takes many years of sensitive, insightful and inspired leadership to change the way people think, the values they hold dear and the way they behave. If they ever forget how vital those factors are to strategy implementation then they will also underestimate how hard it is to change the strategic direction of the business. Leaders need, alongside sound corporate or business strategy, a profound understanding of people. They have to judge not only what the underlying values of the behaviour changes should be but also how to communicate the different and changed behaviours and attitudes that will achieve the new strategy they devise. They then have to decide which of their executives will help right away; who could help (once they are won over) and, finally and sadly, who will always be an impediment and will eventually have to go.

When I realized that I was seeing a constant pattern of similar difficulties with regard to implementation in fundamentally different organizations across a range of industries, I realized that it was time to tell that story.

Acknowledgments

I should like to thank the following people for their help. My wife, Phyllis, who read and reread this work many times and told me when passages made no sense. My publisher, Stephen Partridge, and many friends who have checked the book for content and common sense. Among those who read early versions and advised on improvements are Andrew Callaghan (MD, Suttons plc), John Farrant (Chairman, William Sutton Trust), Richard Gourlay, Ray Gudge, George Hazle, Professor Leonard Minkes (Emeritus Professor at Birmingham University), Bert Morris (Chair of Lorien plc and Macro 4 plc) and Professor Derek Pugh (Emeritus Professor at the Open University). As always, all mistakes remain my fault alone. They have merely saved me from the worst.

Preface to the Third Edition

There is something gratifying when one gets to the third edition of a book, not least of which is that it proves that a few people bought the previous editions. Furthermore, a considerable number of readers (from all over the world) have contacted me to tell me how to improve any further editions. I have taken all the sensible advice into account in this edition. Consequently, I have removed the first simplified version of the workout as many people felt it was superfluous. I have also tried to remove some of the subheadings to make the book easier to read. I have added new chapters relating to the valuation of businesses, creativity in strategy, management and team motivation and some closing thoughts on the old and the new economies.

I hope readers and users of my workout methods find the third edition even more useful than the earlier editions. Thank you to all the readers who helped to improve it.

Dr Cyril J. Levicki, 2003

Part One

Methodology for strategic analysis

Introduction to the workout method

How this book works

The book is intended to be a simple-to-use strategy workbook. It is based on over 20 years of practical strategy development work in organizations which needed to create and install new strategic direction. The workout system is used by thousands of practising managers. Many executives are overworked and find that time is both their most precious and rarest commodity. They never seem to have enough time to think clearly and carefully about the strategic direction of their organization. Anyway, most of them prefer to do that type of thinking by instinct and at the sub-conscious level. Too frequently this causes accidents and wrong directions to be taken by their subordinates and sometimes by themselves in mis-guided takeovers and time wasted when pursuing acquisition possibilities and other apparent opportunities. Had there existed a strategy document to refer to, they would have realized immediately that the idea did not fit the strategic purpose of the organization at all and should be immediately abandoned and no time for reflection wasted upon it.

Part One (Chapters 2–13 of the book) covers the various necessary processes of strategic analysis and helps the reader understand how to conduct a strategy analysis for him or herself. Each chapter contains a

workout on the subject matter of that chapter. The method has been refined by many years of practical work with managers and aims to ensure that you do not forget any important aspect of the analytical process as the strategy is prepared. These aspects change from edition to edition because there can never be any 'final' version of the process of strategic analysis. The subject of strategy formulation and implementation is evolving continually and requires constant updating. The additions also reflect my increased experience at the highest levels of international strategy leadership and observations of how real leaders do it in reality.

Part Two (Chapters 14 and 15) covers aspects of the implementation of strategy, leadership and strategic management of an organization (which is a specific skill that I differentiate from ordinary management). I also offer a few tips on getting strategy implementation right.

Part Three contains a complete set of all the workout audits as they appear in the individual chapters throughout the rest of the book. You might try to complete them before you read the chapters in detail, to decide which areas you understand best.

Many chapters contain short case studies and stories to illustrate the theory and how the practice can go wrong or right. Often the stories demonstrate appalling consequences of apparently simple procedures which have been badly implemented. In other cases I give examples of unethical conduct or even moral turpitude and the reader will not be surprised that the perpetrator was unwilling to give permission for the story to be told. It is hoped that the stories will, nonetheless, give you insights and an understanding of how to implement the ideas contained within the book.

Occasionally you may feel a shiver run down your spine as you read a story and wonder whether it is about you or somebody you know. The truth is that these stories are about all of us because no one can practise strategy, leadership or management without making mistakes. The enduring qualities you need are those of continuous learning and relearning. A leader needs to see in a new light and as frequently as possible ordinary events which take place routinely every day. At the very least, we should remind ourselves constantly of best practice. If you are not doing that minimum, then you have probably already begun to fail.

A definition of strategy

Strategy is the document or set of concepts that form the plan for the future of an organization. Every organization will need a different plan which has to be tailor made for its particular and unique history, circumstances and capacity. Strategy analysis is the process whereby one arrives at a strategy. Strategic management is a way of organizing your business such that you maximize the chances of fulfilling the objectives of the strategy.

The process of strategic analysis looks at the external environment of the organization and the internal strengths, neutrals and weaknesses of the business. These, together with its culture, enable a firm to select and head towards the strategic direction it has chosen. Once you know where you are going, you can 'decide how to get there' (design and structure) and what choices of short-term tactics (budgets and plans) will make it happen.

The concepts of strategy

As you can see from Figure 1.1, the process of strategic analysis is simple. It goes from one rational, sequential step to another. Essentially, you evolve a mission statement, then immediately consider the external environment including a look at known and potential competitors. You then analyze the value chains of the businesses you are in, in case you decide to grow your influence and power in the industry by taking some of them over at a later date when you have set your strategy. You then check objectively the internal strengths, neutrals and weaknesses while not forgetting to assess the culture of the organization, which is the key control mechanism of the behavioural range of the organization. You can then define the long-term strategy you wish to put in place. At this juncture one should design any necessary amendments to the structure. You should have been keeping these to a minimum because they can be so disruptive to the business and people's feelings. Finally, you select tactics and short-term plans for the year or two ahead. This is necessary every year, as is a check on whether anything in the external environment has changed radically enough to necessitate a large-scale change in the overall strategy.

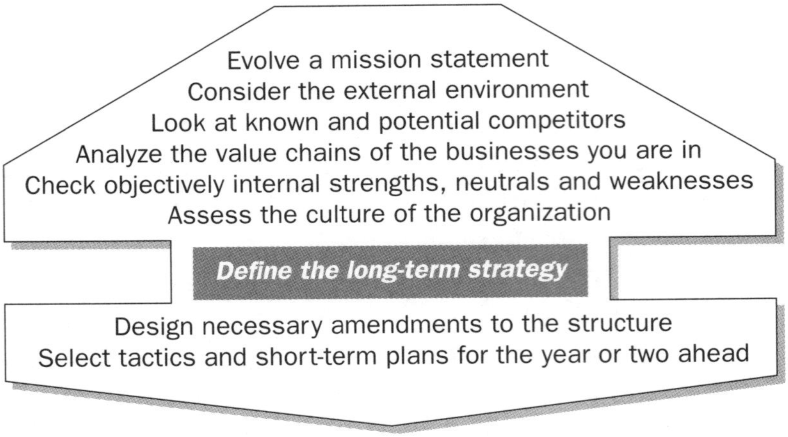

Evolve a mission statement
Consider the external environment
Look at known and potential competitors
Analyze the value chains of the businesses you are in
Check objectively internal strengths, neutrals and weaknesses
Assess the culture of the organization

Define the long-term strategy

Design necessary amendments to the structure
Select tactics and short-term plans for the year or two ahead

Figure 1.1 The strategic workout methodology

The person responsible for the overall delivery of performance of the organization is the person who should ensure that the organization has an effective and deliverable strategy. He or she should, however, strive to let everybody within the business feel ownership of the strategy. Why? Because when they participate in the creation and evolution of strategy they have a greater sense of ownership of it. Furthermore, when employers know about and understand the strategy, they are more aware of what they must do to ensure it is delivered. Their organizational role may be in marketing, production quality, timely delivery or checking customers' credit. Whatever their role, everybody should have a feeling of ownership of the strategy and understand how the job they do is a finite but important part of the implementation of the strategy as a whole.

The processes of strategic analysis set out here are user friendly for any organization. Whether applied to the commercial or the non-profit sector, the same considerations apply and a similar level of knowledge of the external and internal environments is required. All organizations are chasing the limited resources of their sector of interests, be they charitable gifts of money or customers for products or services.

For a commercial enterprise, the components of competition are usually self evident. The problem is the same for non-profit organizations. A charitable foundation is competing for people's 'gift capacity'. If they don't appeal in a stronger and more timely way than other charities, they will lose – and so will the cause they exist to support. It is difficult to be objective about an organization's comparative situation in the marketplace. How does a successful organization decide that its current best-selling, market-leading ideas, products or services are becoming redundant? What percentage of income should be reserved for research and development to seek replacement products? Possibly the hardest area to evaluate is what would be an appropriate level of investment in training and development of people in the organization.

The future is always uncertain but if the organization does not train people for that uncertain future then it can be sure that whatever future arrives, its people will not be ready for it.

Only high-quality strategic analysis can render these difficulties less difficult and the decisions more likely to be correct. The first step is knowing what the strategic analysis process entails.

Who should devise strategy?

Strategy should be devised by the leader of the organization. That may not be the titular head. Many organizations divide their leadership between the chairman and the chief executive. It will depend on circumstances who becomes the strategic business leader. That is the person who should devise the strategy.

Although Bill Gates, the founder and leader of Microsoft, the world's largest computer software business, controls a sizable part of the voting shares, he has long since given up sole control of the strategic direction of the business. He retains charge of decisions about new products and new areas of business Microsoft should invest in. But he largely leaves the strategy setting to people who can make better quality decisions than he can. That does not reduce his power or his wealth. He still owns a large slug of the shares. If he does not like what the strategy managers do he can vote them out. But he knows what he is supposed to do and how to go about doing it.

GEC used to be a multinational supplier to the engineering and defence industries, during the era of its former chairman, Lord Weinstock. The many large businesses it controlled were run for individual business profitability. The leaders of the individual business units were left to devise strategy for their part of the business. After some years of considerable success the chairman, Lord Weinstock, was criticized for not leading the overall corporation, GEC plc, toward an integrated strategy which would enable it to be more than just the sum of its parts. He felt that just making loads of profit with plenty of cash in reserve for the bad times should be enough. Eventually City analysts and 'enlightened commentators' persuaded enough shareholders that it was time the leader went.

The next chairman, Lord Simpson, attempted to find a new strategy for the corporation which would achieve a more favourable share price rating in the City. He moved the business out of the defence industry (where it was firmly and soundly embedded) and took GEC in a new strategic direction, into the telecommunications industry. In retrospect, this proved to be an abortive and catastrophic choice.

Not only did GEC have insufficient core competencies to compete in this industry but the industry itself proved to have limited potential. The value of GEC was destroyed and the cash mountain which Lord Weinstock had carefully built over the previous 20 years was wasted. The company had to fight for its very survival. What Lord Simpson (and his non-executive directors) overlooked was that defence industry contracts run for many years. With a cash mountain in reserve, they could sit out any temporary downturn in the market for a year or two. In the mobile telephone industry, contracts often have a cancellation option of not more than three months. Instead of relying on governments and armies (long-term decision makers, by and large), the company is subject to the whims and vagaries of teenage children and other dependants who will cancel their contracts as soon as the whiff of redundancy or decreased wages loom.

An additional reason for involving others in the strategic analysis process is that one often finds that the most in-depth knowledge of the external world of the competitor is in the heads of people who are not necessarily high up in the organization's hierarchy. For example, salespeople who spend their time out in the field often know more about what competitors are doing than anybody else in the business.

The best strategic leadership teams evolve from special relationships where the chairman and the CEO or managing director find a unique empathy which enables them to cover each others' weaknesses and accentuate each others' strengths. A classic example of such a special relationship was Lord King at British Airways and his managing director, Sir Colin Marshall. Lord King cared mainly about his vision of turning BA into a leading global airline. Marshall was content to be a loyal lieutenant and implement his leader's vision. Between them they built what became, in the early 1990s, the 'best airline in the world'.

Above all, the leader has to decide what are his organization's best, medium and below par skills and resources. People who perform operational (rather than managerial) roles for the organization may have more objective views on these matters than the leaders might care to hear. Leaders will often hear the most accurate truth when they listen to the workers on the shop floor – they often know where the firm's real strengths and weaknesses lie.

Everybody should implement strategy. That is the only way the organization can move cohesively in one direction. It is surprising and regrettable that many leaders are prepared to share their strategy with their shareholders, and even their competitors (by publishing it in the business's annual report), but they do not share it with their workers, to capture their participation.

Part Three of the book contains a complete version of the strategy workout. Examine that and try to complete it first. If you are satisfied that it has enabled you to draw together most of the strands you need to develop your strategy, you might decide you need to read only those parts of the text which your workout shows you need to understand better.

Where you feel you need more enlightenment on the meaning of any part of the workout, the text is designed to help you understand each separate subject area of strategy. Each chapter closes with the workout audit for the subject. If you are attempting to understand strategic analysis for the first time, I recommend that you read all the chapters and complete the workout for each subject as you finish each chapter.

Readers should then re-examine the workout at the end of the book. If you are able to complete it, that will prove you are really strategically fit. Alternatively, you may decide you need to undertake further research and begin the whole process again. You are the customer and should use your purchase for maximum return.

I urge you to fill in the strategy workouts and test your organization's 'strategic fitness'. Please use this book according to the time you have available and the 'fitness' or 'lack of fitness' of your organization. A strategically 'unfit' organization, like any sick, directionless body, will struggle to survive and will die young. I hope this book helps your organization to become or remain healthy.

Summary

The thesis of this book is that strategic analysis is simple. It is the *implementation* of that strategy that is difficult. Further, it is mainly the human element which complicates the implementation process. Strategy is not value free and must, therefore, take account of the beliefs and values of the people involved in the organization. This begins at the very start of the process of strategy analysis and is examined in Chapter 2 under the mission statement. It is considered again in Chapter 7.

Strategic analysis is only the beginning of the important process of leadership of strategic change. Adapting the organization to fit new strategic environmental needs and opportunities defines the process of strategic analysis and implementation. They both require wise and sensitive insight into what motivates both large and small groups of people. Persuading them to adapt their behaviour to achieve new and different objectives is the highest and most supreme aspect of the art of leadership. That is the subject matter of Chapters 11 and 12.

Further reading

K. Blanchard and S. Johnson, *The One Minute Manager*, William Collins, Glasgow, 1990

R. M. Grant, *Contemporary Strategy Analysis*, Blackwell, Oxford, 1995

C. J. Levicki, *Developing Leadership Genius*, McGraw-Hill, Maidenhead, 2002

Mission and vision statements

Introduction

This chapter looks at the starting point of the strategic process. Whatever one does in life and whatever business or organization one wishes to create or run, one must first start with the basic proposition of what one wants to do and what the object of the exercise is intended to be. That is the premise of creating a mission or vision statement for an organization.

Definition

A mission statement is a general declaration of the purposes of the organization and the very long-term objectives that its leaders want to achieve. It is often written in an inspirational style to provide a focused and motivating document for the organization's employees.

An organization's mission statement should aim to be useful to employees, customers and any other interested stakeholders, such as job applicants to the organization (the mission statement may be the first introduction to the kind of operation they are applying to join), members of the financial community, current and potential investors, customers and suppliers.

A leader may want to use different versions of the mission statement to communicate with selected sections of the organization's community. It might be preferable to communicate with the external stakeholders via an 'aims statement to shareholders' or (to suppliers) a 'policy document guiding principal suppliers'. These different constituencies are interested in separate and distinct aspects of the enterprise's existence. The kind of messages contained in an internally focused mission statement may appear to be adverse or contradictory to the interests of the shareholders or suppliers. For example, shareholders may have shorter term investment time horizons than the leader of the organization. They might want profit maximized in the short run and could be put off by a leader's mission statement relating to a ten-year plan, which might involve short-term losses or lower profit margins in order to reap higher returns in the long run.

Setting the mission is the single most important thing the leader does for the organization. In so doing, he gives it a purpose and direction. Although leaders should consult with colleagues about the mission statement to gain acceptance and approval, they should be fairly sure where they really want the organization to be in the distant future.

A good mission should be sufficiently challenging to help people work more purposefully in a focused direction for the organization. However, it should not be so daunting that it makes people feel helpless because the vision seems impossible to achieve.

President Kennedy's mission: get a man on the moon within ten years

An oft quoted mission statement is that of President Kennedy (US President 1960–1963), when he set the mission for NASA, the American space agency: 'We will land a man on the moon within ten years.' This seemed to be an ultimate example of a mission statement because it was focused, concise, had a clear goal, represented a public commitment and had guaranteed funding behind it to make it happen. In those respects, it was an excellent example of the type. However, it also had weaknesses which ultimately led to catastrophic and profound consequences. Within the mission statement there was no particular commitment to quality or to any special obligation to the way employees should be treated. It also made no mention of any valid, economic long-term reasons for the mission. Ultimately, it was a 'leap of faith' **political** mission to keep the USA at the forefront of world leadership.

It could be argued that these shortfalls in the mission statement led to more people being killed in space after the moon landing, as space exploration continued without a particular change in the original mission statement which had been achieved. Political PR seemed to be a higher priority than looking after people or having space exploration represent the triumph of American engineering prowess over physical barriers and hurdles.

The Kennedy mission statement was also too finite. It did not indicate any 'next steps' after the moon landing. Certainly, the NASA organization seems to have gone nowhere since landing a man on the moon. Neither has it managed to find another challenging mission to replace the 'landing a man on the moon' focus of the organization's resources.

NASA has rarely seemed to take advantage of its original lead in the space exploration industry which has now diversified into launching satellites into orbit for communication purposes. Partly as a consequence of the original Kennedy mission statement ignoring (and possibly being ignorant of) this potential future development, Chinese, French and Russian satellite-launching rocket manufacturers are now matching the Americans in that field.

So, a mission statement which was too brief and failed to cover important issues such as care for employees and quality of product lost the USA and NASA an opportunity to dominate a world industry of the late 20th and early 21st centuries, even though it achieved early total technological leadership.

Philosophy and paradigmatic thinking

Learning how to think in paradigms is another way of expressing the need to think within frameworks of understanding. We all do this most of the time. But usually it is unconscious and accidental. When a leader suggests that he is outperforming other bosses in the industry he must be called to account for that claim in the exact measure and paradigm that the comparison is being made to. If the comparison is against figures and results of businesses which are not comparable, the paradigm is wrong and the claim spurious.

The idea of working within fair and reasonable comparisons uses the concept of 'paradigms' of accepted thought. Those paradigms are frameworks or working theories that we all have in our heads. Often they will have formed unconsciously, over years of experience. Sometimes they contain important flaws of logic or errors which, because we have never subjected our paradigm to conscious scrutiny, have consequently not been questioned or tested for reliability or accuracy. That is why, over some years past, many business leaders have run into problems as the standards of governance of their business have proved to be woefully inadequate compared to the standards expected by people who need to judge them, such as institutional investors.

The way such thinking arises warrants a quick glance at the roots of the nature of the thinking process and how concepts arise.

A key philosopher of 20th-century scientific thought was Karl Popper, a Jewish refugee from the German Nazi era who settled down to spend his refugee years at the London School of Economics. Popper (1959) suggested that all science is based on a logic of continuing scientific progress. Science moves forward by means of scientists offering hypotheses which should be expressed, according to Popper, as simply as possible. They should also be set up in a form which enables other scientists to test them by exact replication. Popper argues that scientists should try to make themselves 'transparently falsifiable' so that their theories can be tested the more easily by other scientists. Popper also advocates that when there are two apparently equal explanatory theories on the same subject, the one which is expressed more simply (thus having greater falsifiability) should be the one which prevails. Thus, for Popper, science marches forwards, always getting bigger and more comprehensive, (although simpler), always edging nearer towards the ultimate truth of all encompassing understanding. In Popper's world, theory is truth and fact.

A contrasting viewpoint is represented by the philosophy of Thomas Kuhn (1962), an American philosopher who presents a different view of how science works from that of Karl Popper. He argues that science does not progress forward with theories encompassing more truth. He suggests that science moves in revolutionary stages, neither forwards nor backwards. Science produces theories that encompass the needs of society at that time. During the period when any one paradigm prevails most scientists do small-scale experiments that move science and society forwards in small practical ways. Kuhn calls it, somewhat pejoratively, 'normal science'. Once again, society works within the paradigm.

Towards the end of any period of scientific progress under any particular paradigm or framework it gradually becomes obvious to all working within that particular framework that a new paradigm is necessary. Why? Because towards the end of the useful life of the paradigm anomalies begin to arise from experiments that the paradigm fails to illuminate or help to solve. To break out from the crisis of questions that the current paradigm or framework cannot solve science needs a great revolutionary new paradigm.

Kuhn suggests that towards the end of the era of a ruling paradigm, these anomalies will arise in the scientific results of experiments. Sometimes there are observations of phenomena which contradict the prevailing paradigm or fail to fit within the framework. Kuhn likens this period to any political pre-revolutionary phase. When a great scientist comes along with the new paradigm (a Copernicus, a Newton or an Einstein, a Marx, a Keynes or a Friedman), it is akin to a revolution. He suggests that for a person to change their working paradigm is almost as challenging as for them to change their religion. It is equally hard because it requires those 'normal scientists' to adopt the new paradigm as they would embrace a new religion or a new belief system. Most normal scientists fail to do it and just work out the rest of their lives within the old paradigm.

What are the implications of the two different theories about science and scientific progress? In fact they are the difference between objectivity and subjectivity. Popper's concept is that science and life moves forwards, onwards and progressively upwards. This contrasts to Kuhn's theory that scientific discovery moves only in relative terms to previous positions. Popper is saying that science moves ever onwards towards greater truth. Kuhn is suggesting that it moves in revolutionary leaps from position to position depending on society's needs at that time. Kuhn's philosophical implication is that science and knowledge are not necessarily moving forwards but merely from one place to another. It might represent progress or it might represent, in perspective, a regression to a less favourable position. That represents a philosophical position of relativism. Everything relates to something else – there is no absolute truth or knowledge.

Popper's position is much more objective and strong. Everything relates to everything else and, in the end, to the greatest knowable eternal truths, when science has eventually made enough progress. There is an absolute truth and that is what all scientists are working towards. The philosophical moral equivalent of Popper's position is that there are eternal ethics and morals and that we should all abide by them. Kuhn's philosophical stance from this point of view could be that morals are relative and may change according to need and circumstance.

These viewpoints form the range that must be considered when we try to understand how a leader needs to think and judge when deciding a vision for his or her organization. It is such philosophies that one is using, without necessarily knowing about the thinkers or mode of thought themselves, when deciding what one's organization must do under particular circumstances or when forming a strategic vision for the future.

The ability to think in paradigms or frameworks is vital to any leader of an organization, state or community. A classical example of what we mean here would be the thinking of, say, John Major compared to that of Margaret Thatcher. There can be little doubt that John Major possesses great intelligence. Unfortunately, however, he missed the type of classical education that many of the people around him, namely the top civil servants and many of his cabinet subordinates, had received. His pure intelligence could not make up for the easy leaps forwards they could make in having so many paradigms at their mental disposal, learned from the hallowed halls of Oxbridge and their various public schools. Compare that to Margaret Thatcher who had the benefit of Oxford doctoral-level training. She understood paradigmatic thought easily and knew how to use it to wrap her ideas up in theory-like frameworks which made her ideas seem sufficiently rational to those who were meant to accommodate her wishes. She was thus able to command more respect and obedience from those around her who understand the philosophical game they are unwittingly playing all the time.

There is an unfortunate consequence of all this. The more complex and clever a leader's capacity to use frameworks becomes, the more it drives out their capacity for intuition and creativity. That enabled Major to make imaginative breakthroughs in Ireland and prevented Thatcher from seeing how crazy the results of her frameworks were when they led directly to the universally hated 'poll tax'. Similarly, leaders often use inappropriate comparisons when making claims for the success of their strategies. They compare businesses which are not equivalent, they distort their figures and results or they claim success is coming when in fact their results and potential are barren.

> **The more complex and clever a leader's capacity to use frameworks becomes, the more it drives out their capacity for intuition and creativity.**

It is the role of non-executive directors to ensure that unsound and self-deceiving processes are not enacted and then 'sold' to the owners of the business, the shareholders.

Ethical considerations

Over the last decade or so business managers and leaders have realized that they have duties to themselves, their organization, employees, customers, geographical neighbours, central and local government and many other stakeholders in the organization. These responsibilities go beyond what is legally required and far beyond the narrow interests of just the owners, the shareholders and bondholders.

Matching the realities in the workplace, Harvard, the London Business School (LBS) and many other business schools began to teach some of the principles of ethical thinking. I taught a class at the LBS back in 1980 using texts from philosophy and political theory to try to bring home to MBA students their moral and social responsibilities as managers and leaders.

Why is this important? Because we all live and work in integrated environments. We can never be just a 'worker', a 'mother' or a 'teacher'. If we are to live properly and wholesomely we need to try to be rounded and circumspect in our behaviour and decision making. People are not happy when behaviour in one aspect of their lives forces them to contradict the values which they hold dear in another. For example, you cannot believe in equal opportunities yet work for an employer who requires you to discriminate systematically against ethnic minorities. If you do you are living a contradiction and this will, inevitably, come to haunt you and your organization – sooner or later.

How does this apply to business?

Most employees in business are normal, rounded, ethical human beings. Their decency cannot be switched off just because they go to work. They cannot park one set of values at their front gate and select another, contradictory bunch on their way to work. So, managers and leaders are obliged to think through how to take into account generally accepted mores, beliefs, legal requirements, health issues, safety precautions and product liability issues while they focus on the long-term profitability and (if possible) growth of their businesses.

Arie de Geus (1997) found that the longest living business organizations were usually led by people who had a strong moral sense of their duty to their employees and their customers. This helped them all help each other through the bad times when the business showed loyalty to its people and the good times when they offered loyalty back to the employer rather than leave to take higher paid jobs elsewhere.

The arguments for taking a positive approach towards business responsibilities and ethics are covered under headings such as:

'It is in the best interests of the business.'
'Social actions can be profitable.'
'Being socially responsible is the ethical thing to do.'

The arguments against taking a responsible and ethical approach are covered under headings such as:

'It might be illegal to spend the business's money that way.'
'Government should control the law.'
'My business just has to keep to the law and maximize profit.'
'You cannot measure social and ethical matters. That is not business's role.'
'I have a family to feed. I'll worry about morals when they have full stomachs!'
'The rich have money and time for morals. I'm poor right now.'

How far should employers go in implementing ethical and social values within the workplace? This requires thought about such matters as:

'Would you want to work for a cigarette manufacturer?'
'Would you buy a Ford car if you thought their cars were unsafe with faulty tyres?'
'Would you take a job in a leading consulting company which practises racial bias?'
'If a relative tells you their employer is a takeover target, would it be OK to buy the shares?'
'Is it OK for a poor person to drive a car that is inadequately maintained (and consequently has poor brakes), because they could not afford to have their car serviced properly?'

Corporate governance

Corporate governance rules have become an important issue over the past 20 years. Many institutional investors have realized that many major business corporations have significant areas of management where the rules controlling the potential for selfish greed of some leaders and managers have been too loose and are highly unsatisfactory. In too many cases leaders have helped themselves to excessive rewards for delivering inadequate service and profit. In other instances leaders have used loosely devised rules of takeover and merger accountancy to make mediocre results seem satisfactory for many years. It has emerged that frequently there is no unbiased control of the financial rewards within the business.

Possibly of even greater significance is the system for supervisory control at the level of boards of directors where excessive cronyism has prevailed in preference to the appointment of truly wise and impartial non-executives who are prepared to step in early enough to prevent good businesses being badly led and allowed to fritter away enormous reserves while inadequate leadership gives woeful excuses for appalling performance year after year.

It is beyond the scope of this book to rehearse all the problems and failures or to seek out solutions for the problems. Suffice it to remark here that organizations which have solicited for public funds in the form of share listings on stock exchanges must be governed with a proper decorum. Their non-executive directors must have access to sufficient data about the performance of the organization to enable them to make judgments about whether it is achieving the reported strategic milestones. They must also have recourse to funding to take legal and other advice whenever they feel anything less than the proper standards may be perpetrated in the name of the business. For example, in the case of Equitable Life, the life assurance provider, it is obvious in retrospect that salesmen were selling their policies with excessive promises which could never be met in the long run. They were also selling with reckless disregard to the possibility of customers making fair comparisons with other assurers with statements implying they did not receive similar rewards as other assurance salespeople. The organization was therefore able to invest more of the funds to achieve higher returns.

Similarly, organizations have to appoint non-executive directors who have the courage to criticize fairly but in a timely manner and to ask difficult questions of the executive directors of businesses. They should not be sinecure-seeking has-beens aiming for an easy life offering and returning favours to friends and cronies on other boards with similar dispositions of laziness and insufficiency.

What core competencies does the organization need to achieve the vision?

The concept of **core competencies** refers to an organization's basic know-how skills that encapsulate its capacity competently to provide a service or product in the market. They will usually consist of a mix of long-term accumulated knowledge, natural advantages (such as property assets in geographically advantageous places), technical know-how in production or customer needs, human skills in management, market management or production, or market channel access. For example, Federal Express, which specializes in overnight delivery of small packages, has core competencies in: managing a centralized, physical hub system to maximize efficient package handling; motivating employees to deliver effectively, whatever the barriers; and pure logistical skills in the use of trucks and planes within a hub and spoke structure. Coca-Cola, a leading worldwide brand drink has core competencies in managing a global brand, dominating bottlers without needing ultimate share control and maintaining (through its brand advertising) the mythological power of its 'unique flavour'.

A good mission statement should aim to be stretching. It should usually require people within the organization to learn new core skills in order to achieve it. For a particularly daring and stretching strategic objective, it may require the business to learn an entire new core competency. For example, Microsoft specializes in software architecture to facilitate the use of computers. It decided in the late 1990s that it wished to increase its share of the world market in global communications highways on the world wide web. It had to achieve mastery of new core competencies in telemetry, networks and communications applications before it convinced customers that it was competitive in that field. It had

to take on new types of employee and find fresh ways of handl
It had to restructure its business to manage its telecoms, consult
internet employees whose culture differed from its original :
architecture specialists.

A mission statement will often address how the organization t
people. Some of this will be based on current styles. However, it can also
be aspirational in terms of how the organization wants to treat people in
the future. This is not meant to be idealistic but realistic. For example, BT
(British Telecom) created a new mission at the close of the 1980s, which
made no mention of the staff. This could not have been an accident – its
leaders were too sophisticated during that era to have forgotten such an
important constituency. The leaders knew they intended to reduce the
size of the company from 250,000 to 140,000 people. It would have been
seen as hypocritical and ill-conceived to make statements about how
much the company cared about its people when it concurrently intended
to drop about two in five of those employees.

It has become normal for most businesses to proclaim that: they want
to 'delight' their customer; 'the customer is supreme'; or 'it is only
because of the customer we are in business's. However, few actually
organize their business around the possibility of charming their customer. For example, many businesses mindlessly exploit computerized,
automated customer communications systems. In fact, they make it
increasingly difficult for their customers to talk to them at all. At the
beginning of the 21st century, with major skills shortages around the
world, many businesses are favouring employee care over customer
care. A classic example is offered by many of the world airlines who
treat their customers so abysmally they would almost rather arrest them
for minor displays of appropriate annoyance for bad service than take
their complaints seriously.

Before you can charm a customer they have to know what it is exactly
they want to buy. The range of offers a business can make to customers
can be more subtle than is sometimes assumed. In the air travel industry,
for example, there has been an increase in low-cost basic travel services.
There is a large market which requires less service for lower prices in
commodity air travel. But you have to give the customer a fair deal. If
you want to give low levels of service for a cheap fare, you have to give
the cheap fare first. Sometimes, the old 'luxury carriers', such as BA,
forget that there are meant to be two sides to the bargain.

The mobile telephone industry woke up to this concept in 1998. It added vast numbers of new customers in a short span of time by offering price-controlled, prepaid packages. In other businesses, treatment of the customer may be the main differential between competitors. For example, Virgin Railways, in the UK, is trying to get premium prices for its first class customers by offering 'free breakfasts'. Unfortunately, and simultaneously, it often fails to achieve a prime requirement of most rail travellers, which is to have the trains run and arrive on time.

Many businesses base their research for new products and services on customer focus groups. However, this can sometimes be misguided. For example, the late Akio Morita, former chairman of Sony, often claimed that he would never ask the customer what they want because he considered it to be his job to know what it was possible to create and then to arouse the customer's interest in it. Customers can only tell manufacturers what they know – it is the supplier's job to create what is not known. In leading-edge industries or markets it becomes even more important that the mission statement should indicate to managers and staff which broad approaches it wishes them to adopt.

The mission statement should paint a picture which enables employees to know in what direction the business is driving. They will draw sustenance from this picture of how their own conditions will improve as they provide better services for their customers and make the business thrive. The mission statement should create for the employees the idealized future that the leader wishes them and their customers to enjoy in the long term.

There is a peculiar and odd philosophical paradox, in terms of the overall strategic analysis process, which is enacted when drawing up a mission statement. One is beginning the process of strategic analysis with a mission statement. But it is hard to differentiate a mission statement from the long-term aims or strategy of the business. If the mission statement contains the main objectives of the firm it is anticipating what should evolve from the process of analysis itself. If you know where the firm should be going, as stated in the mission statement, why bother with the analysis at all?

Because in all cases, other than entirely new organizations, one starts the process of analysis with history. The organization existed. It was doing whatever it does up to this point. Leaders (especially new ones)

will usually have some idea of what fresh aims they want th
tion to achieve. The history of the organization will show
opportunities the organization had and took advantage of. It
tell of others where the business was prevented from attemp
enter some opportunity which might have proved more lucrati
new leader with a fresh mission statement offers an opportunity t
off into fresh pastures. But not all opportunities are real. Some are
related to size, scale, real core competencies and aptitude of the firm.
For example, National Cash Registers was small enough to become
IBM, one of the world's largest computer concerns. When it needed to
change drastically, in the mid-1990s, it had the choice of becoming a
partial consulting business. But even the gigantic and rich IBM probably could not have become an oil company or a motor company, even if
it wanted to do so.

It is a paradox that, to some extent, in forming a mission statement one
starts with the conclusions. If subsequent analysis demonstrates that
some of the long-term mission objectives were misconstrued or inappropriate, then this can and should be taken into account at a later stage of
the analytical process.

When all the data have been collected and the organization is ready to
decide what it wishes to achieve in its long-term strategy, one should re-
examine the mission statement in order to judge whether any of the external
or internal environment studies have produced important data that necessitate a change in the mission statement itself. That happens at the end of the
analysis process, when one is ready to formulate a long-term strategy.

Mission versus vision statements

There are some strategy books around which define esoteric differences
between mission and vision statements. This may be a useful distinction
in academic terms, although it is difficult to see quite what the value in
the nuances might be. However, for the purposes of practitioners of strategy, the two terms vision statement and mission statement may be
considered to be interchangeable. Both refer to the very long term. They
are statements of the longest term set of goals and aims of the organization. They represent the concept of what the organization's leaders would
like the organization to become. Mission statements are usually produced

by the leaders of the organization who are there to exercise the best judgment skills within the business; it is their prime responsibility. If they choose to delegate the responsibility to others, there is the danger that the organization will not achieve unanimity on its mission.

An organization's long-term goals have to be consistent. They should contain no contradictions. Neither should they target too many directions at a time. An organization cannot chase a thousand dreams, just a few. Setting the long-term objectives is probably the most important task and duty of the leader of an organization. The objectives may be couched in terms of 'market share', 'highest quality', 'lowest costs', 'ubiquity', or 'dominance' of particular markets.

> **An organization cannot chase a thousand dreams, just a few.**

They may be written in terms of the markets the organization wishes to dominate or the types of products it will specialize in. Whatever the method chosen to encapsulate the message, the mission or vision statement should indicate where the business is heading in the long run.

The mission statement is a dream only in the sense that it requires imagination, ambition and sensitivity from the leader about what is achievable. It should not be dreamlike in terms of achievability. If it does not look feasible, it will not be credible and, eventually, it will just be ignored.

Two mission statements follow. The first is that of BT in the early 1990s as it prepared to become one of the leading telecommunications enterprises in the world. History has subsequently shown that the mission statement failed to inspire or produce the desired result. Although it is easy to have 20/20 retrospective vision, readers should try to deduce what the mission statement lacked and why it failed to elicit the necessary action and effort from employees and customers to achieve the desired world class business that the leader (Sir Iain Vallance) thought he was setting when he created the mission statement in the early 1990s.

The other is that of Trust House Forte (THF), an international hotel and leisure group, which was taken over in 1997 by Granada plc, a larger entertainment, leisure and hotel company in the UK, after having unsuccessfully tried to defend its performance.

The British Telecommunications (BT) Mission

To provide world class telecommunications and information products and services.

To develop and exploit our networks at home and overseas so that we can:

- meet the requirements of our customers
- sustain the earnings growth of the group on behalf of the shareholders
- make a fitting contribution to the community.

Questions

- What do you think about a UK-based business aiming to become 'world class' in one fell swoop?
- What do you think about the use of the word 'exploit' in the second line?
- What do you think about the failure to talk about the employees?
- Do you think the employees will pay more attention to the mention of the 'shareholders' or that of the 'community'?

The BT statement was highly focused. Does it cover enough of the key actions that executives need guidance on so that all the key people in the business know exactly what they need to do to make the vision come true? In 2001 I asked the person who had been responsible for the devising and enacting of much of BT's strategy during the 1990s, where he had been getting his guidance from about enacting the mission statement. He told me it had come mainly from investment bankers and outsiders. He recognized that they always had an interest when they called him because they wanted to sell him some deal or other which would create fees for themselves. That had been the key to the implementation of the mission statement over the decade. Some readers might feel that perhaps the leader should have adopted the responsibility for rendering the mission into concrete form by deciding which companies should be taken over and in what parts of the globe and when.

The Trust House Forte (THF) Mission

- To increase profitability and earnings per share each year in order to encourage investment and to improve and expand the business.
- To give complete customer satisfaction by efficient and courteous service, with value for money.
- To support managers and their staff in using personal initiative to improve the profit and quality of their operations while observing the company's policies.
- To provide good working conditions and to maintain effective communications at all levels to develop better understanding and assist decision making.
- To ensure no discrimination against sex, race, colour or creed and to train, develop, and encourage promotion within the company based on merit and ability.
- To act with integrity at all times and to maintain a proper sense of responsibility towards the public.
- To recognize the importance of each and every employee who contributes towards these aims.

Questions

- Do you feel, as some people do, that it failed to give the organization's leaders and employees a sufficient sense of urgency and focus about its strategic position?
- Did that 'lack of focus' make it more vulnerable to a takeover bid when it came later?

Summary

This chapter suggests that organizations wanting to conduct a proper strategy analysis process must begin that process with a mission or vision statement. The statement helps them give themselves and everybody else relating to the organization an exact set of guidelines of why the organization exists and what it wants to do. It is the starting point of deciding what is included and what is excluded from the legitimate aims and goals of the organization.

Further reading

R. Adams, J. Carruthers and S. Hamil, *Changing Corporate Values*, Kogan Page, London, 1991

A. Campbell, M. Devine and D. Young, *A Sense of Mission,* Hutchinson, London, 1990

A. de Geus, *The Living Company*, Nicholas Brealey, London, 1997

G. Hamel and C. K. Prahalad, *Competing for the Future*, Harvard Business School Press, Boston, 1994

E. Jacques, *Time Span Handbook*, Heinemann, London, 1964

T. Kuhn, *The Structure of Scientific Revolutions*, University of Chicago Press, Chicago, 1962

T. J. Peters and R. H. Waterman, *In Search of Excellence*, Harper & Row, New York, 1982

K. Popper, *The Logic of Scientific Discovery*, Hutchinson London, 1959

THE MISSION WORKOUT

Complete the following mission audit questions.

What is the vision of the leader of the organization?

_____

Where is he or she taking the organization in the long run?

_____

What industry (industries) are you determined to participate in?

_____

What are the current core competencies of the organization?

_____

What core competencies need to be obtained?

_____

What will the organization look like in five years' time?

_____

What are the three key achievements that will be history in five years' time?

_____

Examining the non-controllable environment

Start the strategic analysis outside the organization

Chapter 2 described how the first job in a strategy workout is to decide what is the long-term mission of the organization. The next step is to move mentally outside the organization and look at the external world. The scan of the external environment should include anything that is happening outside the organization within its industry and in other relevant industries. It should also include all the other factors anywhere in the external environment which might affect the organization's interests. First, one must scan one's own industry and any others that might be linked to it in any way at all. For example, an old-fashioned telecommunications business should look at converting its technology to fibre optics and satellite. If it does that it should also scan the television entertainment industry because the same technology lends itself to that industry. If that goes, one might have to examine the programme-making business to see whether that industry's core needs are matched by your business's core competencies.

In addition to these industry affinities, external environmental scanning should examine the range of subjects such as politics (and relevant politicians); the law (particularly in regard to taxation and legislation controlling industry standards); the patterns of sociological change in   relevant client nations; and the dangers of political turbulence in countries where the business operates now or might conduct business in the future.

It is advisable to start the analysis outside the organization because at this stage of the process you *might* still be capable of objectivity in the strategy workout. As you get more involved in analyzing the nitty gritty of your own business, your objectivity is likely to be eroded. It is a short path from losing your objectivity to the natural next stage in human behaviour of seeking out 'data' which corroborate your subjective preferences and preformed ideas rather than seeking objective, and sometimes unwelcome, information which negates your preferred mission. When researchers scan the external horizon outside the organization, most look at it with a subjective eye which seeks corroboration of what they want to believe, rather than objectively examining interesting external facts and events that might really affect the business.

Start the workout on the exterior of the organization. This offers some small chance of avoiding the natural human tendency to look only at those things that corroborate one's own prejudices. Great strategic thinkers avoid this problem by exercising a cold, calculated self control and a ruthless questioning of every key assumption. Unfortunately, few people are capable of such rigorous resolution. Please note here that this is an entirely separate phenomenon from the exercise that a leader must fulfill, *after* the analysis, when he or she has to persuade people that the best strategy has been chosen and the right destination for the organization has been selected. That is a 'selling' job for the leader. He or she has to convince people within the business that they have found the best solution to the organization's strategic dilemma, one that ensures the organization's success. Even when hard selling and clearly delineating the chosen strategic direction, a great leader will always know, objectively, where the greatest weaknesses of the strategy lie.

What external environment do we mean?

The external environment is infinite. You are only interested in the relevant data, predictable events and states of the environment which appertain to your business. But, in looking at them objectively, you need to see what is interesting and important rather than only those phenomena that might be advantageous to your organization. One way of avoiding too easy an interpretation of how these events will affect your business is to analyze the environment from the point of view of your closest or most feared competitor. If it can affect their business there is no reason to assume that you can avoid danger – unless you have specifically constructed a policy to neutralize the exposure. Similarly, if there are objective external economic events (for example, the emergence of

The external environment is infinite.

mobile telephony as a web methodology) or political facts (for example, the strengthening of competition enforcement in the European Union market-place), these have to be taken into account. Sometimes, the facts will be affected by the competitor position.

Consider the situation just mentioned concerning competition law enforcement in the European Union. If one of your competitors managed to take over a mutual rival business, that may, by itself, preclude your business's opportunity to take over another opponent, on the grounds that there may be room for one more large firm but not two.

Whatever method you use to analyze the external environment, try not to interpret or devise strategies and tactics until you get to that stage of the strategic design process. Defining the long-term strategy or short-term tactics is still quite a long way off.

The environment can be classified under the following headings:

- international, national and regional markets
- economic trends
- political events
- legal, social and demographic factors
- particular expectations and tendencies of the industry in which you are involved.

Let's examine the key criteria within some of these classifications in turn.

International markets

A key strategic aspect of managing international markets is the problem of communication. Once an organization becomes international it has to develop special methods of communicating and skills to overcome the potential hazards. The first hazard may be language. That is immediately followed by problems of differences in culture, law and national attitudes.

The capacity to communicate is no longer a constraint given modern telecommunications; however, excessive communication availability may increase the possibility of poor quality management through attempts to control too forcefully. The communication problem is exacerbated in the modern era of massive physical information availability. How does the strategist ensure that key data, market opportunities, political events and competitor behaviours which give genuine forward favourable or dangerous predictability, actually get to him or her at the necessary stages in the strategic analysis process? How does he or she ensure that country managers are aware of what is important, dangerous or benign?

Most traditional international and multinational businesses do it by having the leaders and strategists visit continuously, with a scanning brief for the important data. They also hold regular international company conferences to exchange ideas and receive mouth-to-ear data which may be relevant to the strategic positioning of the business. As I have frequently told clients, it is not the formal sessions which are important at international conferences. It is the informal events, the meals, coffee breaks and the drinking sessions through half the night that really add value to the business.

A further complexity of international strategic growth is the management of physical distribution. Frequently, domestic businesses dominate their home markets through control of the physical distribution system. This might be well disguised. An intruding business from abroad might sink millions of dollars of capital investment before realizing that it cannot penetrate the market. Furthermore, the industry may be at a different stage in its development and have different patterns of competition and distribution. This makes it particularly hard to form valid opinions about the power of domestic competitors, which often have unpublicized connections with government officials and influencers who can distort the rules and regulations in favour of the home competitor. Japan and France offer two of the more obvious and outstanding examples of this phenomenon. Just being on home territory is a powerful aid to the incumbent firm.

When examining international or global markets one needs knowledge and understanding of different national characteristics. These will differentiate the form of demand for products in each country. They will indicate the basis on which it may be necessary to differentiate and 'localize' products and services when trying to penetrate markets. Apparently, the Japanese version of Coca-Cola is sweeter than that in other countries because the Japanese have a sweeter tooth than most of the rest of the world.

Differences between the cultures of countries are sometimes startling and surprising. It is far too convenient in international organizations to take real cultural differences for granted and fail to remember in how many subtle ways one has to manage each country differently. Fons Trompenaars (1993) points out the variety of differences between different nationalities. For example, he found that 91 percent of Swiss respondents to his questionnaire would not write a false personal review, even to help a friend, whereas only 17 percent of Yugoslavs would have a similar inhibition; 97 percent of Australians prefer to be left alone to get on with the job; in Egypt only 32 percent like to work alone. Most Italians (71 percent) would openly express upset feelings at work; only 17 percent of Japanese respondents would share similar feelings.

One should also be asking other important questions about the external environment. Has any country in which your organization is involved become less stable politically? Is it part of a strategic alliance? Should you continue trying to penetrate the markets of a particular country or cut your losses? Are there new growth opportunities which did not exist before? In the 1980s I did some work with a senior officer (now dead) of Ultramar Petroleum. The business had substantial contracts to mine LNG (liquefied natural gas) in Indonesia. He always enjoyed reminding me that Indonesia seemed far more stable than normal democratic states, which had elections every few years causing strategic upheaval every time the government changed. I continued to raise my objections to the business working with a corrupt dictator. He continued to tell me that President Suharto had ruled Indonesia for many years and looked likely to do so for many to come. As far as he was concerned that constituted much greater political stability than existed in the UK or the USA, with our foolish democratic elections every four years or so. His strategic analysis failed to take into consideration that the only way to remove a corrupt, totalitarian dictator, in the absence of a democratic system, is by means of a revolution. It duly came, in 1998. The disruption and devaluation of accumulated assets was much larger than any normal democratic election result could ever bring about. However, the regime had lasted nearly 20 years. The business had made continuous profits at a high level during that time. Outside the moral considerations, that his business bribes to the rulers were helping to keep a corrupt politician in power, on all the economic arguments my client was right and my ethical considerations wrong. What does the reader think?

National markets

The difference between analyzing the strategic environment when a business is national, rather than international, is massive. When considering national markets one needs to take into account the variations in local customs and geographical distances in terms of the costs of distribution. Strategically, the difficulty with being a national specialist is that you are vulnerable to international competitors of whom you may be unaware when analyzing just the local environment. Although the scale of national business is intrinsically different from that of a larger, international business, it is no less important to understand that both national or international legislation, politics and trends (both social and economic) may affect your local business as profoundly as they will an international business. This problem is accentuated with the increase of large political agglomerations, such as ASEAN (Association of South East Asian Nations), the EU (European Union) or NAFTA (the North American Free Trade Alliance).

For example, although you may be running a small country hotel, national and international standards of hygiene and food preferences will still affect your business. Similarly, you may have a thriving small and locally famous business, but that will be entirely irrelevant for a major international hotelier who will see the local and the national market in a different context. The small operation's fate may be rendered meaningless in a national or international context and scale. A business will need to take the potential large competitor into account. This is not reciprocal for a large international business. The large operator will not usually need to reciprocate by taking the small operator into account in its calculations.

Many of the key warnings about nationally oriented organizations' vulnerability to much larger international rivals apply to regional (sub-national scale) businesses. A key advantage for the regional business is to understand local conditions thoroughly, as well as market differentiators and distribution channels. There will also be idiosyncrasies of local politics and planning regulations. There may be special rules about property. There often exist opportunities to close off access to vital resources or rights. The local business must use such knowledge to exploit the few advantages which its smaller size confers.

There are some simple rules about physical distribution too. The key factors here are value by weight and volume. If the products are high value and relatively low weight (e.g. pharmaceutical products) the organization may be able to maximize economies of production in one place and spend on distribution. If the product is bulky but light (such as packaging) it can maximize on the use of large trucks by road or rail, if available. But they will probably need more manufacturing units than the high-value low weight and size objects. If the products are both heavy and capacious, they will probably have to put more capital into local manufacturing units and spend less on the transport and delivery costs of the total supply chain.

Putting the organization into an international context

The leadership of a large national cable concern was having great difficulty in getting its managing directors to understand why they had to become more customer focused; the organization was losing over 40 percent of its customers each year (through customers stopping their subscriptions to their services). It was much harder to win customers a second time than it was to retain them with good service the first time around. The reasons were multifarious. The company tended to recruit customers with poor economic circumstances whose income was subject to more viscitudes than middle-class customers would be. These customers were also more vulnerable to the doorstep-selling techniques the business employed. The quality of customer service was appalling. Consequently, customers used the only threat they had, which was to stop taking the service. The programming was terrible – clients frequently stopped subscribing because, they said, 'they could not bear to watch any more repeats of programmes they had already seen a dozen times!'

The business called a conference of its top 30 directors. The organization's original objective had been to dominate the market for cable services by the year 2001. For this reason, the managers felt there was plenty of time to worry about 'being nice to customers', eventually. Anyway, most of them came from the USA where the cable industry almost always enjoys a local geographical monopoly which had permitted them to offer mediocre service combined with high prices. In the UK everybody paid a compulsory licence for the two BBC channels and also received the two ITV advertising channels free. For the majority who were disinclined to take more television, saying 'no' to cable was relatively easy.

The organization's leader decided to put the matter into context. With the oncoming deregulation of the whole European market, there was an opportunity for the organization to conquer Europe and achieve economies of scale. Rather than have a 20 percent share of a 60 million-person market, he wanted to try to grab a 30 percent share of the whole European market with its 350+ million population (cable was considered more acceptable in continental Europe than in the UK). This completely changed the attitude of his team. They suddenly realized that there was no time to 'play' at learning to get customer service right. They had to get it perfect now. They had to lock up the whole UK market fast, to have any chance of taking advantage of the much greater opportunity in Europe as a whole!

A German discount food corporation became aware of the high profit levels enjoyed in the UK food retailing industry. These margins were high because the market was dominated by two large retail suppliers, Tesco and Sainsbury's. The German corporation tried to set up retail discount stores in the UK, but every time it applied for planning permission, Tesco and Sainsbury's combined to raise objections on planning law grounds with every local authority where permission was requested. Because the domestic lawyers had superior knowledge of all the possible reasons for refusing or granting permission, plus good quality relationships with local planning officers, they managed to frustrate the newcomer enough to dishearten it. The German corporation gave up after several frustrating years of legal red tape. Eventually, the UK government changed its policy of granting planning permission for all new out-of-town supermarkets – thus ensuring the continued domination of Sainsbury's and Tesco's duopoly. That left the two businesses to slog it out between themselves: by the end of 1998, Tesco had won most of the first few rounds.

Economic trends

One of the most important long-term truths in any business situation is that ultimately an organization cannot buck the economic trends of its industry. Bryant & May was originally a Swedish company which set out to try to achieve a monopoly in matches which were used mainly for lighting fires, gas stoves and cigarettes. Unfortunately, by the time it had almost achieved its objectives, cheap disposable lighters had become ubiquitously available, thus rendering the monopoly almost worthless with no extra profits, because a viable substitute product was available. Telecommunication businesses fought hard to lay down fibre and copper networks so they could dominate particular telephony markets. By the time that many of them had built their own networks, they were not worth having because so many spare networks were available that they could be rented more cheaply than the cost of owning!

The concept of the **product life cycle** is often relevant when considering long term economic trends. The product life cycle theory is that all products and services go through a life cycle of four stages:

- Stage one is the *introduction* of the new product to the market. It is likely to be bought only by a few innovative, and probably wealthy, people who like to be 'avant-garde' in trying new products. The first stage is rarely profitable for the supplier(s) because the costs of development are high.
- Stage two is of *rapid growth* when many more suppliers emerge to make the product. These manufacturers have been able to overcome the barrier of the original inventing organization often having patented the manufacturing process. This stage is often unprofitable at the beginning (because there are too many suppliers) but becomes profitable toward the end as some suppliers exit the market.
- The third stage is known as *maturity*. It is usually profitable as the market matures and continues to grow but with far less competition as the less efficient suppliers drop out of the industry.
- The fourth stage is a period of *decline* (sometimes profitable but often dire) as the market becomes saturated with the product and the main sources of custom are people needing replacements or new entrants into the overall market. Figure 3.1 illustrates these concepts.

Consider the trends for your business sectors. Which part of the product life cycle do your products fit? If you wish to grow your business you need the largest possible range of products and services in the second stage for growth and in the third stage for maximum profitability.

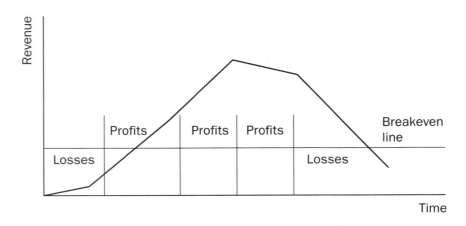

Figure 3.1 Product life cycle

Becoming a global leader

It is possible to migrate your business from having products in old, mature or low-profit margin industries into high-growth, high-value-added and high-profit industries. This takes a great deal of strategic planning and decisive, intelligent strategy implementation. There is never any shortage of capital available for investment, under modern banking conditions, as long as intelligent strategic analysis has taken place and the organization's leaders demonstrate a strong probability of successful implementation of change, growth or migration to the new industry. A classic example of a successful migration is that of Reed International which moved from a low-profit, mature industry of paper and packaging into the high-profit, growth industry of international publishing and data processing.

As most industries (local, national or international) mature, they develop a pattern of having a few businesses dominate the market by market share. Ultimately, one or two outstanding organizations are seen as the vanguard in that industry or field. Furthermore, that market share domination is accompanied by a compatible higher level of profits. In truly large-scale industries, the larger market dominators often achieve net margins of 10 to 12 percent of revenue. The second positioned market share often achieves a lower but still respectable 8 to 10 percent net margin of revenue. Finally, the poor third

market share business limps home with
enue. You often then find a batch of
maintain themselves in existence for ap
of revenue. There are often small devia
sists of smaller niche businesses whi
special share of the market for thems
which represents higher value or ser
local monopoly in distribution or a
allows them to compensate for a lac

In information technology IBM domina
with the computer industry. Now, everybody in the comp
take account of Microsoft. In hotels, Hilton, Marriott and Holiday Inn domina
in the USA whereas Forte and Meridian were dominant in Europe. In international telecommunications, AT&T was a dominant global player with a
particularly strong brand in the USA, whereas Europe has been dominated by
domestic telecommunications groups such as Deutsche Telecom, France
Télécom, and BT. However, in international telecoms, WorldCom has become a
player in just a few years, although it had a severe setback in 2002 when its
accounts were found to be flawed. In Europe, the scene is still dominated by
the domestic PTTs (state-owned post office and telephone systems). However,
the mobile operators, particularly Vodafone, are beginning to challenge the
fixed line company positions. In automobiles, General Motors (GM) has had a
dominant position in the USA and around Europe (under various brand names).
It is closely followed by Ford. However, GM's more than 50 percent share of
the USA market has decreased to just 33 percent in a decade, with mainly
Japanese and German businesses stealing GM's market share, together with
their American competitor, Ford, undergoing a resurgence. Almost certainly
this industry will continue to be dominated by these two major brands, together
with one or two Japanese brands such as Toyota, Mitsubishi or Nissan, and
Germany's VW and BMW probably also surviving as global players.

Between 1950 and 2000 the world has become increasingly dominated
by large global and national brands. At the beginning of the 21st century,
with lower barriers to entry in many industries, increasing availability of
capital and increasing dispersion of technological know-how, we are

t trends. Many more industries are polarizing into
ation by a few leading market share businesses (as just
ultaneously, new opportunities are emerging with the web-
tion in communication and distribution. Thousands of new
s are taking the opportunity to start up and try to compete with
er businesses which have become complacent in their mature sec-
This is creating great opportunities for fresh, new entrepreneurs to
velop niche markets in regional, national and global industrial sectors.

However, there will be a contrast between very large corporations using economies of scale to maintain their size-related advantages compared to small enterprises using nimbleness and energy to compensate for their lack of scale. The large organizations will have the disadvantage of overhead and administration costs which come with the difficulties of administering a large operation; the smaller businesses will have the disadvantage of often fighting for scraps from the giant's table. Occasionally, the small operator will win in the marketplace and begin to develop its own advantages and disadvantages of size. For example, consider what happened to Apple Computers as it became a large corporation in the 1990s. It failed to adopt the policies and norms of management of a large corporation. Because it persisted in trying to run itself inappropriately with the management tools of a small business, it lost most of its market share and its lead as an innovator in computer architecture to its competitor and eventual master, Microsoft.

Every industry has leading exponents of the skills of that industry. Somehow, these businesses are able to make more money out of the same turnover or have lower costs than most others of the same size. It is vital to study those competitors and understand the source of their competitive edge. The words I hear most frequently from losers in any industrial battle are, 'Those fools must be losing money if they are selling at those prices.' I have found from my experience as a consultant to 'the fools' who were losing money that they were almost always making more profit at the same price than the competitors who thought they were fools. Few people or organizations are prepared to lose money when doing business. Some, with extremely long-term strategic vision, are prepared to lose money for a short while, but only in order to gain strategic market share. The plaintive cry that 'they must be losing money at these prices' really means, 'The world is unfair – they are more clever at this business than we are!'

For example, the cable industry in the UK has been losing money for over a decade. It is prepared to make these losses because it foresees a bonanza once the enormous investment costs of installation have been recouped. People in the industry have to hope that the external circumstances do not change too much and that they will be able to make their profits eventually. However, if satellite technology develops interactivity capacity and can squeeze more lines on its bandwidths, the cable industry may be denied the profits it currently sees coming its way.

The first question any good strategic analyst should ask when the 'strategy workout' first begins is, 'Who makes profit in this industry or business and how?' Compile a list of the different branches of the industry and business. Some of these will be profit makers while others just cover their costs; frequently, there will be others which lose money. What is the source of profit? Why are some winning and others losing? What accounts for their ability to make money? The answers will always be different but there will be a pattern. Some will be achieving their profits because they get better prices from customers than others. Why? Do they get richer customers? Does their brand represent better value to their customers? Are they buying their goods or manufacturing them at lower prices than your business can? Do they have a special agreement with the suppliers? Are they getting advantages from import duties or have they discovered a lower rate of tax which gives them a permanent advantage? For example, how many people know that goods imported into the UK which are guaranteed to be 'antiques over 100 years old' attract an import tax rate of 5 percent compared to 17.5 percent for exactly the same goods which are not guaranteed to be in that 100-year-old age bracket? Some countries exporting goods to the USA are allowed special low rates of duty because the US government has decreed that they merit special help to overcome specific disadvantages. Why would a wholesaler buy from another country when they can bring the same goods in cheaper from a favoured manufacturing nation?

When doing your preparation for the workout, be sure to have a clear list in order of profit merit, from best to worst. For example, a typical list for a business in the transport industry would be that set out in Table 3.1.

Table 3.1 Example of profitability in the transport industry

Business type	Profit margin %	ROCE† %
Logistics management	7	30
Warehouse management	6	25
Vehicle management	5	20
Management of drivers	4	24
Contract hire (vehicles)	4	14
Contract hire (people)	3	18
Warehouse space	3	10
Truck rental	3	8
Engineering service	2	14

These figures are illustrative and are not intended to reflect reality in this particular market
†Return on capital employed

Obviously, from the details of Table 3.1, any business in the transport industry would want to move its main source of revenue into the 'logistics management' sector. Many firms in the industry concluded that if they added the word 'logistics' on the side of their trucks it would enable them to make increased profits. Naturally, as most of them did nothing to increase their skills or competencies or to learn more about how to provide 'logistics management services' to their customers, the main effect of their changes was to increase profitability in the truck painting industry. (This subject is covered in greater detail and depth in Chapter 8.)

The prime question should always be: 'Is the business capable of moving to new, more profitable sectors of the industry? Does it have the know-how, will and cash to develop or buy what's missing?' It will depend on the condition of the business whether the organization chooses or is forced to stay in the poorer profit sectors. Furthermore, the difficulties of exit will be key. That is described next.

A key factor governing industry profitability is whether it is easy to enter the business or difficult to exit. To concentrate on entry first, businesses or industries which are easy to enter are normally less profitable and offer low returns on capital. Ease of entry implies that it does not take much capital to start up in that industry; the technological barriers are low; the human skills required are not complex; or,

> *A key factor governing industry profitability is whether it is easy to enter the business or difficult to exit.*

finally, there are no legal barriers to entry (for example, no patents guarding the right to make a pharmaceutical product).

For many years the easiest form of business to enter in the UK was retail confectionery, tobacco and news agency. Consequently, these small businesses had low margins and were run by (frequently) unskilled entrepreneurs. Gradually, throughout the last half of the 20th century, corporate multiples bought up the prime sites in that industry, which has matured into an oligopoly led by companies such as W. H. Smith. Unfortunately, W. H. Smith forgot it was a conglomeration of small businesses. It tried to turn its small stores into large, high street retail outlets. This turned it into a business which had lost its mission in its customers' lives. It had, by the end of 2000, spent several years attempting to find a new strategy.

Another cause of low profitability in industries is the difficulty of exit. This often refers to heavily capitalized industries, where firms have very large amounts of capital tied up in single process machinery that cannot be used for other purposes. The cost of scrapping such large amounts of capital is so high that it is easier and more economic to continue to run at a loss than take an expensive write-off and exit from the industry. The effect applies, however, to almost any long established business with any property assets held on long-term leases. The premises tend to be more or less customized to the specific business's needs. The greater the cost of conversion of the premises to suitability for other industrial uses, the higher the exit barrier.

Some industries are differentiated between countries. For example, distribution systems are rarely the same from country to country. It is vital to understand how your industry differs in other countries if you are intending to undertake international expansion. Often a skill or advantage that you value least in your home market is exactly what is prized abroad. For example, Unilever sells soap in India off the back of trucks as a cash business. This is not much different from methods it dropped in Europe 50 to 70 years ago.

Similarly, there will be areas where a firm has a leading edge in its domestic market which it believes will simply transfer abroad. But the leading edge may turn out to be commonplace in the targeted country, at least in an oversupplied sector. Alternatively, the organization's skills may be seen as too innovative in the foreign market and it would probably cost too much to persuade the new market to accept a different approach.

One of the great fallacies in strategic analysis made by American businesses wishing to enter the European market is the belief that Europe is a unified, integrated market of 350 million people. Federal Express and several American banks have come to Europe with that misplaced concept. Their argument is that if they can run an integrated operation for a population of 280 million in the USA, then an integrated firm looking after the 350 million population of Europe can achieve even better economies of scale and returns on investment. In fact, Europe, even with the European Union trying to make it a single economic entity, is not an integrated market but is highly differentiated from country to country. The differences are caused by language, legal systems and cultural inheritance. Consequently, operators like Federal Express found it very difficult to come to terms with the apparent economies of scale which the European market seems to offer, but which are just not there in reality.

Some European enterprises have made a similar mistake in the opposite direction, believing that America is one integrated market with a common English language or that the USA is so large that any good idea will make money there. In fact, every North American state has its own traditions and distribution systems, as well as idiosyncrasies of language and law. A car can be sold in New York or the Midwest which will be illegal in California because of California's tight emission control laws. Food additives which are permissible under European legislation may be inadmissible in the USA. Above all, employment conditions in both Europe and the USA differ from country to country and state to state. Dixon's, a leading retail supplier of electrical and photographic products in the UK and France, took over an American chain of electrical goods shops, brand named 'Silo', which its leaders thought was involved in a similar industry. Dixon's skills in the UK are discount retailing, branding and controlling distribution chains. It found that few of its UK skills were transferable and it began to lose money to an extent that was becoming a haemorrhage. It had to take a large loss on its investment and exit with its tail between its legs from the USA, retaining but a minority share in Silo Holdings.

Even more serious is the way in which some European business leaders underestimate how sophisticated and skilled some of the apparently rough and ready American business methods are. For example, the property development industry in the USA makes many of its profits from the accumulation of financial advantages over many years from special local and national laws governing the rates at which buildings may be depreciated. These concern different lengths of lease, the type of body owning the assets, special transfers of ownership between different legal entities and the opportunity to develop different heights and sizes of buildings based on agreements with planning authorities about public spaces and improvements to localities which save the local government from providing similar landscapes. It takes many years of study and sophisticated development before one can compete with property developers in the USA even though it looks to be a simple economy of scale competitive environment, viewed from 3,500 miles away in London or Paris.

Federal Express

Federal Express has built a USA-wide business with a hub and spoke system, providing an express small parcel service overnight from any part of the States to any other part. It flies all its goods on its own planes into the hub in Memphis, Tennessee (chosen for its excellent flying weather). They then fly everything out the same night to every city and town in the States and finish the delivery by truck. Federal Express came to Europe thinking that a similar hub and spoke system would work for Europe. It even hoped for greater efficiency as it calculated that the European market was larger than that in the USA. Unfortunately for Federal Express, Europe is not one large nation like the USA but a collection of highly individual nation states which have many means of not cooperating, no matter what European Community law dictates. After a few years trying to make the UK the centre of a European hub, Federal Express had to exit from the UK with an exit loss of over $80 million, as well as accumulated losses of many millions more. It continues to trade country to country in Europe but has, for now, been forced to forego the dream of a European replica of the American system.

Politics in any country normally reflect the social trends being adopted by the population in general. After all, politicians are only selling people's hopes back to them, in return for the right to exercise political power over the voting population. It is therefore vital to be thoroughly aware of the social and political trends which could affect your industry. Social trends, such as the aging of the population, an increase in demand for a pollution-free environment or a social ethos demanding more ethical behaviour toward employees and customers, are merely the more obvious manifestations of political legislation reflecting social demand and fashion.

Furthermore, social trends and political legislation can become tools available to the organization as a means of achieving strategic intent. Persuading politicians to pass legislation to set standards and rules in an industry is one of the tried and tested methods of eliminating weaker competitors from the marketplace. It is a practice often engaged in when an industry enters the high growth phase of the battle for market share (see section on product life cycles on p. 37). Most fast growing, emerging industries indulge in such behaviour.

Once an industry becomes mature, we often find that the survivors are particularly adept at influencing public and political opinion. In Europe, the pharmaceutical industry has traditionally been adept at lobbying. In the USA, lobbyists for the car industry are renowned for their capacity to achieve legislation which raises barriers to competition.

Further reading

R. M. Grant, *Contemporary Strategy Analysis*, Blackwell, Oxford, 1995

G. Hamel and C. K. Prahalad, *Competing for the Future*, Harvard Business School Press, Boston, 1994

P. Q. Quinn, *Intelligent Enterprise*, Free Press, New York, 1992

F. Trompenaars, *Riding the Waves of Culture*, Economist Books, London, 1993

THE EXTERNAL ENVIRONMENT WORKOUT

What are the most important economic factors in the organization's domestic market?

1 _____ 2 _____
3 _____ 4 _____

Where are the business's most important markets?

1 _____ 2 _____
3 _____ 4 _____

What are the most important economic factors in those markets abroad?

1 _____ 2 _____
3 _____ 4 _____

Who are your most important spheres of political law making and lobbying?

1 _____ 2 _____ 3 _____

What are the most important political factors likely to affect the organization?

1 _____ 2 _____
3 _____ 4 _____

Which legal factors affect or could affect the organization?

_____

Which laws would you want to see enacted which would most benefit your organization's competencies?

1 _____ 2 _____
3 _____ 4 _____

Which current demographic trends may affect the organization's workforce?

1 _____ 2 _____
3 _____ 4 _____

What are the trends in demand for the organization's main services or products?

1 _____ 2 _____
3 _____ 4 _____

Is there any key political legislation which could affect your industry (industries)?

1 _____ 2 _____
3 _____ 4 _____

Studying the competitors

Introduction

Competitor analysis became almost a generic term during the 1970s and 1980s to replace the more complete strategic analysis which the rest of this book outlines. Some other writers on strategy include competitor analysis under the 'general external environment' analysis. I consider it important enough to merit a separate chapter on its own.

The analysis of who you consider your competitors to be can also define the industry and business you think you are in. Thus, if you are in the insurance business, but only look at broking companies, then you are really defining yourself as a broker, not an insurer. Similarly, if you are in the business of air travel in and around Europe, you may choose to consider your competitors to be just the other airlines working the European routes. However, if you define your business as 'the service of getting people to and from different points around Europe', you will have defined yourself as belonging to the transport industry in Europe. You will therefore look at competitors supplying services by boat, train, road and rail. Every one of these can deliver the service of getting somebody around Europe who needs to travel. Once you have done this you can consider properly the criteria on which the real industry is competing. That is 'the service of enabling people to make timely and convenient journeys'. Thus, for example, once the Channel Tunnel was complete and people could travel from the centre of London to the centre of Paris in three hours or less, it behoves the airlines to find some ways to minimize the time getting to and from airports, as well as the delays from arrival at airports to actually travelling. Those elapsed time periods mean that plane travel between London and Paris has, in fact, become slower than train transport.

If you are considering a strategic transformation of your business to a new industry, then you should be able to name the organizations with which you will compete in that new sector. The competitor workout at the end of the chapter will show you whether you really understand that industry and its key players, at the company, business and industry level. Do you know them as deeply and profoundly as you should if you are about to enter the industry? One of the more difficult concepts to measure in business is the value of 'the experience curve'. This is the valuable know-how that businesses accumulate as they gain experience within an industry. Often business leaders underestimate what their employees know in their operations. Even more dangerous is underestimating what you do not know, especially when moving into a new industrial sector. Consider the transformation of GEC, the UK-based defence industry specialist. As its new leader, Lord Simpson, transformed it into a telephony specialist he should perhaps have asked himself why so many telephony business leaders were so willing to sell him their businesses at inflated prices. The vital clue that he missed was that they knew the industry might be heading for some setbacks. Even if they did not know, the assumption that the defence industry could prepare GEC to compete effectively with businesses which had long experience in the fast moving consumer goods (FMCG) business that mobile telephony had become was supremely inane.

One of the sillier mistakes that many organizations make about their competitors is to underestimate how good they really are. Competitors don't become bad just because your leader excoriates them. Contrariwise, they are rarely as formidable as one's wildest dreams suggest them to be. All surviving businesses have good qualities and weaknesses. None is paramount forever. In the 1970s in the UK it was thought that the German economy would rise forever. But it didn't. In the 1980s it was thought that Arab oil wealth would enable them to buy every valuable piece of property in the USA and the UK. It didn't and they couldn't. They eventually ran out of money and even had to sell some estates back. Equally, in the early 1990s, it seemed that the Japanese and the Asian Tiger states were invincible and would drive out all manufacturing skills and growth from the advanced industrial states and impoverish them. Their impetus blew out and their inexorable forward drive halted. At the beginning of the 21st century it seems that China is in an unstoppable ascendancy. China is a large, entrepreneurial and great nation. It could easily become greater than the USA and dominate the 21st and 22nd centuries in economic power and influence. Let's wait and see. The point is that all economies and all businesses have

their great eras and their weak ones. In competitive spirit terms, a good rule is to have enough respect for all competitors to take them seriously and not underestimate them. But neither should you *over*estimate their skill, power or prowess. They all have their Achilles' heel and will weaken one day. Just ensure that your business is

> *One of the sillier mistakes that many organizations make about their competitors is to underestimate how good they really are.*

in a strong enough position to take advantage of their weakness when they do falter. When they do lift their Achilles' heel and render themselves vulnerable, be ready to attack the weakness with a suitable strength from your business's armoury. If you attack merely with a neutral skill or an inappropriate one, you will fail to win the competitive strategic battle.

Most organizations have areas which they consider to be sacrosanct, where they are not prepared to give ground or allow competitor intrusion under any circumstances. If you wish to attack a competitor, it is wise not to arouse that competitor's most aggressive competitive spirits by invading its particular, sacrosanct territory. If you do decide it is appropriate, then it should not be an accident. When attacking especially sensitive strategic territory, it should be a deliberately aggressive act. You do it when you consider your organization to be so strong that you choose to deal your competitors a psychologically mortal blow – and you should be utterly sure it will be a knockout! If they have a high market share, attack on price. If their brand is their salvation, attack on service. If their manufacturing skill is their strength, find a killer innovation. Look at Dyson vacuum cleaners. James Dyson attacked the generic brand leader on the effectiveness of their product – with a totally innovative way of delivering the same cleaning effect with greater power. When they copied his designs he sued them in the British courts and humiliated them. They were not allowed to copy his designs and had to revert to their inferior technology. It is unlikely Hoover will ever recover. However, they still retain a great generic brand. If their leadership were wise, they would either buy a licence from Dyson or invest in massive R&D to find a technology which they can patent and protect which begins to deliver as effective a cleaning capacity as Dyson's products.

As one of the first steps in your competitor workout you should be able to name the top few performers in the industry in which you are competing or wish to compete. By and large, the top one or two will be well known, but do not ignore numbers three and four, especially if you are not among them. For example, in the grocery industry in the UK most people would name Sainsbury's and Tesco but what would be your guess for numbers three and four? In the USA most people would say IBM is still the leader in the delivery of computer hardware and among the leading players in the delivery of computer software. But, who ranks next? Is it Dell, Compaq, Apple or a host of generic Taiwanese and other ASEAN states manufacturers? By the way, take note that Jack Welch, in his famous autobiography (2001), always instructed his executives to aim for the number one or two position in any industry they competed in. If they could not manage that, he would threaten to sell the business off. He was right. Those are the only positions worth holding because they usually are the only ones that make decent levels of profit.

The global entertainment industry is particularly fascinating at the beginning of the new millennium, because it is becoming one of the world's largest industries. Businesses within it are merging, devolving segments, forming new alliances and searching for opportunities. Each business is deciding on its specific range of interests in the creation of entertainment and other media materials, in the ownership of the means of distribution (cable, television, cinema, satellite) and in the need to achieve geographical coverage of some or all of each of these aspects of the industry. For example, Rupert Murdoch, a global mogul and owner of News International, a media company, has decided to specialize in one form of distribution (satellite) but is trying to do it in every geographical segment of the world. He is also specializing in two segments of infotainment (information and entertainment), i.e. production with newspapers (Australia, Europe and the USA) and film production (Fox Studios in the USA). This makes his businesses difficult to compete with because he is strong in every aspect of the media industries. Furthermore, he has established a reputation for strong and aggressive tactics, with high levels of skills in lobbying and relationship management with political leaders all over the world. Anybody in any part of the media industries must take account of News International, wherever they are established.

An organization does not necessarily have to be a leader in its industry for it to be important at national level. Thus, although the organizations just cited were, by dint of their global size and reach, leaders in the computer industry in the UK and abroad, Amstrad Computers was for some time an important UK national player in the provision of personal computers to the British retail market. Similarly, British Airways (BA) was, for a while, a large player in the international air travel market. It had several national level competitors, each of which may be important on only a few international routes. For example, British Midlands is a national player, with just a few international routes. However, BA has to decide whether British Midland expanding into destinations around Europe is a specific threat which needs dedicated competitive action. Defining who the important national players are and profoundly understanding their competitive profile is important. ValuJet is a UK-based air journey business based on low costs for low prices. It started life as a national carrier but has rapidly moved into the European market, gaining market acceptability. This has forced BA, the UK-based global airline, to respond with its own 'no frills' economy line. BA now has the problem of running a service-laden, high-price/high-service airline in one part of its business together with a contradictory, low-price/low-service airline in another. Which culture will prove to be the stronger? One possible outcome could be BA's reversion to the high-price/low-service air carrier it was in the 1970s.

In all circumstances organizations are much more important than any individual within them. This is more true the larger the organization grows. Nevertheless, one should also recognize the importance of specific individuals in some organizations or industries. In some industries particular individuals are gifted, dominant and dangerous. Recognition that they dominate their industry is probably a sensible approach to analysis. It is important to know these dangerous people, both for their aggression and their intelligence. You may decide to work in ways that do not draw their attention towards your organization. That is usually the wisest course of action. You might attempt to buy them onto your side by offering them tempting positions in your own business. Whatever strategic approach you choose, it is always dangerous not to recognize them or take their predictable attitude into account. And if you attack them competitively, it is usually wiser to do it quietly and surreptitiously.

> *In all circumstances organizations are much more important than any individual within them.*

Most national and international organizations take their strategic decisions on the basis of objectives such as market share domination or lowest price operator. They sometimes forget that local markets can be dominated by small regional enterprises with important local skills. Local companies may be better connected to local infrastructures, have better access to more resources, know the local politicians and/or journalists better or merely have a local reputation which is more important in the region than the national or international brand which the larger company may use to dominate most of its markets. It is important, at the very least, that the local managers of the larger companies be aware of the local enterprises which are firmly established in their own regional territory.

The many sources of competition

The home base of the most famous writer on competitor analysis, Michael Porter, has long been Harvard; his most circulated book *Competitive Strategy* (1980). His analysis always advised strategists to focus upon the 'Five Competitive Forces'. The first and keenest competition comes from all the other organizations recognized to be competing within the industry.

There are three further sources of potential new competition. The first comes from those businesses which are already customers of organizations in the industry and which might be tempted to try to buy their suppliers or create their own supply service (usually because they believe their supplier is making too much profit). This is known as **integrating backwards**. A typical example of this would be Sainsbury's or Tesco in the UK integrating backwards and managing their own goods deliveries or buying and running their own farms to cut out the farmers' profit from their business equation.

A second source of new competition could come from current suppliers to the industry. To continue the last analogy, a haulage or logistics company could find itself competing against truck manufacturers. This, in fact, happened during the recession in the early 1990s. Truck manufacturers, which had the manufacturing capacity to produce a high number of trucks (no matter what the demand curve), entered the haulage industry to develop a commercial outlet for the trucks which they were unable to sell directly to their customers in the logistics industry. This type of strategic behaviour is known as **forwards integration**.

Third, one has to look across the entire commercial horizon for competitive danger and scan the entire business environment for any operator which might want to enter the industry. There is a vast amount of **spare capital** sloshing around the world all the time at the beginning of the 21st century. Any good business idea will find capital funding. There are also many mature, high-profit companies which are accumulating cash faster than they can invest it in their own industries. Such companies, with large cash balances, are loose cannons and could enter any growth-oriented industry they choose.

For example, Microsoft, now a global computer software business, has accumulated so much wealth (in 2001 it was holding around $30 billion in cash), that it has bought stakes in businesses in cable hardware, property, internet and film industries. Even if it doesn't stay in them all, it can use its capital and its shares (which have a higher value than most competitors) to buy into almost any business or industrial or service sector it wishes. Even if it bought mistakenly, it could also create havoc before it exits from any position it decides not to persist with.

Similarly, in the United States, AT&T and the Baby Bells, spun off after the breakup of the monopoly in the 1980s, had positive cash flows of several billion dollars a year. Many such organizations are using this cash to enter the 'megamedia' industries of the 21st century. Consider what AT&T did to the cable industry at the end of the 1990s. It has been unsuccessful in breaking back into the local telephony markets that were controlled by the Baby Bells. It decided that a valid strategy to get back into that sector would be buying cable businesses which had local loop technology for the delivery of entertainment. In addition, such tactics would also get AT&T into the emerging internet and new media industries it found more appetising than 'old economy telephony'. Unfortunately, after it had spent over $100 billion buying Media-One and Liberty Media, it found itself in considerable debt and discovered that these businesses did not have the right technology for AT&T to do what it wanted with them as local loop telephony supply mechanisms, until and unless it spent some further $10 billion and two to five years improving their networks. That was enough to break the camel's back and the mighty AT&T was reduced to selling parts of them off again to fund its normal business development.

Most organizations with spare funds are likely to:

- purchase businesses which they perceive to be making excess profits
- move into industrial sectors where their core competencies can be exploited to take advantage of growth opportunities
- buy businesses which add synergy to their strategy.

Competitiveness within industries

Rivalry within an industry comes from many sources. It may be because the industry is very young and the future dominant firms have not yet won their market share or found the specific source of competitive edge which will ensure their dominance in the future. Rivalry often persists in an industry which has low technology or technology which cannot be protected by law (where the designs are not patentable). Rivalry also comes where the distribution system is open and available to anybody at low cost. Rivalry can be reduced by making the business's products or services more unique, branded or effective, in the minds of its customers/clients. For example, there is almost certainly little real difference between brands of clothes washing products. Yet their proprietors spend large proportions of their revenues each year trying to convince their customers that their product washes whiter, cleaner, or with greater luminosity, sometimes maybe even with a bluish whiteness (something that most users are anxious to avoid – it usually means that a colour has run).

Competitiveness in an industry is increased if there are few barriers against other new suppliers entering the industry. This may be because distribution channels are easily available or as a consequence of similarity between products. If there are many suppliers in most countries of the world it increases competitiveness. Likewise, if the components of the product are widely and easily available. It is a pity that the few countries in the world that can produce cocoa do not form a cartel because they are woefully underpaid by their customers who make huge markups of profit on the basic raw material when they retail it in the sophisticated outlets of North America and Europe. Compare that to the few oil-producing

Competitiveness in an industry is increased if there are few barriers against other new suppliers entering the industry.

states in the world which have learned to achieve agreement on controlling supply and thus maintain high levels of revenue and profit while extracting less of their valuable raw material than their customers would like.

Sometimes industries are more competitive because customers can move backwards or forwards along the supply chains if the suppliers ever become too greedy and demand excess profits. A simple example would be that people could easily buy fabric to make their own clothes if retailers overcharged. More likely, in that industry, would be the entry of new suppliers from other markets to supplement or replace any retailers that had gone off the boil. Thus, Marks & Spencer, which had an enormous share of the UK retail clothing market, lost out to Matalan, a rival retail group, when their clothing became dowdy, unattractive and too expensive.

How can you build barriers against substitution? Every business needs to fight continuously to build barriers to copyability and substitution. Sometimes this involves making the product a fashion item with changing styles every few months or years. For example, the camera industry has become fashion conscious. Customer preferences change from small to bulky cameras. They have moved, with computer chip technology, into the digital age and many cameras now offer quality procedures and finishes that were only previously available to professionals. Of course, this good news for the camera industry has been bad news for small suppliers of print and artwork as this can now be accomplished within businesses' own marketing departments rather than put out to a small art and design business.

The last source of competition comes from the threat of substitute products. In a new age of technological innovation, no product or service is immune from the threat of substitution, even when a business thinks that it has a patent to protect its unique features. Pharmaceutical companies are notoriously litigious in their attempts to protect their patents. However, their competitors frequently find some substitute to compete with the best selling products of their rivals.

In the USA, Wal-Mart appears to have merged the skills and techniques of the best retailers and physical distribution businesses. Others will find ways to replicate what it does and offer a substitute. Microsoft appears to have created a virtual monopoly with its 'Windows' architecture for personal computers, but its monopoly will be broken one day, by a substitute product. It is inevitable when a business is evidently making high, virtual monopoly profits, that it will attract rivals who wish to share or grab its excess profits. Microsoft is currently fighting a battle in the US courts to protect itself from those competitors. They assert that Microsoft is using its wealth to destroy rival products' chances in the marketplace – even giving away like-for-like products to prevent rivals from getting a grip in Microsoft's market.

You will see at the end of this chapter that the workout consists of two pages. The first covers the content of this chapter under the heading 'competitor analysis'. The second is headed 'individual competitor profile' and will enable you to test your understanding of particularly important competitors by completing a workout audit of a few simple details about them. You should complete a separate 'individual competitor profile' sheet for at least the top four performers in your industry, whether you are international, national, regional or local.

The questions in the competitor workout are simple. However, you might be shocked when you discover how many of these simple questions you may not be able to answer accurately. In that case, you should take the trouble to research the details, either from the competitor's annual general report, in-house knowledge within your organization (particularly from your representatives and salespeople) or from other sources in the industry, within local or national government records, the academic world, the news media or professional data providers.

It is advisable to keep the company's competitors records fully and continuously updated. A key feature of this part of the workout is knowing the competitor's leader. This does not automatically mean the chairman or the chief executive. There may be other influential people in that organization who are affecting its strategic direction. This is why you should know their psychology, vulnerabilities and whether they are satisfied with their current position in the industry. If they are going to take new strategic initiatives, you need to have considered what they are likely to be. Even more importantly, you ought to know what that most influential person cares about most deeply. Armed with that knowledge, if you are going to make any strategic moves, you will be able to predict whether and how your competitor is likely to retaliate.

Finally, you always have to make judgments about your competitor's most important strengths in its business approach to the industry. You also need to know what your competitor's most important weaknesses are. If you are going to mount a strategic attack, it should be aimed at exploiting those weaknesses rather than combating the strengths. The general rule is that an organization should only show strategic aggression when it is sure to win – and preferably against the weaknesses, not the strengths, of their competitors.

A successful example of this behaviour was the attack by BIC, a French firm which specializes in 'throwaway' everyday goods, such as pens, lighters and safety razors. It attacked the American market for cheap razors, much to the annoyance of the mighty Gillette, which dominated the American razor market. Gillette threatened to start making cheap pens to flood the French market. It was an idle threat. The real retaliation came when Gillette launched its own version of a cheap throwaway razor, which it then introduced to the European market. However, BIC has remained the dominant supplier, based on its special competence in making relatively low quality but fair value-for-money products.

A less successful example of such an attack was that of Amstrad Computers in the market for personal computers in Europe. Amstrad never understood the need for quality and professional backup in the PC market. Consequently, it was unable to sustain its attack and after a short-lived success was beaten back from the market by much more customer-oriented manufacturers, wholesalers and retailers such as Compaq, Apple, IBM and other low price but adequate, Far East 'own label' suppliers.

When you have completed the competitor analysis for your organization, think about what your competitors would write about your company if they were doing a similar analysis on you.

Further reading

M. E. Porter, *Competitive Advantage*, Free Press, New York, 1985

M. E. Porter, *Competitive Strategy*, Free Press, New York, 1980

P. Q. Quinn, *Intelligent Enterprise*, Free Press, New York, 1992

J. Welch, *Jack: What I've Learned Leading a Great Company and Great People*, Warner Books, New York, 2001

THE COMPETITOR ANALYSIS WORKOUT
Current industry competitors

Under each of the following categories, put in the names of companies or people where appropriate. Regard this as a simple measure of your knowledge of the industry.

Which are the top performers in your industry?

1 _____ 2 _____

3 _____ 4 _____

Are there any other important national competitors?

1 _____ 2 _____

3 _____ 4 _____

Who are strategically the most dangerous people in competing organizations?

1 _____ 2 _____

3 _____ 4 _____

Which are the important regional or local competitors?

1 _____ 2 _____

3 _____ 4 _____

Which are the current customers most likely to integrate backwards?

1 _____ 2 _____

3 _____ 4 _____

Which are the current suppliers most likely to integrate forwards?

1 _____ 2 _____

3 _____ 4 _____

Any organizations that might enter the industry?

1 _____ 2 _____

3 _____ 4 _____

THE INDIVIDUAL COMPETITOR PROFILE WORKOUT

Complete one of these for each important competitor mentioned in the previous workout.

What is the competitor's company name?

What is their annual revenue? Their annual profit?

What is the name of the competitor's leader?

What is their psychology?

_____

Is the competitor satisfied with their current position in the industry? Yes/No

If not, what strategic moves do you think they will make?

_____

What action from your organization will provoke the fiercest retaliation?

_____

What are the competitor's most important strengths?

_____

What are the competitor's most important weaknesses?

_____

5

Market and business analysis

Introduction

Before I started my career as a strategic adviser to corporations, I had spent many years starting up and running my own small businesses. I thought that experience would be of little use in my later career as a university teacher and strategic adviser to large corporations. Actually I was mistaken. It was highly valued by them. It took me many years to realize why.

I was fortunate, from early on, to have an instinct for knowing how to find profits from business situations and transactions. That same instinct was to prove invaluable on the large scale, advising large corporations. The same capacity for finding profits of a few thousand pounds in my small businesses worked just as well, following PhD training at the London Business School, to find profits and business opportunities at the multi-billion and multinational level in gigantic corporations. I was surprised that the same rules applied – it was just the scale that was different. Furthermore, I realized that very few leaders or senior managers possess this instinct. The process which gets them into leadership positions is usually based on their capacity to get a group of people and resources organized to achieve strategic instructions, not the process of creating or finding profitable opportunities from given situations.

This chapter is my attempt to help the strategic thinker to put his mind through the processes that I use by instinct to try to find opportunities for profitable situations for clients. It should also enable a strategist to check when the business s/he is analyzing has lost its way or its market position. At the corporate level, there are always divisions fighting for limited resources. Running the constituent parts of the business through the processes outlined here will enable the reader to ensure that the organization's scarce resources go towards the parts of the corporation which are likely to use them most profitably.

Industries and markets in general

Porter's competitor analysis (in Chapter 4) began the process of understanding the markets your business is involved in. The analysis can be used to examine the market circumstances of the business in general. However, I prefer to look at markets as a concept in themselves. This enables a rich set of concepts and views to be examined which may, eventually, when looking at strategic opportunities, suggest new avenues of growth and alternative uses of the corporation's wealth.

Which industries are making large profits?

Industries which use brain power and ideas tend to make more profit than those which use brawn and pure physical muscle. For example, at the simplest level, the earth-moving equipment industry, in general, makes lower levels of profits than does the oil line industry which uses small machines and sophisticated analysis of computer data to help fuel supply businesses find new sources of supply. This profit level is helped by the fact that one firm, Schlumberger, an oil industry service giant, has developed a whole series of technological breakthroughs which enable it thoroughly to dominate the market and charge monopoly-type prices to the few world class competitors left in the oil industry. One should note that all Schlumberger's customers are more than big enough to develop comparable technology for themselves. But because

> *Industries which use brain power and ideas tend to make more profit than those which use brawn and pure physical muscle.*

Schlumberger provides such high standards of excellence and strives continuously to retain its competitive edge with high expenditure on R&D leading to continuous innovation, it is just not worthwhile for oil majors to integrate backwards and grab Schlumberger's business while it is being sold to them so effectively and efficiently.

Barriers to entry and exit

The first important filter in any industry is the barrier to entry and exit. What are the important aspects of an industry which prevent others from getting in or current businesses from getting out? For example, if one wanted to enter the automobile industry, one should take into account the cost of setting up a dealership or dedicated distribution system because all the current competitors in that industry have signed exclusivity deals with their current retailers. The cost of entry to the industry of automobile retailing used to be so prohibitive it could not be contemplated by any business other than with the backing of an already established and successful manufacturer. In fact, with the onset of the internet it has become possible to have direct selling arrangements with retail vehicle customers which not only circumvent the difficulties of retail systems but also enable the client to order exactly what they want with all the various extras directly from the manufacturer. This may represent a major opportunity in that industry – or it would if it did not still require a major brand to begin to fight in the industry as well as a distribution system.

The reason why some organizations stay in an industry is because they cannot get out. There are simple economic models which explain this diagrammatically (see Figure 5.1).

Some businesses in particular industries have high exit barriers built into the nature of the industry. Some come from being locked into high property costs, perhaps an excessively long lease which cannot be sold on to another business. Another barrier may result from having to equip the building in a special way which prevents it from being used by other businesses without large expenditure for refurbishment. For example, consider trying to use an electricity generating station as a retail grocery outlet. It might be in the right geographical location but it would take an immense amount of rebuilding.

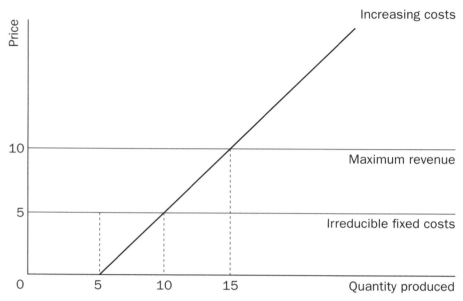

The business is locked into losses of 5 units
Between 0 and 5 units of production it should just pay out the costs and await bankruptcy if no other matters change
Between 5 and 10 units it pays to produce, even though it still loses money but not as much
Between 10 and 15 it makes real profits right up to 15 units of production
Over 15 units it starts losing money again because it costs more to make than it can sell for

Figure 5.1 Breakeven and exit cost barriers

When a business has been around a long time, it may face prohibitively high costs of exit if it wishes to make its people redundant (in Germany and Sweden this is very expensive even when the business has not employed people for very long). Other, increasingly high built-in costs may lie in long-term contracts to pay for fixed minimum licence or rights costs whether or not the customers exist.

For example, News International, Rupert Murdoch's business vehicle for his satellite television business, gains much of its revenue from supplying its cable industry competitors with channels of software such as films, cartoons or news. They agree to pay for a minimum number of customers (usually a fixed percentage of the potential total). Thus, if NTL (a leading cable television business in Europe) could have, theoretically, 10 million customers, they agree to pay Sky Television for a minimum of 80 percent of those 10 million customers at 5p a customer a week. This minimum applies even though NTL only has a 30 percent penetration of its customers base. At its simplest, it is paying three times for every real customer it has. Sky's argument in favour of the deal is that this is the only way to force NTL, its customer, to try to increase the number of viewers which means that both NTL and Sky can then sell their advertising at higher rates because more people are watching the television. Astonishingly, the cable companies agree to these extraordinary payment systems. It is possible that this has not a little to do with the fact that there is practically no other source for many of the programmes they want to transmit. For example, Sky has virtual monopolies on many sports, films and cartoons.

Barriers to entry over long periods can also be the source of high profits. The barriers to entry change over the life cycle of an industry. At first they may consist of technical knowledge as the first suppliers in an industry hold patents or conduct the R&D on the service before the business begins. A classical example of this was Xerox in the photocopying industry. Later they lost their first starter advantage to Canon. Similarly, EMI, a media business, was the first with body scanners, a major medical breakthrough. Ultimately, when a business stumbles across an invention which does not lie within its own area of customer expertise it would be well advised to look to a partner with specialist knowledge of the appropriate industry to help it take advantage of and maintain its competitive edge.

One of the greatest sources of profitability in any industry lies in its capacity to control competition through legal barriers such as obtaining a patent or a licence to run a limited supply of a particular service. For example, the right to broadcast on the ITV channels is sold off by auction every few years. Companies wishing to be in this industry have to calculate how much profit they might make from holding the licence and how much they are prepared to work for (in terms of the level of percentage profit). Their bid will be a function of this equation. Sometimes the government (if they are in charge of the auction for the rights) have to judge the veracity and potential success of a bidder. For example, in the last round of bids to run the National Lottery in the UK, Richard Branson was part of a team which put in the highest bid. He asserted that his group would not take profits, unlike its competitor bid. But, even if one took seriously their claim that they would plough back all the profits they made, Branson still had to make a judgment that they would run the lottery as efficiently as their competitor, Camelot. But the government decided that Camelot, the commercial bidder, would still raise more funds for charitable purposes, even if it did take a profit, than would Branson's group, even if it did not!

Distribution channels

Control of the means of getting any part of the production chain from one place to another is always a source of great potential profit and a barrier to entry. When Cadbury-Schweppes, a leading UK drinks manufacturer, wanted to enter the US market for soft drinks it found it impossible to get around the distribution channels that were tightly controlled by Coca-Cola and Pepsi. Ultimately, it had to agree to set up a joint soft drinks distribution system in the UK, known as Coca-Cola Schweppes, in order to persuade Coca-Cola to allow it some distribution in the USA.

With the advent of the internet, many changes are taking place in distribution channels. However, although the effects are revolutionary, they are not always evolving as predicted. For example, in retail grocery, it is proving hard to persuade people to change their ways of buying food. Further, the economics of home delivery, which the internet makes theoretically possible, are massively high. How many customers will be willing to pay the real price of home delivery is not yet calculable. It may be that the industry will use the internet in some other delivery mechanism to reach a compromise with costs shared between the customer and the supplier. What is obvious to the supermarkets is that if they do not discover and get ownership of the new distribution channel they will be in danger of allowing a newcomer to enter their industry and possibly steal forever some of their long-term and devoted customers.

Many industries feared the effects of the internet because they could not predict how it would affect their distribution channels and what it might do to their long-established relationships with their suppliers and channel managers. Many businesses in the retail sector particularly feared that many of their customers might switch overnight to ordering all their purchases through the internet and never go again to a mall or a retail high street. In fact people all over the world have proved to be more conservative in their willingness to change as well as more cautious in the way they spend their money. In the earliest days of the internet people thought that all branded and therefore safe and predictable goods would emigrate to the internet in their distribution patterns. That has not happened. People still enjoy the shopping experience. It is now realized that people gain a social value from shopping as well as their enjoyment from the act of purchase and the prize of ownership of the good. It is going to take a lot longer than the few years of internet we have experienced up to now to see what goods people are willing to trust to previous knowledge and buy 'physical sight unseen' and which they wish to see, feel and touch (and therefore not entrust to the anonymous internet) before they purchase.

Large and small industries

There are specific aspects to every industry which govern its size and profitability. For a start, one must ask whether the industry delivers an important service to its purchaser and whether it represents an important and valuable part of their expenditure. For example, housing, vehicles, food and clothing are fairly key personal expenditure items. It is a remarkable fact of evolution that societies which have become rich and sophisticated place less importance on their purchase of commodity foods and far more on their expenditure on refined foods and 'serviced food purchases' such as meals in restaurants or food brought to their home already cooked and prepared. In many societies certain industries tend to be controlled, regulated and sold in the public sector, such as roads, rail travel, water supply, waterways, electricity and gas supply. The arguments for this are multifarious and debatable. For strategists the importance is noting which sector purchases in each separate political system and the different rules which are applied in each. For example, in many Far Eastern states it is perfectly normal and morally acceptable to pay introduction and arrangement fees to third parties for enabling a corporation to meet the right people in the public sector or government offices who can actually give and sign the purchases. In the USA this is regarded as a form of bribery and corruption and is expressly forbidden in law and practice. Although all American companies try to adhere to the letter of the law in this regard, almost all of them have had to find some means of circumventing the law when trying to do business in states where such buying manners are practised.

Different countries and groups of countries evolve in utterly surprising and unexpected ways. In England antiques and old homes are highly prized. In France it is the new and modern that is more esteemed by most people. In the USA people are willing to move state and home searching for work and lifestyle at any time. In Western Europe people move far less frequently and prefer to stay fixed and even unemployed rather than leave home and go looking for employment. The Indian government insists that all foreign businesses must have an Indian partner who controls and owns a majority of the shares. In the USA, in most industries any nationality can own as much as they want unless it is related to the media or defence industries. In those cases positive discrimination by the government agencies in favour of American incumbents still resolutely takes place.

Factors such as these may control the relative size of any industry. The patterns of evolution govern more tightly the relative profitability of an industry. For example, how competitively did market share evolve? Some industries are natural monopolies or oligopolies such as large-scale commodities (gas, electric, water and fuel). Every government has choices about whether it wishes to have just a few or only one supplier in those industries and how it wishes to regulate their levels of profits. In too many African nations a natural monopoly is just an invitation to a relative of a politician to maximize wealth for the personal gain of the family. In other countries, for example Western Europe, almost no competition is allowed in a few state-controlled businesses, such as small letter and parcel post, terrestial television or road construction and maintenance. Often the state retains control over the industry through strict regulation and (when it is owned by the state) profits are repatriated into central government funds. In Eastern Europe, there is a longer tradition of state ownership of natural monopolies. These are gradually being privatized but not regulated as strictly as in their Western European counterparts.

Capital requirements and cash flows

Industry size is, to some extent, measured in terms of the capital requirements of participants in the industry. Large-scale industries require huge capital. Only the larger scale corporate setup will deliver the necessary levels of capital and organizational structure to deliver the long-term objectives. For example, one cannot quite imagine the 'small electric turbine' being a valid concept in America or Western Europe. Even miniature steel plants are big. Other industries grow larger in market scope and scale through time. For example, colour television has become far more widespread throughout the world. Further, in sophisticated markets, customers often have several sets, one for each important room in their home and often one for each child too. Although it atomizes their family viewing it purchases peace in a household.

Quite often the cash flows of any particular industry are separate and different from its capital requirements. Although the subjects of capital and cash are entirely idiosyncratic to themselves, they are intertwined in that they can affect each other powerfully. When capital requirements are large, it is often because the industry requires infrastructure before it can actually raise any cash. This concept is easily understood in terms of, say, the rail transportation industry, where you cannot run a train for cash inputs until the vast outputs to pay for a rail, signalling and safety system are installed. In the cable industry, one has to lay down a great deal of fibre underground, set up 'head ends' to transmit the programmes for the television channels in the homes of customers, purchase expensive software (films, sports events television rights, etc.) and manage a timely marketing campaign to customers before any revenue can be expected. However, once the cash does start to flow, there are many positives to its nature. The cash flows in from such a business on a weekly and monthly basis. Many customers pay deposits which are held at the company's discretion. All this cash flow may bear little resemblance to the system of payments. For example, one can only settle payments for use of other telecommunications telephone lines after they have been calculated every three months. The residues due to the supplier of software are usually only paid annually. Similarly, suppliers of IT services, marketing, billing and other 'business-to-business' services can usually be paid on commercial terms after 60 or 90 days.

Industry levels of profitability

A factor which controls the profitability of an industry is the product's relative importance as a contribution to the total product or service being consumed. For example, the price of parking in a railway station car park is relatively inelastic because the much larger purchase is usually the train ticket. The parking price may grow quite disproportionately to the train ticket for years. Similarly, if the product represents just a small part of a much larger industrial process. One client of mine made inordinate profits for many years as a specialist dyer of cottons and threads for the weaving industry. The cost of his small part of the total production process was minor and formed a very small percentage of the total. Consequently, by giving good service and no cause for the clients to look elsewhere, he made exceptional profits for many years.

Cash flow affects an industry substantively. If cash flow is highly positive, one can often use the cash to reduce debt or even to make loans and indulge in new strategic options akin to banking. In the USA Sears Roebuck built a large banking business on the back of its positive cash flows from retailing which resulted from the industry terms of trade requiring payment long after the goods supplied had been sold. This applies to many retail businesses. However, it also has applied to large manufacturing businesses. Ford, the global car manufacturer and GE, the global defence, electronics and media conglomerate have both built large credit and loan businesses from the strength of their positive cash flows.

It is worth noting that the older the business, the better the cash becomes. The first years of most businesses are spent building infrastructure, obtaining expensive buildings, accumulating capital machinery and developing a human resource capable of creating and delivering the services and products the business wishes to provide. As these capital requirements diminish, cash starts to flow more easily and more of it remains within the coffers of the business.

Room for a tiddler?

Although many industries are naturally big, there is often room for a specialist tiddler – a small business which carves out some niche which it makes it own. In the UK furniture industry Ercol did that with plain country-style cottage furniture. MIT has done it in combining engineering and business education. In automobiles, for many years, Land Rover did it in four-wheel drive vehicles. In shoes, in the USA, Allen Edmonds have done it in high quality footwear. In Italy, Ferragamo have done it in ladies' handbags, scarves and shoes. All have become large businesses. The niches that these tiddlers have carved out are nearly always based on high quality products, backed by a brand which personifies the product and which becomes part of the product itself. For example, Marks & Spencer, a leading British retail business, established a niche position in high quality prepared foods against a massive dominance of the food market by two duopolistic market leaders, Sainsbury's

> *Although many industries are naturally big, there is often room for a specialist tiddler*

and Tesco. It managed to achieve this highly profitable niche by investing in high levels of R&D to develop unique products. It branded them so well that people were using the brand to market themselves. Thus they would invite people to dinner. On arrival they would say, 'I was too busy to cook from raw materials. So I spoiled you by buying the best ready made food from Marks & Spencer.' It also had the happy subtext that it implied that they were also so successful they could afford to spend on their guest and buy the best and the most expensive food. Of course, Marks & Spencer were the happy recipients of this 'up-market chattering class self-approval'. Every business should be asking itself, strategically, is there a further niche for us? Is there some market sector or segment we are missing? If there is, and we don't occupy it, will it be the thin end of some newcomer's wedge?

Quality management doctrine evolved as the determination to maintain continuous improvement in all processes within the business. There is no end to the process and task of continuous improvement and keeping the competitive edge well honed. Strategic intention nearly always includes some time and effort on price competitiveness and control. That is an aspect of quality and continuous improvement.

When assessing the industry a business belongs to, a strategist has to ask whether the business either needs or wants to stay in the industry. There is no rule which says one is locked into a particular business or industry forever, no matter what the influence or traditions. Arie de Geus showed that the most long-lived organizations were not wedded to the idea that they have to stay in any particular industry. The owners of such organizations felt more a sense of duty to their staff and their customers than they felt to 'the market' or 'the industry'.

Of course, before you exit any market it is advisable to have some strategic idea where else could you go. Consider the example of Graham Wallace, who, at the end of the 1990s, became the leader of Cable & Wireless Group, a UK-based telecommunications and network business. He recognized that telecoms shares, like those of his own business, were at a peak in 1999, 2000 and 2001. He therefore, astutely, sold off many of his corporation's telecommunications assets at very high prices. Many of the purchasers of his redundant companies later deeply regretted their purchase as PE ratios on telecommunications companies halved and halved again. Yet Graham Wallace kept building his cash mountain. He had also developed a real alternative strategy as he told it. He was going to enter the internet protocol wholesale network supply business, as well as provide telephony networks for business customers. However, by 2002 it was becoming evident that the reality of market scenarios for these businesses was not developing as quickly or as profitably as predicted and that they might not be as lucrative as expected. Business-to-business markets are rarely lucrative – the business leaders who buy in them are usually too astute. That meant that Graham Wallace's chosen new vision could not use all the cash and capital he had stored neither had it the potential to replace the high profit businesses he had exited. The clamour for him to hand some back to the shareholders became overwhelming. Thus, the freedom he had gained by getting cash in hand when almost no other businesses had foreseen the opportunity was lost.

Industry longevity

Every product has a natural life cycle which can last from a few weeks in the case of 'fashion' toys for children's markets to centuries in the case of, for example, the television market or telecommunications. Business strategists have to ask themselves what time scales suit their mind and their organization's skills and competencies. A terrible example of a failure to do this was witnessed in the case of GEC, a UK-based multinational defence industry specialist. The essence of the defence industry is that it makes products for large and rich organizations like national armies and governments. Lord Simpson was appointed its leader following a long reign by the previous incumbent, Lord Arnold Weinstock. In his strategic wisdom, Lord Simpson decided that the telecommunications industry looked more enticing than defence, largely because, it would appear, it was popular and fashionable among the young tipsters on the stock exchanges of the world and among the merchant bankers (who, of course, made a great deal of money taking their potential purchases to him for perusal). Lord Simpson decided to exit the defence industry and move into the telecommunications supply industry. To do this he had to buy businesses which were then highly fashionable and, consequently, expensive. This meant that he had to pay high prices, unlike those he achieved for the businesses he sold. Worse, he spent cash to buy the telecommunications businesses rather than issue shares. However, the more appalling mistake was not to realize that in the defence industry contracts last for many years. Rainy days are forecastable many years ahead and can be avoided and prepared for. In the telecommunications industry forward contracts are for a maximum of just three months. The contracts are easily rescindable and they are in the hands of ordinary members of the public, not leaders of government agencies who tend to take decisions in much longer term horizons than retail consumers. The cash flow effect of the difference is vast. When the telecommunications industry slowed down in the year 2000, it took just a few months for Marconi (as GEC had become known) to catch pneumonia, run out of cash and became a corporate basket case.

Competency management and extension

Any business which wishes to survive must acquire the special competencies and core skills that it takes to meet minimal requirements to satisfy customers. For example, in the restaurant industry, maintaining high levels of hygiene must be a core and vital skill. Any business which fell short on those criteria would necessarily find itself leaving the industry under legal attack or deserting customers. Railtrack, the enormous business responsible for maintaining and renting out track to the various rail passenger businesses around the UK, fell woefully short of the necessary minimum standards for safety and customer care in its custodianship of that regulated monopoly. It consequently handed the political power to the government minister to renationalize the business and destroy the shareholders' value from ownership of a potentially lucrative regulated monopoly.

During his renowned long period of leadership of GE, a global conglomerate in the USA, Jack Welch insisted that every one of the many leaders of the substantial businesses in the GE empire should aim to ensure that all their products or services stood in the number one or number two market share position. If they were not in that position and did not have a plan to gain the necessary competencies to get to that position rapidly, he warned them that their business was likely to be sold off as a 'dead duck' at any time it suited the pocket and cash flow of GE. His strategic logic was impeccable and faultless. I used to advise managers and leaders when I was training them in my earlier years as a consultant that they had to be number one, two or three position in their industry. I was wrong. Welch was right. When any industry is dominated by three major players (or any number above that), only the top two make any level of profits worth having. Number three is always struggling to keep its head above the water. It is always fighting to gain market share, at the expense of profits or revenue or both. If it is not doing that it will be spending capital fruitlessly on R&D or service enhancements which tend only to differentiate and not to win the coveted number one or two slots. The inevitable conclusion must be to get a strategy to be in the number one or two slot within a relatively short and certain amount of time or get out of the business. It is just not worth the long and ghastly pain and agony of being forever the bridesmaid of the industry and never the bride.

Any small monopoly will do

I always expressed amazement when recently privatized industry leaders used to tell me how much they appreciated being out in the private sector where they could encounter competition and use that as a spur to greater efficiency. I always considered that to be a nonsense. Every business, whether large or small, has an inherent tendency to seek to maximize profits. That can be best achieved through monopoly. Monopoly gives the opportunity to maximize any profits available in any industry. When the monopolist is spurred on by the possibility of even greater profits by being efficient and a fear of losing the monopoly if their standards are not kept at the highest levels, then, hopefully nobody will be tempted to try to break the monopoly. That is the essence of the argument put forward by Joseph Schumpeter in *History of Economic Analysis* (1954). Schumpeter hailed monopoly as the great impetus of capitalism.

This argument applies to any business. Whatever the skill range or set of competencies, the strategic objective should always be to use them in as monopolistic a manner as possible. Whatever can render the assets and skills that a business offers more monopolistic in appearance or reality, the greater will be the profit and excess that the goods or services of the business can be sold for. Consider the industry of business consultancy. Why do they all tend to compete by selling the same tools that every other consultancy is fighting with? Those which have evolved new tools to make themselves unique are able to then sell them as the only source. That deserves and achieves excess profits. I always found it astonishing, when competing with large consultancy businesses, that they all offered the same old range of programmes, planning, audits and risk aversion techniques. It is unsurprising that the only source of excess profits for them was the exploitation of their brand, which frequently belonged to their accountancy brethren from whence they sprang. Unsurprisingly, they were as good as their auditor brethrens' most recent lucky escape from scandal and audit failure. One knew that as soon as any of them got involved in a truly large scandal or audit failure, there lay the next big accountancy/consultancy merger. Consider what happened to Andersen's, the global auditing firm, which moved out of existence almost overnight, as it became embroiled in the scandal of poor, if not derelict auditing, of Enron, the global American-based energy business, which went bankrupt in the first quarter of 2002.

Product ranges and natural mixes

The concepts about organizational competencies mentioned earlier relate equally to a strategic understanding about what extensions to current products and services are feasible, sensible and fitting. One accumulates competencies through the accretion of know-how, contacts, distribution channels and relationships with sellers and employees. One also assembles relationships with buyers and knowledge about the types of further products or extensions to current products they might buy. In the 1990s many banks realized that they had a subgroup within their general customers who were wealthy individuals who might buy different products and services from them, if they assembled the correct mix of managers and services for those clients. Unfortunately, most commercial banks had so lost the concept of high quality customer service that they were quite unable to provision the market they had identified.

Service and market extension can also go spectacularly wrong. During the 1960s and 1970s the UK-based Saatchi brothers slowly and painstakingly built up the world's largest advertising empire. They carefully extended its scope into many rational strategic niches, such as buying advertising airtime on television channels. By amalgamating all their own and other agencies' buying power under one specialist buying agency they were able to exercise extensive buying power over the advertising media sellers and also capture extra profits for their own business as they retained a slice of the reductions they secured on behalf of all the buying agencies' clients.

Unfortunately, the Saatchi brothers lost the plot in terms of how far their strategy of providing agency services might be extended. They had taken advertising further than any other agency had ever gone before. They advised the Conservative party in Great Britain on how to win elections by understanding what people really wanted to hear from politicians and by carefully analyzing people's fears about the competition that the Labour party represented in the electors' minds. It seemed a short step from such clever analysis of buyers' minds to analyzing the whole business of their clients. That meant a logical step into business consultancy and advice about the total business. From there they made the next radical and deadly thinking progression that said, if we can advise them on everything, why not run anything? It's surely all just a matter of 'management'? So they bid for the Midland Bank, which looked cheap at the time. It was one strategic move too far. Analysts realized that the brothers really saw no strategic limits to what could fit synergistically and what made no sense at all. They became a 'sell' recommendation on most brokers' lists and their empire went into steep decline. Eventually they lost control of their business and had to start again. The next time they adopted a strict policy of 'stick to the knitting'.

Businesses in particular

Up to here in the chapter I have focused on industries in general. From this point I will home in on particular aspects of businesses that are especially important in the process of strategic analysis.

Relationships with political organizations

It is never too early for any business to get connections with local political organizations which are relevant to its business interests. This may apply at the local, national or supranational government level. Such relationships have very few negative connotations. But they always have large positive potential. For example, at the local level, you never know when you might need help with planning permission for an extension to your business. At the national level it is good to know which civil servants or government ministers are in charge of the law, administration or regulation on all matters concerning your industry. When these people are looking for knowledgeable people to advise them on new regulations for the industry, they can only ask the people they know. That means they will ask you or anybody in the company you wish to nominate. Much regulation of global and multinational businesses is taking place at the international level of continental political alliances. In Europe the influencing body is the EU (European Union). In the Far East is it is the ASEAN (Association of South Eastern Nations) and in the Americas it is NAFTA (North American Free Trade Agreement).

It is unhealthy for your business to be meeting officials in these bodies for the first time when you are asking them to approve a takeover or merger which has political, competition or monopoly potential or dangers. Even a highly competent leader such as Jack Welch, the recently retired boss of GE, the American conglomerate, failed to persuade the administrator in charge of competition regulation in Brussels on behalf of the EU to allow him to complete his last takeover before retirement.

Service and service element additions

Within any particular industry there is always the strategic possibility of extending the service levels or building in performance factors which will differentiate your product from its rivals and persuade your customers to accept higher prices for better value. It is astonishing that so many businesses expend valuable capital buying new businesses or products they know nothing about when their time and capital would be far better used thinking more about the products they have already. For example, Amstrad, formerly a leading supplier of electronic gadgets in the UK market, later moved into computing and later still to telephony. Although the business achieved high levels of market penetration at the beginning, it always looked for new products to launch rather than improving the quality and service of the ones it had established. Consequently, the brand became devalued and was treated with suspicion by consumers on most of the products that the company tried to launch.

It is equally important to remain focused on any aspects of uniqueness that are already established within the products and services under your control. Although the rules of continuous improvement should always apply one must never forget what persuaded customers to buy the products or services in the first place. IBM became the generic and leading supplier of information technology devices because they listened to what customers wanted and supplied them. When the customers began to tell them that they wanted small desktop computers IBM, for the first time in its history, told the customers that IBM knew better. They almost lost all their business because they didn't. The BBC, Britain's unique high quality radio and television broadcaster, has been doing the same thing to its Radio 4 customers for some time. They are fortunate that they have a virtual monopoly. The customers would have moved to the competition much sooner if they could find an opposition to move to.

Almost as important as guarding your uniqueness is to protect any scarce resources you possess. These may consist of a unique distribution channel to important customers. You may have an important geographical location that customers have become accustomed to over a long period of time. You may own a freehold property which enables you to lower the nominal rents you charge to your accounts, for example, when it suits the business to lower costs during times of recession or high competition, or just to be flexible and able to quote lower proposals to customers when its suits the business to do so. Sometimes your unique competitive edge resides in the form of human resources. For example, you may have the best managing director of research leading the research division of your multinational pharmaceutical company. Look after him or her carefully, protect them fully and generously. If he or she leaves, not only are you losing your best brain but also the competition is gaining it.

Protection of integrity

Many years ago, when I was first teaching this workout system to senior executives at British Telecommunications, I always asked people attending the seminars what they thought was the most important asset of the corporation. Many answered 'the telecommunications network'. Others responded 'the local telecommunications loop'. A few, who had understood that businesses needed to be focused on customers said 'it's our customer base'. I used to tell them that I thought it was the high level of their reputation for integrity. I reminded them that many of their operators, engineers and other staff had access, through the nature of their business, to the most important secrets of customers' personal or business lives. If British Telecom ever lost its reputation for honesty or its integrity, its very survival could not be guaranteed, even in the short run.

Although integrity is obviously vitally important for a company that has access to so much confidential material the argument applies equally to every business. Once your customers decide you cannot be trusted they will always be cautious about anything you might wish to sell them. Consider all the customers for pension plans who bought from Equitable Life, the UK-based life assurance firm which discovered it had miscalculated the cost of its promises to its customers over many years. Consequently it had to ask the courts of law for permission to go back on its promises to its customers. The judges refused, thus forcing the leaders of the company to put it up for sale to any bidder they could find.

> *Once your customers decide you cannot be trusted they will always be cautious about anything you might wish to sell them.*

Psychological imprisonment

For many years I have bought all my socks from Marks & Spencer, the UK retailer. I have probably been doing that for at least 35 years. Possibly my mother was buying my socks from their stores many years before that. A few years ago I noticed that socks were wearing out much more quickly than they used to. I stopped buying them at Marks & Spencer. For about three years I looked around for an alternative regular and reliable supplier of good quality cotton socks. I never found another store that seemed reliable. I did once buy a pair from another shop. Although the socks were good I never went back to buy more. More recently, fortunately, it seemed to me that Marks & Spencer socks had regained a look of quality. I trusted them enough to buy another six pairs of my favourite navy blue cotton socks. The reliable high quality of socks at Marks & Spencer had made me into 'a psychological prisoner'. In other words, I would almost rather do without fresh supplies of socks for many years than face up to the task of breaking free from the habit of buying quality and reliability which was built in to the behaviour patterns of my body. That made me a 'psychological prisoner'.

I mentioned earlier the natural tendency of business leaders to try to make his or her company into a virtual monopoly in order to maximize profits. It is equally important to make all your customers 'psychological prisoners'. To do that means developing a dependable balance of qualities within the product and its surrounding services. It applies to the man delivering on time, serving the goods pleasantly, reaching continuously high standards and the best value for money you can profitably supply.

Once your customer has become accustomed to your quality they will become addicted and psychologically unable to begin the search or indulge in any needs to find similar products elsewhere. With your customers as psychological prisoners your future is guaranteed.

Sunk costs are a concept which strategists take from economics as a valuable insight into lost opportunities and possibilities which must be abandoned. Every business undertakes journeys along wrong paths. It is the nature of strategy and business that the future never works out as one predicts. The expenditure of investment capital must be considered as sunk costs when you have realized that strategic path is going nowhere. These are irrecoverable expenditures. Letting go of past expenditure when it is getting you nowhere is very difficult. One always feels, psychologically, that some good must be dragged out of the bad investment. Sometimes the costs are all completely wasted and no good will ever come from that source. Letting go is hard but essential. Hanging on, trying to make the lost sunk costs into useful inputs, is a total waste of time. Even worse is the waste of even more money for no good. Learning to let go of sunk costs is an important strategic behaviour.

Barriers to entry

Legal protection of entry systems are the best guarantee of protection from competitors. If your legal protection is comprised of a legally enforceable patent or is guaranteed through the ownership of licences from a government body which has banned full competition then, as long as the regulations allow good levels of profit, your business should have a licence to print money. It is rare that governments or regulators allow such uninhibited profit making. However, as long as the business is allowed reasonable flexibility in the way it charges its investment costs and appreciation of capital, then it should be possible for the business to demonstrate reasonable profit margins to the shareholders while keeping the regulator satisfied that excess profits are not being made.

Branding is another technique to prevent competitors entering the industry against you and your business. It takes time and much investment in both product development and intelligent marketing to develop a brand to a level where it is good enough in itself to dissuade people from competing against your business. But it can be done. Consider, for example, brands such as McDonald's in fast food, Marlboro in cigarettes, Sony in the electronic gadgets field, Kodak in camera film, CNN in instantaneous television news, Kellogg's in breakfast cereals, Rolls-Royce in luxury cars or Tiffany's in high class jewellery.

Finally, the barrier to entry that is easiest to underestimate and the most powerful in terms of its effect upon the cost curve of those that have it is the value of the **experience curve**. What is it and how does it work? When a business has been around a while it gradually learns more and better how to do what it exists to do. A simple example illustrates. Most people, when they first learn how to drive, find it difficult and tiring. After a fairly short time they pass their driving test and find it easy and relaxing to do what used to tire and worry them. That goes for every job in any business. It is known as the experience curve. Some academic studies have shown it to be as valuable as 40 percent to 60 percent off the starting costs of any production process. In other words, any product which used to cost 100 units to manufacture will, with experience, cost only 60 units within a given period of experience. The existence of the experience curve is something that new entrants often fail to take account of. That is dangerous to a newcomer because the cost of acquiring an experience curve is incalculable. Once it has been acquired by the business it offers a permanent advantage. It can be applied equally to services as to products, to retail as well as to manufacturing and to any aspect of business life. It explains why so many apparently sleepy old firms go on existing forever, seemingly without trying. They get to a stage where they don't have to try any more. They know how to get it right so easily, they always offer near perfect service or product.

Further reading

J. Schumpeter, *History of Economic Analysis*, Allen & Unwin, London, 1954

THE INDUSTRY ANALYSIS WORKOUT

Is your industry large or small scale?

_____

If small, can you see a clear route to transform it to a larger scale?

_____

What products or services command the highest profits in your industry?

_____

Are there any barriers that prevent you from entering that market area?

_____

If so, what are they?

_____

Who controls distribution channels in your industry?

_____

If it's not your business, how will you ensure you get or maintain control?

_____

Does your business have access to sufficient capital to grow into number 1 or 2 in your industry?

_____

Is cash flow positive or negative? If the latter, can this be changed and how?

_____

Where are the niche markets in your industry?

_____

What would it cost to leave the industry?

_____

Is your industry long or short lived (in tens of years)?

_____

**Does your business have all the necessary competencies to compete
successfully in this industry?**

_____

If not, what skills do you have to acquire and how?

_____

**How will you enhance your strongest selling products/services to increase
their potential profitability?**

_____

**List the key political figures and senior administration bureaucrats your
organization has access to**

_____

**What is the value of the experience curve in your industry to the best
business in it?**

_____

**If that is not your business, how long will it take your business to achieve
similar levels?**

_____

What is your psychological hold over your customers?

_____

**If you do not have a psychological hold, what _should_ it be when you get
one?**

_____

6

Organizational self-analysis: strengths, neutrals and weaknesses

Strengths, neutrals and weaknesses

SWOT analysis is one of the best known tools in the strategic or market-ing tool bag. Almost everybody seems to know the phrase and many use it. It stands for:

Strengths
Weaknesses
Opportunities
Threats.

There is one problem with this analysis. In spite of its beguiling usefulness, it is just a bit too simplistic to be of profound value. It may be a particular problem when it is used by strategists. The tool is usually used by applying the **opportunities** and **threats** analysis to the external circumstances of the business and the **strengths** and **weaknesses** descriptors to examine the internal skills of the organization. The method can give a fast insight into the external and internal environments which affect the organization in terms of strategic opportunities.

I believe that the simplicity of this dichotomous way of analyzing the world can be misleading in its lack of refinement. It tends to make the world look black or white and it may be inappropriate to take strategic decisions on that basis. I therefore recommend a slightly more complex way of conducting the internal audit of the business. This can be achieved by adding an extra line of analysis under the label 'neutrals'. This is an entirely novel way of analyzing the SW part of a classic SWOT analysis. It is, therefore, a small claim of originality by the author that one of his key contributions to strategic theory has been to change the concept of SWOT to SNOT (or, to be technically correct, SNWOT).

Why bother? Because many businesses find that among their weaknesses may well be one skill or quality which they need to use as a critical success factor in pursuit of their strategic thrust. For example, many business leaders nowadays believe they could not run their business properly without an effective information technology system. This can be particularly important when a company has set an ambitious growth strategy. The IT systems will be vital to measure sales, marketing effects, revenues recorded, customer segment types, predictions about the business environment and so on. When one asks most business leaders whether they believe their IT to be of world class standard they respond that they do not believe it is.

If any particular strategic thrust of the organization is dependent on the information system being world class it is even more obvious that the organization as a whole needs a more sophisticated set of criteria when deciding its strategic direction than just strengths or weaknesses. I also recommend, when analyzing the internal skills range of the organization, that the headings **strengths**, **neutrals** and **weaknesses** be further subdivided into five subsections headed A, B, C, D and E with A as the best and E the worst in each section. Thus an E on a strength column will be very close to an A on a neutral. This makes a relatively simple categorizing tool into a sophisticated instrument of analysis. Although one should never use any weakness as part of a strategic growth objective one might consider using a B neutral if one had the luxury of a few months to try to make the neutral into a strength and then build on that.

How can the addition of one extra line add so much to a comparatively simple analytical tool? Because it removes the possibility of a classic mistake that many executives make when devising the strategy for their business. It may be clear to them that the organization is weak in a particular skill which is vital to the successful achievement of the strategy. They, therefore, 'wish' the weakness into a strength. Thus executives often find themselves including a weakness as a key part of the strategic plan, even though this may cause the whole strategy to fail. For example, one should always consider that all the Ds and Es in the weaknesses column are major points of reference for strengthening and improving and should never be left in that condition. Look at the following brief case study.

ABZ Truck Rental: turning a weakness into a defeat

ABZ was a market leader in the truck rental business in the UK. However, it had poor information technology systems and mainly used a manual system. Its managers knew that a simple business such as truck rentals should be able to take advantage of computerized booking and administration systems which were commonplace in slightly more complex businesses such as airline ticketing. Unfortunately, the leaders decided to develop their own 'in-house' software rather than buy it as a ready-made package. Seven years and £20 million later, ABZ had failed to install a single information technology (IT) system; its competitors, such as Ryder and Transfleet, had caught up and were overtaking it and its market dominance was gone.

Seven years earlier the strategy had included IT excellence as part of the assumptions for the strategic plan to remain market leader. The premise that with good IT they could dominate the market and grow, was false. It was only with improved customer service they could really expand and dominate the market even more than they did at that time. That mistake led, inter alia, to the corrosion of the whole strategy. First, they threw money at the IT problem, money which which was entirely wasted (because they did not know enough about IT to know how to spend their money); second, they could have chosen a different, more apt, set of criteria on which to base their growth (like customer service training and better quality trucks); and, third, they lost seven years during which their competitors lapped up all the growth which ABZ could have had.

Competencies and deficienc

In academic circles there is some debate whether the con
tional competencies was first put forward by James Quin
Hamel (Hamel and Prahalad 1994). However, it's the n
useful. Every business has accumulations of knowledge ar
long-term advantages and insights that are particular to that
leaders and its workers. The accretion of these competencie   ..most
invisible and takes place over time.

Competencies often develop unseen and do not appear on the
balance sheet. For IBM it became summarized (in the 1980s), with the
expression, 'Nobody ever lost their job for ordering IBM computers.' In
the air travel business, Boeing has grown dominant because it knows
how to extend standard models safely and to secure imaginative
finance packages for its customers. In accounting software, SAP grew
to global dominance because it had a pure competence in tailoring
its system to any client's particular needs. In global merger and
acquisition, Goldmann Sachs became dominant because they knew
better than others how to find, reward and motivate the best personnel
in an industry which is uniquely dependent on the quality of the
people employed by the merchant banker.

Strategists need to define carefully their organization's particular
competencies as well as understand those the business will need for it
to win in any new markets or ventures they recommend. This also
applies to the problem of deficiencies. Missing competencies, which
may be vital for the achievement of any particular strategy, can be
regarded as deficiencies. They have to be eliminated by acquiring
people who carry those skills with them, by outsourcing or by taking
over another business which has them. If one follows the latter route,
the acquiring business will also need the competence to manage a
takeover without destroying the essential qualities and values of the
business it is taking over. It could be that the reason it is a deficiency in
the first place is because the culture of the acquiring firm destroys the
very competence that is being acquired.

Benchmarking

Over the last 20 years many of the best firms have set up a benchmarking capacity. By this means they measure themselves against the highest standards in their or any other industry. Benchmarking can be used to measure anything from capacity for people development to people turnover; from accountancy skills to revenue per capita. To some extent it could be said that what a business measures will be what a business becomes. (It will certainly be what its managers pay attention to.) Many traditional airlines measure themselves in terms of operational efficiency in the use of their airplanes and rarely in terms of their customer satisfaction. It should not have been surprising when an old airline invented a new way of looking at its industry: that was Scandinavian Airlines (SAS), which measured its effectiveness in getting customers to their destinations on time, something they discovered passengers cared about a great deal. Suddenly they shot from mediocre to world best in customers' satisfaction terms.

It is surprisingly easy to acquire the right benchmarks to measure the business and its people against. Nowadays many governments are organizing the collection of data across industries and can make the benchmarks available. Similarly, industry federations and similar organizations within the industry can furnish the numbers against which everybody can compete. Chambers of commerce and world trade organizations also often arrange the collection of valuable data about industry standards.

To summarize the best benchmark concepts briefly, they are about the organization's leaders' and managers' determination to measure the business's standards against the best in order to set the firm on a path of continuous improvement. Whenever it appears that the organization is reaching any goals, they are strongly advised to move the goalposts rather than allow the danger of complacency to set in. If the business fails to make substantial progress against its benchmark criteria it has to brainstorm and find new methods of attacking the problem rather than assume that it is the benchmarks that are wrong.

Information technology

Information technology is a common weakness. Of course, those ABZ managers were not fools. Neither are the many hundreds of leaders and managers who have tried to build strategic intent onto their organization's IT weaknesses during the 1970s, 1980s and 1990s. They realized that they had made assumptions that were not based on fact. To compensate, they would throw large amounts of corporate resource at the IT weakness, in terms of both personnel and capital, to try to remedy what they knew was a fundamental flaw in the strategic analysis and their ambitions for the company.

Unfortunately, business weaknesses do not change that easily. If turning weaknesses around were just a matter of throwing money at the problem, no profitable businesses would ever go wrong. What tends to happen is that weaknesses develop over time and go on being just that – a fundamental weakness in that business's skill range. Why? Because organizations, like people, get so used to compensating for their weakness or coping with the consequences of their frailties, they forget what a smooth running organizational strength would feel like. For example, in the ABZ Truck Rental business mentioned earlier, I was doing a tour of a branch where the new IT system had been installed. I noticed that the clerk was still filling in the old paper record books when the new computing system could be used to hold all the records instead. I asked her why. She responded, 'Well, the computer system does not really work properly. If I complained I would be told that I'm not really trying. So, I complete the computer system, even though it distorts and loses the data. But to ensure I really know how many trucks I have available and where, I carry on doing it by hand in the old paper bookkeeping system.' Thus a new, supposedly labour-saving IT system has actually resulted in an increased workload rather than the contrary. Why? Because the company's communication and listening skills were so poor that they would have reprimanded her rather than congratulate her for telling them the truth about their appalling new system. The executives thought they would rather listen to the consultants and advisers who were installing the system at enormous expense to the business. Eventually that business failed to hold its UK domination and was sold off as an unnecessary and non-core business.

The wider lesson is that when businesses make the key mistake of basing their new strategic thrust partly on a weakness (in IT or any other) the overall strategy is bound to fail. That is why the simple but necessary addition of a 'neutrals' line to the strengths and weaknesses analysis is vital, together with this absolute rule:

When deciding the strategic thrust of a business, it must never in any way be dependent on turning around a weakness in the organization's skills base. At best, it can include one neutral skill and then only if a credible plan to turn that neutral rapidly into a strength has been prepared and the resources necessary to achieve it voted into action.

This simple but vital rule has saved the strategies of many companies. The weaknesses of most organizations do not arise overnight. They develop because the organization has always neglected a particular area or just never managed to understand that subject. We have mentioned IT already, but there are many other areas that some companies get wrong continuously. Some never master the art of selling. Their products may be so good they sell themselves. But if the company had selling skills, it could be twice as big. Other firms always lag behind in research and development (R&D). They copy other businesses when they issue new models or technological improvements, but they are never the first. Yet for many years the Japanese thrived by copying any innovation developed in the USA or the UK.

Weaknesses are endemic in most organizations and they are very difficult to change into strengths. Indeed, the best that a business should hope for is to turn its weakness into a neutral. Even then it may take a considerable period of time. Similarly, it is possible to turn a neutral into a strength but, again, only with great effort and a considerable amount of time and, often, capital.

The implication of this rule is that a strategy can only succeed if it is largely based on the recognized, real strengths of the business. When it is based on a weakness it is highly likely to fail. Even when based on a neutral, there should be a realistic plan in place to turn that neutral into a strength.

Turning around weaknesses and neutrals

Most businesses underestimate how difficult it is to improve weaknesses and neutrals. Managers do not just ignore the weaknesses. Usually they are aware of them and they often put major resources into improving them. However, there appears to be a psychological effect which results from putting heavy resources into turning around a weakness. Once an executive has committed the resources, it becomes increasingly more difficult to recognize if the effort has had no effect. Organization ABZ had spent over £25 million on the IT project over the course of seven years. It became hard for its people to accept that they had made little or no progress at all. I was brought in because they asked a recently retired executive to appraise their progress for them and he decided it was zero. But, even though he had left the organization and had no axe to grind, he felt it was wiser to have my consulting organization come in to make a truly objective appraisal of the state of their IT (which was appalling) in order to get their leaders to realize they had wasted nearly £30 million and seven years of their time.

Sometimes trying to improve an organizational weakness makes it even harder to grapple with the problem. Subordinates begin to 'rearrange the truth' so their leader does not discover how badly the turnaround is going. Facts get distorted and soon the organization loses track of where it is. Executives then start taking decisions based on false data and the organization's really serious problems begin. One corporate client who sought my advice spends millions of dollars every year investigating customer attitudes toward its somewhat mediocre service. When the results were particularly poor in any one month, the senior executives actually used to give false data to the chairman, rather than show him the worst results. Of course, this also tells us something about this chairman, who obviously exuded more fear than was useful if he had really wished to obtain honest information from his people.

It takes a long time to make a difference

Another equally important reason not to try to incorporate weaknesses as a key aspect of a strategic objective is that managers often underestimate how long it takes to turn a problem around. Most problems take a long time to develop. It is unwise to believe they will not take an equally long time to cure. Often a manager gets moved to another area of responsibility before the cure is effected. The problem then goes back downhill to where it began. Another cause of failure in turning around important weaknesses is that they are culturally based. Unless the culture is changed, the problem will not be solved.

If we continue the IT example started earlier: the first thing most organizations do to change this weakness is to appoint an IT director. He, in turn, will persuade the CEO to put a computer terminal on his desk to show the others that he cares about IT. However, almost nothing the IT director does will persuade the CEO to switch on his terminal, and that is what the CEO's subordinates will notice in the sense of cultural example. They will think that IT is still not important and, therefore, not worth taking trouble to learn to use themselves.

The turnaround specialist

One promising young executive I worked with was put in charge of the turn-round of a £100 million revenue loss-making business. He completed a great brand and name change. He had even analyzed what organizational behaviour changes were needed to ensure the business stopped making losses. But he never had a chance to make it happen. He was promoted to the main board of his business and allowed to leave behind responsibility for the organization he had been improving. Sadly, that business immediately slid back to where it was before he was there. He himself learned a dangerous lesson. He had got himself promoted on the rebranding and the name change – not on a substantive change in the results of his business. He spent the rest of his career replicating the same trick. He went into sick businesses (he claimed to be a 'turnaround specialist'), made superficial changes and moved on. He never made a substantial difference to any business he touched. He frequently left them highly damaged and weakened. As far as I could perceive, very few people (other than a few of his closest colleagues and executives) ever realized how useless he really was.

Internal change should be at the rate of change of the external environment

Some weaknesses are only perceptions. This may have often been the case with IT just discussed. IT has been developing at an astonishing rate for 40 years. The rate of growth has left everybody not intimately involved in the industry feeling that they are out of date every time they invest in any computer hardware or software. Thus, organizations always felt that they were missing opportunities that may never have been real for their

industry anyway. Take another example. Equita⌐
assurance business. It used to be a market leader. Ho⌐
judged guarantees it made during the 1980s to some ⌐
put itself into the dangerous and certain position of ev⌐
was forced to change its entire leadership as a consequ⌐
judgments. The new leadership devised a plan whereby
ing the guarantees were forced either to give them up v⌐
agreed enhanced lump sum in addition to their pensioɪ   ɪisk
putting the entire organization into a position whereby it ⌐ould have to
declare bankruptcy, which would have endangered their holdings far
more. It is not surprising that most voted to take the lump sum and avert
the greater uncertainty. The weakness had been turned into a strength.

If leaders are to make rational judgments about their organization's
weaknesses, they must also keep an eye on the external rate of change.
Most businesses now have the kind of information-monitoring systems
which would have looked highly advanced just ten years ago. This
enables them to understand how the external market, political systems,
competitor firms and innovation rates are progressing. Leadership must
monitor to ensure the business is always progressing faster than the average in their industry and preferably, faster than any others. As always,
the only worthwhile positions in any industry are first or second and the
former is infinitely better than the latter.

Your greatest strengths could be the source of your worst weaknesses

Although we have emphasized the difficulties of turning weaknesses
into, at best, neutrals, the same does not apply to strengths. There is no
reciprocal arrangement. Thus, although you cannot turn weaknesses
into strengths rapidly you can certainly turn strengths into weaknesses
with great ease, in almost no time at all. Look at Enron, going from the
world's leading energy company to bankruptcy in less than a year,
through overindulgence in certain accounting tricks to enhance profits.
Andersen's, their auditors, went from membership of the world's top
five auditing firms to notoriety in three months. NTL, the leading UK
cable firm, went from a $20 billion star on the NASDAQ exchange to

the business to its loan and bondholders in less than six months. Texaco was worth $35 billion just prior to its bankruptcy. Global Crossing became the world's leading cable laying firm by 2001 and went bankrupt from a position of value just a few months earlier of more than $25 billion. Bethlehem Steel Corporation was worth $4 billion just before it filed. In the USA, following the 2001 11 September catastrophe of the attacks on the Twin Towers and the Washington Pentagon, 224 companies worth a combined $180 billion in assets filed for bankruptcy.

L'Oréal

L'Oréal is a French-owned multinational which is a global leader in the beauty care and treatment industries. It has a major strength in its ability to sell, through its sophisticated salesforce. One of its important distribution chains is through high-class hair and beauty salons where it is well regarded because it invests a higher percentage of its revenue in research and development than most of its competitors in the industry.

When L'Oréal salespeople announce a new breakthrough treatment, staff in hair and beauty salons (where L'Oréal first tries out most of its innovative products) buy large quantities on the strength of L'Oréal's previous excellent performance in making innovations in the industry. Occasionally L'Oréal gets it wrong, for example by marketing a product that just does not take as much hold of the public imagination as it estimated. On those occasions it would be easy for L'Oréal's strength to turn into a weakness with salons finding themselves loaded with bad stock that is unlikely to sell.

L'Oréal's reputation would be destroyed and its selling strength would have caused a weakness. L'Oréal is aware of this danger. It has a built-in safety device whereby the marketing department always controls the sales teams. If the marketing department recognizes that a mistake has been made because the sales to the public are not matching the promises of the salespeople to the retailers, then all stocks are automatically withdrawn and credited to their customers' accounts.

Choose internal strengths that are enduringly useful rather than ephemeral

It is important to work on strengths, neutrals and weaknesses that are enduringly important and not ephemeral and merely fashionable. For example, continuously training staff to maintain high levels of customer service and responsiveness is more important than changing the corporate logo or staff uniforms to add a fashionable gloss to staff appearance. The same applies to other ephemeral fashions.

It was fashionable, in the mid-1990s, to 're-engineer' businesses. This 're-engineering process' was being sold as a product by many leading consultancy firms. It was fashionable and may prove in the long run to have created more problems than it solved. Re-engineering solves short-term cost problems. The difficulties it creates are less clearly perceived. Many companies joined in this fashionable cost control short-term solution to poor trading, accepting and believing they had a weakness in terms of excess management layers. The early 1990s recession touched almost everywhere in the world at some time. There were, apparently, too many people in most companies. Re-engineering the business was seen as 'an appropriate thing to do'. It seemed to reduce costs in the medium term. Less obvious was the scar tissue that re-engineering left in its wake, especially the loss of knowledge and know-how among the human resources who were let go and who would never maintain their knowledge or return to the business which had dismissed them. Those cultural negatives would endure long after the benefits of the cost savings had disappeared. The cost disadvantages of the loss of knowledge and loyalty from the human resource base of the business were incalculable.

At the beginning of the 21st century, it would appear that another global recession is taking place. This has been exacerbated as a consequence of the 11 September 2001 terrorist attack on the Twin Towers in New York and the Pentagon in Washington. (We should note carefully that although the recession of 2001 applies to many of the advanced nations such as the USA and the member countries of the European Union, it may well not apply to Russia and China which appear to be relatively uninvolved with the anti-terrorist global war.)

The reaction of many leaders of companies which are seeing recession facing them in 2003 is to undertake similar patterns of behaviour to those they applied in the early 1990s. For example, they are using 'downsizing' as the latest jargon to reduce human resource totals. This is almost certainly an ill-advised reaction to the new recession. Economic history, like history itself, never repeats itself exactly. The basic difference between the previous recession and that in 2001 is that the latter is taking place against a background of low unemployment (rather than high unemployment); it is accompanied by low inflation (rather than high inflation); and there is a global shortage of technically skilled human resources (the opposite was the case in the 1990s). It is therefore obvious that behaving in a similar way in the 2001 recession as in that of the 1990s would be ill-advised. In fact businesses should cut down capital expenditure, marketing costs and reduce international expansion. The best strategic advice in the new millennium recession is not to cut back on people. Indeed, the best policy would be to conserve them in any way possible.

Communications is another constant problem in most organizations. All management questionnaires find communications are deemed insufficient in organizations; a manager can rarely give just the right amount of information to everybody. Different people have different needs, whether it is to carry out their role for the organization or based on their personal preference for more data. Communications also have a habit of becoming distorted as they travel up and down the hierarchy – or even along the ranks (the 'Chinese whispers' syndrome).

The best advice on solving organizational weaknesses is to decide carefully which of the trends is long term rather than temporary. It is not worth spending valuable human resource time turning around temporarily unfashionable or dysfunctional parts of the business.

Not science but good quality checklists

Business leaders find it difficult to find time to come to seminars and listen to lectures by learned academics because they are frequently 'people in a hurry'. What they usually want is solutions to problems, not a lecture. They are prepared, if necessary, to listen to the whole seminar. But what they really want is simple 'how to do it' advice on application of the theory.

Readers will have seen advertisements in newspapers offering guaranteed winning formulae for football pools and lotteries or, even more ludicrous, advice on how to beat the bookmakers' odds on horse races.

Few people would be foolish enough to fall for this sales pitch. We all know that if they could really do it, why would they sell it rather than gather all the winnings for themselves? Business managers, however, want to believe academics, especially when they tell them 'the answers'.

Real business life cannot be subjected to the same scientific study that provides revelation in more developed sciences such as biology or mathematics. Human beings involved in business do not conform to scientifically predictable patterns. The science of business management is in its infancy. We will only know how immature it has been throughout the 20th century in 100 years or so when some objectively minded academic will look back and properly evaluate the inadequacy of what today passes for 'business science'.

If there is little science, what have all the academics been doing for the past 50 years? Well, they have not been wasting their time completely. In order to prepare their statistical analyses, they have had to gather data. The great benefit of collecting data is that they had to think about what data would be relevant to each subject. Therein lies the great benefit of their work. The relevant sets of data collected for analysis provide excellent checklists. These checklists can be used by business managers to ensure that they do not make mistakes when they think about their business. The audit sheets provided in this book are an example of just that – simple, comprehensive checklists which are intended to ensure that no important subject gets overlooked as you put your strategy together.

Checklist for strengths, neutrals and weaknesses analysis

Accounting skills (financial)

This refers to the skills with which the accounting and financial managers of the business manipulate money, credit, loans, equity, debt, bonds and all the instruments of financial management of the company. Skilful manipulation of the various means through which the organization raises and handles money can make huge additions to profitability or vulnerability. How well does the finance director conduct relationships with the company auditors, bankers, debenture holders, preference shareholders, other financial institutions, company rating assessors, merchant bankers or the stock exchange?

Does he know where to get finance when it is needed? Does he understand how to link the results of the business with its strategic development, thereby keeping the institutional backers confident in the future?

Accounting skills (management)

Does the accounting function of the organization merely collect data or actively provide information to managers to help them manage the business better? Are the data it collects accurate? Is there a flexible accounting system which means that the leadership is able to run the business in the best way for the needs of the market?

A strategic observation

In the cable industry it has been demonstrated that clients who opt to pay their monthly accounts by direct debit from their bank accounts are far less likely to switch to another supplier of telephony or entertainment than others. Furthermore, this form of payment is less costly to collect and more sure of collection than other systems. With information like that, it becomes important to assess what discount it is worth giving to customers who opt for direct debit, to ensure good overall customer management.

BT has, for many years, collected the subscription part of its income three months in advance. It does not take long to calculate the value of such an immense 'loan' of three months' free credit to BT from the subscription income from 25 million customers. Every £10 is worth £250 million free cash loan. If average rental charges per quarter were £50 that would total £1.25 billion free cash loan.

One company I worked with completed its strategic analysis and decided that it would be in the best interests of the company to change from running its international businesses with a country structure to a structure based on market sectors, in order to match the increasingly global approach of its customers. The state of its management accounting department was so ill-organized that the company was unable to install its preferred strategy because the accountants just could not supply the accounts in the required form. Consequently, the company had to put back its strategic objectives and structural change for two years until the accountants could reorganize the accounting and reporting system. In the meantime, its global competitors were grabbing business and its opportunities were disappearing fast.

Another company I worked with had an accounting department which was so devious in its capacity to move revenue and profits around the businesses to maximize the company's avoidance of tax that even the public limited company (plc) board directors could not recognize their own division's results when they emerged from the accounting department. The result of this was that the directors could never manage the corporation strategically from year to year because they were never really sure what was the true state of affairs in any of its businesses!

Access to finance

This may be confused with financial accounting skills. This category simply refers to whether the company is able to raise the necessary working capital to finance all its growth plans. Equally, if the company needs to carry out a substantial takeover of a competitor is there access to sufficient finance to complete the deal? These are the considerations of this category.

Business or divisional strategies

Divisional strategies in isolation are of little benefit and can be positively harmful if they happen to contradict the corporate strategy. The objective here is to see whether the separate divisions or businesses have their own strategies and, if they do, how well do they fit under the umbrella of the corporate strategy? Have the strategies been communicated to all relevant parties?

Corporate strategy

The judgment to be applied here is not just whether the organization has a corporate strategy but whether it is known and understood throughout the organization. A strategy which has not been communicated is barely more useful than no strategy at all.

It is necessary to differentiate between a strategy for the whole corporation and the previous category, which refers to the strategy for each of the businesses.

Corporate strategy also refers to the 'acceptability' of the strategy to the institutional and other investors. If it isn't credible to them, it probably isn't acceptable to the non-strategist, either. It is therefore probably not worth implementing because the institutions will withdraw their patronage. For example, Tomkins plc, a UK-based conglomerate, was told by its institutional investors that they did not believe in conglomerates any more. Greg Hutchings, its previous boss, kept telling them that his diverse businesses were countercyclical to each other and that it was his good management that was making all the difference. Unfortunately, for him, they voted with their share holdings. They chose to hold a minimum of Tomkins stock, thus keeping the Tomkins plc share price at a low value for many years. Hutchings eventually announced that he would break the company into its constituent parts to increase value for the shareholders. This move was, unfortunately for him, too late to enable him to get back into the strategic good books of the analysts and the owners. He was dismissed in 2000.

Cost structure of the business

Different businesses within the same industry can have different cost structures. These may be the consequences of the history of the organization or a direct result of strategic practices. For example, did the founders buy outright the business properties which are in the books at the original costs and which carry no or low annual costs? Or does the organization rent all its property at current prices which may impose higher variable annual running costs on the business than the competitor in the former situation? Marks & Spencer, a leading UK clothes and food retailer, owned most of its properties freehold. When it ran into considerable marketing turbulence at the end of the 20th century, it could turn its properties into leasehold and use the cash to buy itself some time as it tried to find a fresh approach to please the customers it had switched off in the previous decade.

Many cost structure differences may be the consequences of accounting policies. Does the organization write off capital costs over the true life of the capital or the fastest time permitted under the relevant tax laws? How does it value semi-manufactured stock? Are there reserves against bad debts or are they an annual hazard? An accumulation of small past decisions and policies on subjects such as these may mean that two competing organizations in the same industry have substantially different cost bases. This may prove to be a major liability for an organization with a high cost base in the market. For example, for a business which writes five-year contracts with its clients, the property charge policy could make an enormous difference to its contract costings and thus the contract price to the customer. A salesman could consistently lose out on bids for new business because the cost structure of the business is managed differently from that of its competitors.

Distribution network

A firm's distribution network can be strategically important in giving it the ability to control entry into its industry by competitors. For example, Coca-Cola has an immensely strong grip on the distribution network of the soft drinks industry throughout the USA. When Cadbury-Schweppes, a UK soft drinks company, wanted to enter that market it was unable to make any headway for many years. Finally it gained some penetration by agreeing to allow Coca-Cola equal access into the UK through the joint marketing company they formed to distribute both Coca-Cola and Schweppes products in the UK.

In the desk and laptop computer industry Hewlett-Packard and Compaq chose to go a traditional route through wholesale and retail. Dell Computers chose to market direct to the final customers through direct conventional marketing in the 1990s and later, after the turn of the 21st century, via the internet. At the time of writing, it looked like Michael Dell, the founder and leader of Dell Computers, might be winning the battle of market domination, partially as a result of his choice of distribution system.

Entry barriers

How difficult is it to enter any particular industry a business is involved in? For example, is the business capital intensive or is it possible to enter the industry with low startup costs? It is hard to imagine how to start up a small-scale car manufacturing plant. So the initial startup costs would be an effective entry barrier. Contrariwise, it may be relatively easy to start a manufacturing line of washing powder. Many of these products, however, have strong brand loyalty. In the case of powder detergents, although it might be easy to enter the industry from the cost of manufacturing angle, it would take large amounts of capital to build the high level of brand loyalty already enjoyed by the two giants which dominate this world industry, Procter & Gamble and its rival, Unilever. Incidentally, the next entry barrier for powder detergents is to capture space on the shelves the incumbents control because their brands are already bestsellers. One always has to ask whether an industry is mature and dominated by established brands. They take a long time to create and instill. A new entrant would have to prove to a retailer that its product would guarantee equal or better profit per square foot of space to have any chance of getting onto the shelves at all.

Exit barriers

This category is the opposite of the previous one. How hard is it for a business to leave the industry it is involved in? The longer a company has been in business in most countries which have laws protecting employees' rights, the more expensive it will be to remove staff when closing down. Other prime exit barriers are long leases or freeholds of property which cannot be used for anything other than the occupants' use. This may lock an organization into a loss-making business where, in spite of the losses, it is still cheaper to stay in and lose money rather than pay the cost of exit. Consider all that fibreglass the cable businesses have sunk into the ground all over the world. If the market for cable television entertainment sinks there is little alternatice use for all those ducts full of cable.

However, a misguided assessment of long-term strategic weakness and apparent high exit barriers can sometimes lead to false economies. One corporation I worked with reckoned the exit cost from its parcels business was £25 million. It calculated that it was better off staying in the business and trying to get it right, even though it was losing up to £5 million a year on revenue of £90 million. Over the course of the eight years that I observed the business, it endured another £40 million in trading losses. On that calculation alone it would have been wiser to bite the bullet and close the business or sell it to a competitor who might be able to create some synergies and make it pay.

Even worse, this parcels business formed part of a larger logistics corporation. The parent company had always sent its best managers to try to solve the problems of the parcels business. When they failed it blamed them and asked them to leave the corporation, forgetting that it was the business which was no good and not the executives trying to turn it around. It became known as a 'managers' graveyard'. Ultimately, the cost of the financial losses was severe. But the exodus of excellent executives who were lost to the corporation via this catastrophe area was a much more expensive haemorrhage than the pure financial cost of exit would have been eight years earlier.

Information technology skills

We have discussed IT extensively enough elsewhere in this chapter for the reader to have sufficient criteria to judge whether IT is a strength, a neutral or a weakness.

Lateral communications

This refers to communications at any level in the hierarchy between people on the same level. One often finds managers who are happy to communicate with their superiors or with their subordinates but who are, conversely, highly reluctant to communicate with each other. Sometimes they do not realize that their information is relevant to their colleagues' work. However, more often it is because they see members of their peer group as rivals for their next promotion. Withholding information is a source of power and control. They believe it will ensure that they keep the upper hand.

Communications is a problem in any organization. People always find it difficult to understand how other people will interpret what they say. The reasons are multifarious. First, we all use words differently. Next, we all express what we want to say differently on various occasions according to mood, temperament, physical or mental situation. The same may be applied to the recipient of the communication. People might say the same thing for different reasons or motivations. For example, some people may be using information or communication as a means of expressing their power over others. Others, because they have an inferiority complex, may interpret an entirely neutral communication as an attack on their integrity or their position. The causes of wrong and errant communications are so large they could fill this book. Suffice to say that communication is the single most damaging weakness of almost all organizations.

Leader's ability

This is one of the hardest categories to judge. The leader is meant to manage the longer strategic time horizons of the business and can, therefore, only be properly judged over, say, a three- to five-year term. The problem is that one can only find out how good a leader really is long after he has left the organization. Then it is too late to get back the bonuses the business paid him or her for what looked like good work. However, this does not mean one is unable to make judgments, merely that it is difficult. A good leader will inspire confidence that he is getting it right. People will understand what he is trying to do. They will feel confident that the company is going places and those places are worth going to. Similarly, one knows intuitively when a business is going wrong and being poorly led. What one needs is a board of directors with the courage to act on that intuition.

One should not confuse charisma or personality with leadership skills or character. Sometimes leaders have charisma or they develop it. But it is not a *requirement* of leadership. Sometimes it actually gets in the way because the people paid to make judgments about the CEO, such as the non-executive directors or the chairman, may be prevented from seeing what an appalling job is being done by the leader because he is able to confuse their judgment by charismatic behaviour which dazzles, but ultimately achieves nothing.

The annual long-term strategist

The leader of one organization I worked with (a UK plc) regularly changed his strategy every year to explain why last year's results were below par and claimed that the new strategy would resolve that year's problems and set the company on a new, more successful direction. That chairman–leader had great charisma and presentation skills. Even so, it must be considered astonishing that the brightest and best brains of the City of London analysts allowed him to pull the wool over their eyes for the 20 years he has been pulling this stunt. Every year I watch him do it again. Last year he thought car retailing might be a great strategy. This year it will be truck servicing. The year before it was some great new franchise he had won from some obscure foreign car manufacturer.

Why is he never asked the hard questions like: 'Why did the strategy of last year and the previous year fail, when it was explained as rationally and charismatically as this one?' Or, 'Why should anybody believe you this year?' He gets away with it on pure personality. Unfortunately, underlying this abuse of charisma, is a history of his making hundreds of people redundant each time another tactic fails. The chairman himself is a wealthy man after so many years at the top (and he inherited his share holding from his father anyway).

Leadership skills in general

Aside from the main corporate leader's skills, do the managers in general demonstrate leadership qualities? In another book I have described the differences between management and leadership. The most important differences are outlined in Table 6.1.

I also believe that over the course of a career a person will be using different aspects of him or herself in both sets of skills at various times at variant rates as they fulfill different functions and roles in their career. Figure 6.1 illustrates what I mean.

Table 6.1 Role variations between leaders and managers

Leaders	Managers
Visionary	Interpreter
Strategic	Tactical
Inspirational	Motivator
Communicator	Messenger
Good with people	Enabler of people
Corporate view	Business oriented
Organizational	Political
Moral fibre	Ethically passive
Equilibrium (structure neutral)	Hierarchical
Transformational	Transactional

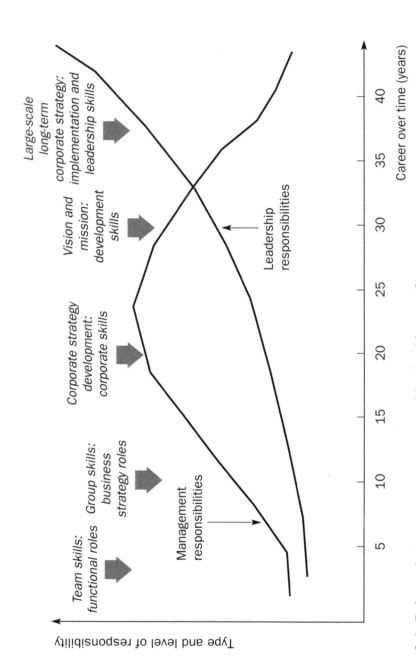

Figure 6.1 Balance between management and leadership over time

Management responsibilities start early for leaders, in the management phase of their career and peak between the twentieth and twenty-fifth year for those who are climbing towards a top leadership role. Leadership duties and skills should overtake management tasks, on average, some time in the last 20 percent of their career.

Loyalty of the workforce

How loyal are the employees? Would they rather work for your company than any competitor in the industry? What premium in salary would it take for your rivals or your customers to head hunt your best managers? How many senior executives have you lost in the past year and did they go to work for your competitors or merely exit the industry? Did you want them to go? Would you have preferred that they stay? Are you telling yourself the truth or just rationalizing their departure with comments such as, 'I'm not sorry to see them go'?

Management ability

A similar set of questions applies to the management. Do the managers really control their part of the business or do they merely obey instructions? Do they know how to get results from their people? Do they understand how to delegate? Do they get things done through their team or do they really do most of the work themselves? Are they so busy managing that they have forgotten how to get their hands dirty in a crisis? How often has one seen a manager walk past a queue in a store entirely oblivious to his seething clients' feelings as they watch him walk idly past?

One measure of the quality of management is given by examination of the company's management development programmes. Is management training evolutionary, developing a manager over the whole course of his career? Or is it a one-off skills programme? Are managers continuously retrained even if they have not been recently promoted? Does management development stop at senior levels with the underlying assumption that they probably know it all by the time they achieve senior levels in the organization?

Manufacturing skills

Does the business know how to make the things it claims to be able to provide in a timely manner with high quality? Even more important, does the business ensure that clients and customers really feel full satisfaction with their purchase rather than just relief that it was delivered at all? So many businesses fail to appreciate that purchasing, whether of industrial or consumer goods, has an emotional as well as a pure 'use' aspect. Even though the customer bought a music centre for his or her own entertainment, they want to feel it was the best value for money, it will give them a degree of satisfaction and the transaction took place in a pleasant atmosphere. That rarely happens. The same also applies to industrial goods. Too many businesses behave strictly to contract and believe that is enough to create a satisfactory working relationship between buyer and supplier. They expect the customer to refer them to the parts of a contract which apply when complaining of some service they expect to have been delivered. For example, one client of mine, Exel Logistics, a leading international transport and logistics business, was supplying warehousing and logistics services to Tesco, the leading UK supermarket chain. Exel used to present Tesco with monthly additional invoices for items such as light bulbs and extra plug adapters. In response Tesco were unremitting in their demands that the contract be fulfilled to the letter. Unsurprisingly, the relationship went through many rough passages before they learned to behave more gently and decently to each other.

One is reminded of the legendary 'quality story' of the UK firm that had decided to outsource the manufacture of one of the components which it had previously made in-house. The UK firm had much lower standards of quality than the Japanese supplier which it asked to supply some components. The UK firm set what it considered to be a stringent quality standard of three faulty components per 1,000 supplied. The components were delivered in two boxes, with an accompanying letter. The letter said, 'Please find the 1,000 components ordered. In the second, smaller box you will find the three faulty components you also requested.'

Marketing skills

One should consider here the general marketing skills of the company. Does it have relevant data about its markets? Does it use all the tools of advertising, promotion and PR fully? Does the company handle its product life cycles actively or passively? Does the marketing department collect data about competitors and their products and does it disseminate the information to the relevant managers? Does it conduct focus groups and continuously provide data to improve the product or services of the business to increase market penetration? Above all, does the marketing department control sales (the way it should) or vice versa? Does it ensure that the total approach of the business starts with delivering total value-for-money satisfaction to the customer? Does it monitor the customers to check that the customer feels the promises have been delivered? Does the marketing department have the authority and power to do something about it if customers are dissatisfied? I remember an incident at British Telecom, a short while after a new so-called marketing director was appointed. He discovered a case of a pensioner who had been over-charged £500 by an unethical BT salesperson when the customer had not really understood the commitment she was making. She could not pay and had to have the device removed. He asked sales to return 50 percent of her money as a gesture of goodwill and to deflate any potential if the story hit the press. Not only did the fairly minor sales manager refuse the senior director's request, he also told the regulatory department to send the marketing director a letter explaining what a dangerous precedent it would be to be so nice to customers. 'The regulator might force them to do it every time!' they told him blithely.

Organizational structure

This refers to the way the company is organized. Does the organization structure get in the way of the implementation of strategy or help it? Are customers confused because they receive visits from more than one sales-person for different parts of the product range? Does the structure facilitate marketing and selling? Is it easy to communicate with other members of the firm? Are staff easily promoted between divisions, businesses and departments as their careers develop, so they can gain wide experience or does the structure get in the way? Structure needs to be relatively stable.

Over the course of the 1990s many businesses believed that, because industrial change was coming at a faster rate, it was necessary continuously to redesign the structure of the organization to mirror the external environment. This destabilized employees' lives and maximized the anxiety of the whole workforce. It did nothing to help people focus on their work or their problems. It merely made them more political, frightened and unstable.

Structure indicates to people the hierarchy or organizational power system. It tells people where they could go if their skills or inclinations indicate it. If the system does that it is good. If it fails to do that, it is misguided.

Products

The portfolio of products or services the organization offers to its customers is a key strength or weakness. Is it comprehensive? Is there a vital ingredient or product that is controlled by a competitor? Does the organization's range compare favourably with those of competitors? Where does the customer shop first? Considerations such as these will define the quality of the organization's service or product range. Are the products branded and less substitutable? What market share do most of them have? Does it average first or second position in the market?

Quality of brands

Although this category generally applies more to retail businesses, many industrial businesses have important brands that add value to their products, provide barriers against imitation and help maintain price differentials against rival products and services. The value of brands has received increasing attention from the accounting profession in recent years. The costs of building a brand to rival a competitor's established product brand name is often sufficient to deter strategic leaders from competing at all.

Quality of human resources

The quality of people plays an immense part in the potential strategic opportunities facing the organization as well as in the choice of routes an organization might adopt to get there. The quality of staff will be dependent on past human resource policies, the amount of investment in training and developing people and the general attitude of management to people (usually with guidance on style from the leadership of the organization). In the course of time all these elements become a force for strength or weakness.

In addition, the type of workforce may be dictated by the industry itself. For example, in the information technology software industry, the workforce tends to be well educated, sophisticated and relatively independent minded. The methods needed to manage a sophisticated workforce such as this will be substantially different from the strategic style that would be effective in an industry with more manually skilled employees such as the automobile manufacturing industry or restaurants.

Reputation in the marketplace

A company's reputation is vitally important to all aspects of its business. A company often needs a good reputation to achieve its objectives. A poor reputation can prevent it from achieving its purposes because it won't be able to recruit the right people (who won't want to work for it). It may be that all the best people already work for the highest reputation firm in the industry – why move? Some companies acquire a good reputation for a few limited aspects of their business, while retaining a poor reputation concerning other parts. For example, some years ago, BT had a poor reputation for the quality of its basic telephony service. At the same time market research demonstrated that its reputation for the standard of its products (such as telephones and switching systems) was high.

The power of reputation

One executive I was training told me how he had been sent, as chief executive, to sort out a catastrophic situation in his company's Australian subsidiary. The previous chief executive had fiddled the books for three years before being caught and dismissed. The customers were up in arms because the quality of product had deteriorated and they were suing the company for failure to meet contractual obligations – quite justifiably.

When the new boss arrived in Australia he decided that the only thing to do was to face the music and meet all the complainants to sort out the

problems. He further decided that he had better meet all the non-cus-
tomers and find out what they thought about the company. He discovered
that every important buyer in the industry was prepared to meet him to tell
him what an appalling condition they thought the company had been
allowed to descend into. They were even ready to give the company new
business, eventually, if he could turn things around. The story demonstrates the power of reputation. Even though the recent past had been
dreadful the customers were still willing to talk and, eventually, forgive and
forget. That was the power of the business' residue of great reputation.

A good reputation has many benefits and a bad reputation has more
power for ill than first appraisal might show. For example, when
the organization's reputation is sound, customers make strong, good
assumptions about your products and give the organization the benefit
of the doubt when things go wrong. Contrariwise, a company with a
poor reputation can do nothing right in the eyes of its public.

An important consequence of reputation is the quality of recruits the
company attracts. Does the company get the best pick of the graduates
from universities or other sources of labour? Does it have to pay in the
upper quartiles by industry norms or can it pay mid-level salaries and
still attract and retain the best people?

A leader has to question whether his or her company is reputed for
excellence or mediocrity. Do the employees feel they have to apologize
for where they work or, even worse, avoid mentioning the company's
name in polite society? These are the measures of reputation.

Relationship with government or regulator

Some organizations work hard to ensure they have relationships with
politicians or, sometimes more influentially, with the advisers who guide
legislators on policy and legislation. This can be an important source of
profitability and control in an industry. The ability to influence standards
and rules governing an industry can be a powerful tool to prevent competition or control the costs of entry into the business.

Many new industries, after a few years' trading, set up an industry
federation which then tries to persuade the government to pass legisla-

tion to ensure rigorous standards in the industry, sometimes regarding safety, other times relating to ethical safeguards, occasionally just setting standards of customer service. In fact, what it really does is to pull up a drawbridge behind those safely ensconced in the industry to ensure that they can divide up the profit spoils among themselves. These standards act as deterrents and barriers against potential entrants into the industry.

The same considerations apply to many privatized enterprises which are controlled by a regulator who largely replaces the role previously fulfilled by a cabinet minister. In the UK, British Gas (the corporation controlling the supply of all gas in the UK) was privatized with a virtual monopoly of its industry. Its customers received poor service and its relations with its regulator deteriorated into a virtual slanging match. Subsequently, it lost its monopoly and, probably, its long-term profitability. It has now become a multiple billing service business of commodity products and services.

Relationship with suppliers

Old-fashioned views about relationships with suppliers have traditionally been that they were servants to the customer and were broadly obliged to do what the customer wanted. As many more industries have become oligopolies and the choice of suppliers diminishes, it becomes more important to have an excellent relationship with suppliers based on mutual respect and self-interest.

One needs to ask whether one's organization is the supplier's preferred customer. Is the supplier willing to fund or enter a joint venture to assist with research and development in your organization? Would you be the first customer the supplier would think of if he received an inquiry for your product and was asked for a recommendation? If there was a downturn and supply became limited where would your business stand in the queue? It happens. For example, political reasons ensure that the supply of storage for nuclear waste is an extremely tight market. Would a UK supplier of that service rather service a loyal, long-term French nationalized industry customer or a private German company which was prepared to pay the market price for the secrecy and careful security that would be involved?

Selling skills

How effective is the salesforce? Can they sell the maximum quantity or are they content merely to meet non-stretching targets? A salesforce should be proactive, looking for market opportunities and continuously nagging its managers to bring out new designs and informing them of the demand for new products.

One industry which has some of the best salesforces in the world is the pharmaceutical industry. This strength has led the industry into an interesting strategic dilemma. They were so successful in selling drugs to doctors and hospitals throughout the 1980s that they had created, by the 1990s, a swell of public opinion which believed they were too successful and profitable. This adverse public opinion is handing power to politicians who can then change the rules governing patent protection. This may lead to decreases in profitability for the pharmaceutical majors – a clear case of a strength being used so indiscriminately that it becomes a weakness.

Vertical communication

Communications is probably the one subject that almost every group of leaders and managers believes it does less effectively than it wishes. Similarly, it is the one common complaint from all workforces that they do not receive enough feedback and information about the parts of the organization they know little about.

Both sides are probably wrong to some extent for there must be limits to how much information is sent up and down the line, if only to prevent excess information leading to less rather than more actual communication.

However, there are objective measures available and these can be used to measure whether communication is effective or not. Most organizations that are good at this tend to use employee attitude surveys on a regular basis. These can give sophisticated feedback on how much information employees are actually receiving as well as how they feel about their managers and leaders. Such surveys are best used on a regular basis and monitored carefully for changes in key measures.

A note on the profitability of industries

Some industries have chronic excess supply problems. This may be due to particularly low barriers to entry, attracting excess supply to the industry as soon as some firm in the industry reports higher than usual profits for the year. It could be due to having 'lumpy' technology, meaning that the economies of production in that industry are large. For example, one cannot build a small steel manufacturing plant. If a firm in such an industry builds just one major new plant the whole industry could be tipped into oversupply from marginal undersupply. Such a condition will keep a tight cap on potential profits and possibly push the industry into chronic losses.

If you decide your business is in an industry plagued by this 'supply lumpiness' problem, when you come to make your decisions about the strategy you may wish to consider whether you have any opportunities to move your business into more profitable sectors, either upstream (closer to manufacture) or downstream (closer to retail). You may decide you want to exit the industry completely, over time.

The problem of objectivity

The hardest aspect of conducting an audit of the organization's internal strengths, neutrals and weaknesses is the difficulty of retaining objective judgment. This is hardest of all when assessing areas of known weakness where the organization has made a special effort to improve. One must accept that there can be no absolute objectivity. All judgments in the areas we are examining are, of necessity, subjective. However, when making such judgments the value of belief can actually impede progress rather than act as a catalyst for positive good.

Belief in the organization and in the results one is aiming for is usually a key way to achieve the extra edge over competitors. However, when it comes to assessing the SNW situation of the business, belief must be set aside in favour of the most absolute objectivity you can manage. If a category is bad, admit it and face the change implications! Ruthless honesty is the key to achieving an accurate SNW analysis. After all, the only person you can fool in this internal analysis is yourself!

Further reading

G. Hamel and C. K. Prahalad, *Competing for the Future*, Harvard Business School Press, Boston, 1994

C. Handy, *Understanding Organizations* (4th edn), Penguin, Harmondsworth, 1993

J. Hunt, *Managing People at Work*, Pan, London, 1981

J. Kay, *Foundations of Corporate Success*, Oxford University Press, Oxford, 1993

C. J. Levicki, *Developing Leadership Genius*, McGraw-Hill, Maidenhead, 2002

T. J. Peters and R. H. Waterman, *In Search of Excellence*, Harper & Row, New York, 1982

P. Q. Quinn, *Intelligent Enterprise*, Free Press, New York, 1992

S. Slatter, *Corporate Recovery*, Penguin, Harmondsworth, 1984

STRENGTHS, NEUTRALS AND WEAKNESSES WORKOUT

Check each of the following categories in terms of its being a strength, a neutral or a weakness. Sometimes it helps to allocate a number from 1 to 5 indicating high (5), medium (3), or low (1). Thus, a neutral with a 5 on it would be very close to a strength with a 1 on the same category.

Organization function   Strength   Neutral   Weakness

Access to finance

Accounting skills (financial)

Accounting skills (management)

Business strategy

Corporate strategy

Cost structure of business

Distribution network

Divisional strategy

Entry barriers

Exit barriers

Information technology

Innovation (turning research into products)

Lateral communication

Leader's ability

Leadership in general

Loyalty of workforce

Management ability

Manufacturing skills

Marketing skills

Organization structure

Personnel administration

Products

Quality of brands

Quality of staff

Relationship with government

Relationship with regulator

Relationship with trade unions

Relationships with suppliers

Reputation as employer

Reputation in market

Organization function	Strength	Neutral	Weakness
Research and development			
Selling skills			
Services			
Technical engineering skills			
Vertical communication			
Additional categories (relevant to your particular business)			

SUMMARY OF SNW WORKOUT

Select the top four strengths, neutrals and weaknesses from your analysis on the previous workout and set them out with a brief note on how you might use, neutralize or improve the effects of each for the success of the organization's mission.

Strengths

1

2

3

4

Neutrals

1

2

3

4

Weaknesses

1

2

3

4

Organizational culture

What is organizational culture?

Culture can be thought of as the aggregated behavioural characteristics of an organization that define the way it is likely to behave and react to most stimuli which affect it, of whatever nature. It is typified as what an organization tells itself about 'the way we really do things around here'.

The culture of an organization is the corporate equivalent of the personal psychology of a human being. An individual's psychological makeup defines his personality, how he behaves, what he looks like to others and how he or she will respond to any circumstances. The culture of an organization functions in a similar way and defines the kind of things the organization can and cannot do. It becomes a predictor of what changes are likely to succeed or fail. An organization's culture defines its potential capacity to achieve success (and its likelihood for failure) in the same way that an individual's psychology largely controls his accomplishments and defaults in life.

Culture is a strong force because it is a combination of history, trauma, people and accident. It is the story of accumulated habits over the history of the organization. The longer the history, the more habits will have evolved and the less easy it will be to change. Sometimes the habitual behaviour will have become disconnected from the original reasons for the behaviour. Take, for example, the waiter in a restaurant who carefully brushes the bread crumbs from the table before serving dessert. There may or may not be crumbs to clear, but he will brush the table anyway.

More substantially distorting, habitual behaviours oft
ries and offices when new systems arrive but behaviour
to match them.

The longer an organization has been in existence,
trauma it will have suffered. Trauma leaves indelible sca
face of the business. They disappear from sight, but this
the scars from having an effect. For example, British Ga:
the 1980s had a long tradition of arrogance and a thorough lack of flexibility of response. It found it almost impossible to change its culture and
become customer responsive. Consequently, it lost shareholder value and
ruined its relationship with its UK regulator because of its inability to
achieve a flexible working relationship.

Possibly the most important feature of culture is that it is a measure
of the state of things as they currently exist, rather than as one would
like them to be. A most powerful culture exercise is to get the senior
managers of a company to conduct a culture audit of their present culture – 'the way we do things around here now'. Then get them to
imagine themselves in their company five years hence and conduct a
culture audit of the future company and 'how we ought to be doing
things around here in five years' time'. What will be the important historical events in the future? What will the physical and mental
environment be like then? Who will be the 'past leaders' in the future
and what lessons will they have left behind? Who will be the present
leaders in the future? What technologies will be prevalent in the future
company? Most importantly, what myths, stories and legends will they
have left behind to guide people in the future about how we do things
around here now? It is a powerful exercise and demonstrates effectively
the paths of behaviour change that will be necessary in the company, if
the strategic future is to be attained.

Components of the culture audit

History

The key cultural lessons to be learned from an organization's history can
only be assessed once one has decided which have been the important
and behaviour-forming historical events. One has to decide which events
have left patterns that still affect the way people in the organization do

igs. Sometimes history leaves traditions that people continue to live up to but which prevent them from doing things in more fashionable or effective ways. For example, Marks & Spencer, the one-time leading British clothes retailer, had a tradition of not wasting valuable floor space by providing fitting rooms or toilet facilities for customers. For many years customers accepted this as a strange quirk. However, after Marks & Spencer's popularity as a retailer decreased and people were judging their service for overall value for money, such idiosyncrasies were no longer tolerable in customers' minds.

In general, the longer the history of the organization, the more important its effect; the longer people within it have been doing things in a particular way, the more ingrained the behaviour becomes. The cultural effect gets stronger as behaviours become removed from the reasons for the action. In England, for example, some organizations still retain a 'tea lady' who goes around the building mornings and afternoons dispensing tea and coffee. There are adequate mechanized ways of providing the same service to staff from beverage dispensers. People in organizations which retain the old-fashioned method often insist that this woman is part of the furniture and that they would never replace her. She is part and parcel of the culture, for good and bad; she contributes to 'the way we do things around here in this organization'. BA (the global airline group) still issues air travel tickets which it then exchanges for boarding passes at the airport. They still have staff tear them up into a stub to take on board and a piece they retain for the airline's use. In the age of a potentially paperless society, the whole process is utterly redundant and owes much to long buried atavistic behaviour patterns.

Another important way that history can affect an organization's culture is through major historical events that cause 'scarring' in the collective memory of the organization. Such events may be the burning down of an important depot or some time when the organization nearly ran out of cash. Consider the cultural scar tissue on Railtrack, the monopoly owner of all railtracks in the UK, from the four major train crashes between 1997 and 2000 which left many passengers dead and injured and led to Railtrack's eventual virtual renationalization.

Particular events create historical scar tissue. Ingrained habits come from carrying out processes in a regular way so that employees no longer have to think about the process any more. Thus, habitual behaviour and history create a mental environment which affect the way things are done in the organization and create particular cultures.

Mental environment of the organization

The mental environment is caused by the attitudes and management styles of managers in the organization. Thus, if they are autocratic, the mental environment will reflect this. If they are participative, their subordinates will mentally ingest this and mirror their behaviour. There are many other styles which all leave their ingrained behaviour patterns behind in their stead. There may be more subtle mental atmospheres. Some organizations have an atmosphere of fear or dishonesty whereas others transmit integrity. Some are open and welcoming to outsiders while others have a closed attitude. There is a natural intellectual ambience in some organizations (sometimes related to a high percentage of graduates among employees) which may contrast with a deliberate, vulgar stupidity in others. Some firms build in respect for everybody, within and outside the firm. Others see employees and customers as victims or bait. The insurance industry of the 1980s in the UK seems to have had an atmosphere of suspended ethics wherein it was difficult to ask openly about the moral tone of the way clients were being sold pension schemes which were against their interests.

The effects of mental atmosphere

IBM in the 1980s had an utterly closed outlook on the world. IBMers knew they were excellent; the world cited them as the supreme example of how an excellent company should be run and they believed it themselves. They arrived at a state of self-perceived supremacy. They even used their own state-of-the-art internal electronic mail so they could talk to each other at any time (usually in preference to talking to outsiders).

The personnel of IBM were universally well educated and of a high calibre. They wore similar clothing. They understood each other and were comfortable with each other. It was a complete internal world and they needed no other. It was so internally complete that they failed to notice that the external world was moving on and no longer needed what IBM was offering.

Dell, Compaq, Hewlett-Packard, Microsoft, Novell, Intel and countless other computer hardware and software companies had seen the changes taking place in the real world and were invading the marketplace that had belonged traditionally to IBM. The mental atmosphere had moved IBM too far away from market reality – and it almost cost IBM its economic life.

Past leaders

Past leaders can leave a style and pace of doing things which lives on many years after they have left the organization. It is a useful exercise to ask managers what they think they will be remembered for in ten years' time when they have long gone from their current roles in their organization. Most will look blank faced and reply that they have not thought about it. They should. Possibly they will not be remembered at all (which, for some, might be a blessing) or they will be remembered for things they would prefer to be forgotten. Most managers who make a difference are remembered distinctly for the same two or three simple principles which they decided are important in any job they do.

Sir Don Ryder at Reed International

Reed Elsevier (which used to be called Reed International) transformed itself from a business involved almost entirely in the packaging industry to one involved almost exclusively in the publishing industry (see Chapter 2). The pattern for these large-scale manoeuvres was set by Sir Don Ryder who had been a leader in the organization many years before.

Sir Don had a reputation for turning up outside large factories all over the country and confronting their owners with 'an offer they couldn't refuse'. He rarely received an immediate 'yes', but equally, he rarely departed without bringing into Reed International ownership the factory he had set his heart on, even if he had to pay too much – another cultural tradition that Reed Elsevier appears to have inherited.

Sir Don always retained a style of large-scale buying and selling. He loved massive organizational transformation in grand moves. This was the pattern of behaviour he set in the organization. Decades later the leaders of the 1990s were obeying the cultural imperatives set by the early leadership style of Sir Don Ryder when Reed left the packaging industry completely and entered the publishing industry.

Present leaders

The same considerations that apply to past leaders apply even more strongly to present leaders. Everything chairmen and chief executives do is studied by subordinates and is frequently imitated. Leaders should always be aware of the effect of their style and manner, for they never know when they are starting a trend. They cannot help some mannerisms or idiosyncrasies of style but it is surprising what is copied: heavy drinking, swearing, kindness or indifference are all styles that are easily imitated. Do they choose to be driven by a chauffeur or do they drive themselves? (One well-known leader was famous among his directors for getting out of his Rolls-Royce and exchanging it for a Ford a few roads away from his office, believing that he was setting an example to the rest of the team. Actually they all knew what he was doing. What was the final effect?) Some leaders speak politely to subordinates, others are gruff and rude. Does the leader care about cash flow or merely encourage people to find profits in any crooked way possible? Any of these patterns will be picked up and imitated by managers throughout an organization.

Dauphin Distribution

I was once working with a CEO in Pennsylvania. He was the leader of a food distribution company and he was showing me around his warehouses. As we walked around, I noticed he would stop every few feet and bend down and pretend to pick up a piece of paper or litter. When we arrived back in his office, I asked him why he had been picking up imaginary pieces of litter. His response was telling. I just like to keep reminding my people that in the food business we have to be obsessive about hygiene. They are so good that I rarely find any litter. But when I keep bending down like that – and I know they are watching me on the cameras in the office – they think I have really found something and they remain as obsessive as I am about hygiene!

A key question for the reader is whether there is a fundamental flaw in setting a desirable standard of hygiene by means of manipulative (and, therefore, undesirable) behaviour.

Physical environment

The physical surroundings of an organization can play as large a part in 'the way people do things around here' as does the mental environment. Physical circumstances have an insidious effect on people, for both good and ill. Sometimes the worst effects are caused by the contrast between the environment of different parts of the business. Frequently one finds that corporate head offices are housed in beautiful buildings with stylish furniture and luscious plants abounding. When one visits the manufacturing sites, where the real money is being earned for the company, one finds a contrasting element of squalor, neglect or dinginess. Some HQ people argue that 'the workers don't notice such things'. Do you believe them? What effect do such contrasts really have on workers? What should the policy of your organization be on such cultural factors?

Many factors contribute to the overall physical environment, for example, whether the organization has computers on desks or whether people still use paper and pencils.

Case Study

One organization I worked with had installed a computerized system for logging clients' rentals of its equipment. Previously it had a card index system to log what equipment was being used and where. I asked one assistant to demonstrate the system to me. When she demonstrated the computer system to me, I noticed the numbers on the computer were all blank. I asked why. She explained that, although she had been ordered to do it, she really did not trust it – so she continued to fill in the physical card system. She did the minimum computer filing to satisfy her superiors who were very committed to making the computer system work. She admitted that she had been doing unpaid overtime because of all the extra work the computer was causing! Thus a new (theoretically) labour-saving technology had caused a massive increase in workload, as well as inducing an incredible display of service loyalty from an employee who cared more about the business than her own time or wasted efforts.

Another facet of the cultural effects of environment must be considered from the point of view of the new 'virtual organizations'. These are sometimes new dot.com businesses which have no physical headquarters or offices. The employees work from home and only meet when they go to a sales meeting on a client's premises or have an occasional employee meeting in an hotel or conference centre. Few studies had yet ascertained the cultural effects of these new abstract business forms on the culture of the organization and on the behaviour of the people working within environments which have never existed before. Do the physical circumstances of the employees' home now play an important part in the impressions they have about their company? Do the computers they use to run the business have their own effects on the way they work? Where do they engender their feeling for 'the way we do things around here'? How does a leader transmit such ideas through the ether of a virtual organization?

Technology and its effect on culture

The technology a firm employs can also play an important part in the development of its culture. What the firm does, and how it does it, create habits of thought and behaviour which eventually become entrenched. Does the production process need thought or can it be carried out automatically? Are the offices paper based or do they use computers? Is the business high technology or low technology, giving a tradition of modern against more traditional modes of work? One thinks here of the difference between the quiet efficiency of, say, the electricity supply industry compared to the traditional ways of doing things represented by the coal industry; contrast that, again, to a software company like Microsoft with dedicated brain workers quietly creating wealth at their work stations.

Is the business involved in process or batch work? Joan Woodward, an Oxford University academic (1970), carried out studies to see the effects of technology on businesses. She found important differences between batch and process technologies. What we are asserting here is that each of the subtle differences of technology has its own culture effect.

The effects of a change in technology

Some years ago the managing director of Berol, a company then specializing in the manufacture of felt tip pens, decided that it was missing large profit opportunities because it only supplied wholesale clients. He decided to change its distribution policy and supply direct to large retailers.

Unfortunately, the company did not quite foresee what a vast difference the change would make to the business and it nearly failed as a result. Prior to the change in distribution policy, it had been a process company. To supply its wholesalers it used to take scale decisions to manufacture (say) 10 million grey felt tip pens; then, 10 million red ones and so on. These were supplied to wholesalers and the wholesalers had the worry of holding stock, making mixes of different colours and satisfying their retail clients.

After the company decided to supply direct to retailers, a totally different situation suddenly applied. Retailers sell packs of mixed colours of felt tip pens in a highly seasonable pattern, with peaks at Christmas, Easter and in the summer. Furthermore, they do not like to hold excess stock at other times of the year. When Berol's new retail clients ran out of stock, they would telephone Berol and scream for more supplies and immediate delivery and they did not want 1 million grey ones; they wanted 100,000 packs of ten mixed colours.

This completely changed the culture and profile of Berol's business. It could no longer just make production a function of the production manager's budget; it had to become an instrument of customers' demand patterns. Berol had to change its manufacturing away from a process system to a batch system to meet the demand for mixed colour packs with seasonal peaks, rather than wholesale orders for single colours.

It may seem surprising that these matters were not all foreseen by the managers when they took their apparently simple decision to make a change in their distribution policy. But the traumatic changes were cultural rather than just procedural. Berol nearly went under as a consequence and was lucky to survive the decision.

Myths and legends within the organization

Myths and legends have an enormous effect on the way people do things in organizations. They are used as exemplars to encourage the kind of behaviour wanted in the organization. They guide people on what to do and how to do it.

Myths and legends differ from anecdotes and stories because their origins tend to be based more deeply in the distant past and they may bear less resemblance to actual events that may have taken place. They become twisted over time to form a shorthand summary of 'the way things developed here' or 'a warning lesson'.

The difficulty in using myths and legends is that, to a large extent, they have a life of their own and cannot be created. Thus, one may choose to emphasize some and de-emphasize others to stimulate an effect one desires.

BT's missing mafia

A powerful myth used to have negative effects at BT. I once asked some senior managers at BT why they had so much trouble keeping their street pay phones working when there was no such problem for Nynex in New York.

'That's easy,' they responded. 'In New York the Mafia use street phones to communicate with each other to bypass the phone tapping of the FBI. If anyone is caught vandalizing pay phones in New York, the Mafia would cut their hands off – so the vandals leave them alone.'

The implication was that BT did not have the benefit of the Mafia in the UK to prevent phones from being vandalized. How could it be expected to keep its pay phones in working order?

Even senior managers allowed this myth to excuse them from trying to keep pay phones in working order. The problem was later sorted by an innovative young manager who refused to let the myth beat him. The pay phones are now working well and make good profits for the company.

Stories and anecdotes

The difference between myths and legends and the next category of culture variables – stories and anecdotes – is that the latter are based more in fact than are myths and legends. Usually, stories and anecdotes are more recent; they can be a more powerful cultural tool than myths and legends because they can be created by leaders to achieve particular or general purposes.

For example, to encourage customer care, a manager can choose to do something very special for a customer that forces people to take notice. It could rapidly turn into an exemplary story demonstrating 'how we treat customers'. Naturally one can create similar exemplary behavioural stories toward staff. If one is deliberately setting out to create stories as exemplars it requires great care. It is not always easy to foresee the effects a story might have.

I once did some work for Selfridges, the famous UK general retail store. I noticed a series of photos in the human resource director's office of him shaking the hands of members of staff. He explained that whenever a staff member was paid a compliment by letter, e-mail or word of mouth, by any customer, he would call them up to his office and give them a gift. I suggested to him it would be ten times more efficacious if he went down to the shop floor and gave them the reward publicly in front of all their fellow workers.

Robert Maxwell and Oxford United Football Club

The late Robert Maxwell created around him more anecdotes than the average leader. An outstanding one had great effect. It tells of the time Maxwell bought a soccer club called Oxford United. Apparently his interest in football was not profound and this level of interest was on a par with his knowledge of the sport. He hardly knew that each side had 11 players. The legend goes that he attended the first game after he bought the club. Oxford United lost 2–0. Maxwell, who was not noted for his evenness of mind, stormed out of the ground complaining that he seemed to have bought a club of idiots!

The following week he attended another game, only to see his team lose by an even higher margin, 4–0. This time he was apoplectic. He screamed with anger, 'That's enough! If they can't improve by next week they're going to be playing with just nine men!'

The effect of this anecdote was that when anybody joined one of his many businesses that person would soon learn that Maxwell did not believe in excess employees. So managers were wise to the need to remove excess labour before Maxwell found out.

Robert Maxwell and the lounging smoker

On one occasion Maxwell was striding down a corridor in his office building when he saw a man lounging against the wall smoking a cigarette. He immediately called him into his office and asked him how much he earned. When the man replied £1,500 per month, Maxwell took the cash from his pocket and told him he was dismissed for smoking and lounging around. The cash was in lieu of notice and he was to vacate the premises immediately! The story goes that as the man was leaving the premises, he was heard to mutter: 'That's very generous, I didn't even work for him. I work for the office cleaning company!'

Marks & Spencer's focus on customers

Marks & Spencer used to be one of the world's leading retailers. Although its base has been mainly in the UK, it had an international reputation for prowess in maximizing turnover per square foot of sales space and for giving the customer value for money. A story which played an important part in the effectiveness of Marks & Spencer's high level of customer care was one which went the rounds about Lord Sieff, a grandson of one of the founders of the business. He was standing at a checkout counter in the group's flagship store in London's Oxford Street when he noticed a long line of customers building up at the checkout while several staff members were nearby discussing how to complete a particular piece of paperwork from head office.

Lord Sieff realized that the head office managers were responsible for those employees being distracted from their prime function of looking after the customers because they had asked for the information the paperwork was intended to supply. The next morning he began a revolution by insisting that everybody should throw away every piece of paper in head office. From that day onward he wanted a zero-based approach to all bureaucracy. Any request from head office for information would have to be shown to be necessary before a request went to a store.

The story had two important effects. It saved millions of pieces of unnecessary paperwork being completed by staff in the stores. Even more importantly, it brought home to sales staff that their first job was to look after the customers who made it possible for the company to make profits. Filling in pieces of paper was only a necessary evil and should never take precedence over customer care.

Further reading

R. Adams, J. Carruthers and S. Hamil, *Changing Corporate Values*, Kogan Page, London, 1991

T. E. Deal and A. A. Kennedy, *Corporate Cultures*, Addison-Wesley, Reading, Massachusetts, 1982

C. Handy, *Understanding Organizations* (4th edn), Penguin, Harmondsworth, 1993

T. J. Peters and R. H. Waterman, *In Search of Excellence*, Harper & Row, New York, 1982

F. Trompenaars, *Riding the Waves of Culture*, Economist Books, London, 1993

H. Vroom and E. L. Deci, *Management and Motivation*, Penguin, Harmondsworth, 1979

J. Woodward, *Industrial Organization: Behaviour and Control*, Oxford University Press, Oxford, 1970

THE CULTURE WORKOUT

Complete each of the following categories with the most important features under each category. It is important to note the effect of each subject, e.g. for past leaders, put their name – but also what behaviours remain in the organization because of the way they did things when they were leader.

HISTORY

Event 1 _____

Effect of event 1 _____

Event 2 _____

Effect of event 2 _____

Event 3 _____

Effect of event 3 _____

What is the most important feature of the mental environment?

_____

_____

What is its cultural effect? _____

LEADERSHIP ISSUES

1 Name the most memorable past leader _____

What behaviour is still attributable to him/her? _____

2 Name the current leader _____

What particular qualities do you associate with him/her? _____

_____

What is the physical environment of head office? _____

_____

What is the physical environment of the rest of the organization? _____

_____

If your organization is 'virtual' and you work from home, do you feel you belong to a real organization?_____**How?**_____

_____

How do you understand what the business stands for and values? _____

_____

TECHNOLOGY OF THE ORGANIZATION

Which of the following technologies applies to the organization?
(Check whichever one of the following pairs applies to your organization.)

Paper based	**or**	Computer based
Batch technology	**or**	Process technology
National scale of operations	**or**	International scale
Mature industries	**or**	New industries
Product	**or**	Service

What cultural effect does each of those you have checked off have on the organization?

The way people behave in the organization is learned through the stories and anecdotes they hear when they join and while they remain. Try to think of those which have affected the way you behave.

MYTHS
(These are stories which are probably untrue but which get told anyway.)
What is the best known myth in the organization?

LEGENDS
(These are stories which have sources long buried in the past, but which get passed on anyway, with variations.)
What is the best known legend in the organization?

STORIES

(These are probably true stories you are told to explain how to do things around here.)

What is the best known story in the organization?

ANECDOTES

(These are entertaining stories which also teach.)

What is the best known anecdote in the organization?

Value chains and how to analyze them

Definition of value chains

The creation of any product involves a similar set of actions no matter what the product or service. One has to find raw materials, fashion them into components, assemble the components to make the finished product, distribute the product or service to a final point of sale and, lastly, somebody has to sell them to the final user. This applies whether the item concerned is a service or a product.

Consider the provision of any data such as those provided by the proxy sales business lastminute.com, the UK-based business which sells the goods of any service provider that is seeking incremental revenue from services it has to run. Lastminute.com is in an industry which may be defined as 'the disposal for incremental revenue of otherwise total loss service providers'. It would sell any empty seats for air, road, sea or other journeys, holidays, performances, sports events and theatres – essentially anywhere where there are time limited spare places or goods where there is a possibility of attracting incremental revenue which is higher than the incremental cost of supplying the service or good. Such a service business still has the normal stages of setting up an infrastructure, seeking out those businesses that need the service (supply), setting up a database of likely customers (demand), telling them what is on offer on a regular basis and ensuring what they buy is delivered and they are satisfied with the service they receive (distribution).

The five stages of what I call the **value chain** of any business are:

- Stage One – Finding raw materials
- Stage Two – Manufacture of components
- Stage Three – Assembly of final product
- Stage Four – Distribution to retailer
- Stage Five – Retail to final user.

Every product, service and industry has its own unique pattern. This is formed from the qualities of the product, the businesses that manufacture it and the customers who buy it. All the ingredients, from finding raw materials to selling to the final user, are known as parts of the value chain, a concept first developed by Michael Porter (1980).

Each part of the value chain has its own unique set of skills. Each will have a unique distribution system and most will have a different profit level. Each part of the chain will also have competitors and any business at any part of the chain may choose to carry out that piece of business for itself rather than buy it from another supplier. This is what is referred to when businesses consider moving up or down the supply chain and is the most common form of strategic growth. It can be viewed as the **horizontal value chain** (see Figure 8.1).

Almost every product or service has a competitive product which customers compare it to when deciding what to buy. In every segment those products and services extend upwards or downwards. The concept of the value chain refers to those other products and services which are similar to the business's own portfolio. An organization can also move upwards or downwards along the vertical portfolio to find growth opportunities. This is called the **vertical value chain**.

Value chain analysis is, fundamentally, a creative and robust way to formulate a growth or market expansion strategy. It may help an organization exploit its traditional or core competencies or suggest ideas for growth which set an agenda to acquire competencies it may need to own or control.

The stages indicated earlier describe what can be called the horizontal value chain. It is called a value chain because each stage of the process 'adds value' to the final product. Each part of the process often has a

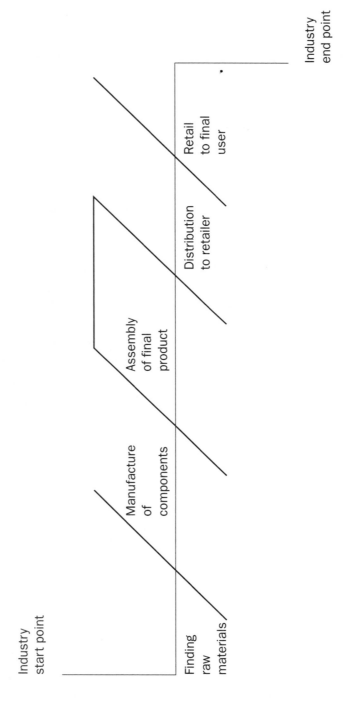

Figure 8.1 The horizontal supply chain

different set of constituent processes and skills and makes a different level of profits. An examination of the complete chain of production of a product, from creation of a service or product via a search for raw materials right through to the sale to a final user, actually facilitates an extended look at everything to do with one's own business's interests in the product. The importance of the concept is that it often also offers any business an easy, relevant means of expanding itself, improving its profitability or discovering where it is vulnerable to strategic attack. If readers work through the following examples, they will soon understand the concept.

For the moment I invite the reader to think about any single stage of the five stages described in Figure 8.1. At each stage there is likely to be a range of competitors, each of which supplies the same or similar products to the same or similar customers. Take the raw materials stage, for example. It might refer to the farm production of wheat. In that particular business there are many suppliers, each of whom produces almost exactly the same product as every other supplier or competitor in that production stage. Those other suppliers are the competitors in the vertical value chain. In most cases they will all be other farmers.

Move on to consider Stage Two, the manufacture of components. Continuing with wheat as the Stage One product, the meaning of Stage Two might be the milling of the wheat into flour. Once again, there are many suppliers who will provide this service. Some might be farmers, from Stage One, who have decided to expand by moving into Stage Two milling. However, other businesses in this stage may buy in their wheat from farmers and consider it to be a stage in the process of making and selling bread. A Stage Two miller could grow, vertically, by taking over other millers. When we come to Stage Three, there may be many different businesses which buy flour from Stage Two businesses. To keep it simple, there will be bread, cake and roll manufacturers. These may be specializing in Stage Three of the process of manufacture of their product. It is obvious that somebody making cakes can probably make bread with the same equipment. If they did so, that would be a move along the vertical chain of the industry. The business may accomplish this by taking over the other businesses in the same stage or competing with them by using its own machines for two purposes or by buying new machines specifically for this purpose. It is worth noting here that if one considers oneself in the bread-making business, one might regard the milling stage as Stage One of the bread manufacture business with milled flour being the raw material.

If we then consider Stage Four, each of the Stage Three businesses may sell their bread, cakes or rolls to Stage Four specialists in the wholesale or transport industry or they may choose to own trucks and do their deliveries for themselves on their own transport. Thus they would cover the Stage Four needs for themselves. However, many will have decided that wholesale distribution is best left to specialists with truck, road and delivery skills. They will buy this stage from the transportation business specialist.

Finally, there would be Stage Five wholesalers and other specialists, which will break up the large quantities of the cakes, rolls and loaves from warehouses for delivery into shops for sale to the final consumer. In Stage Five there will be many different competing firms, supermarkets, corner shops, caterers and sandwich bars in major cities. The businesses in this stage all specialize in knowing the different final retail users who get the product to the 'eating' consumer. There, once again, vertical growth could come from a big business which usually only sells loaves and cakes to the public, deciding to also open, in its back room, a sandwich bar, in order to increase its profits and find new customers. Once again, that would be vertical growth within the same stage of the industry.

The different starting points of value chains

The reason to refer to value chains and not to product manufacturing chains is that the exercise has the objective of covering all types of businesses whatever their stage in the process of business life. The analysis aims to enable the strategic analyst to:

- understand the vulnerability of their own business
- discover, examine and evaluate opportunities to expand the business
- look for increased margins
- understand more profoundly one's suppliers, customers and competitors
- be aware of dangers of takeover from businesses in other stages of any industry.

Table 8.1 shows the layout for a value chain analysis of the entertainment industry. A brief study of this figure demonstrates that the highest margin in the entertainment industry (according to my highly

Table 8.1 A simplified value chain of the entertainment industry

	Stage One	Stage Two	Stage Three	Stage Four	Stage Five
	Finding raw materials	*Manufacture of components*	*Assembly of final product*	*Wholesale distribution*	*Retail to final user*
	Film	Outdoor sets	Film processing	Physical distribution to venues	Multiplex cinemas
	Lighting	Studios	Film cutting	Packaging for film channels	Single cinemas
	Cameras	Film making	Film copying	Sales to outlets (cinema groups, individual cinemas, etc.)	Cable TV
	Trolleys		Dubbing	Packaging for aerial TV	Satellite TV
	Training of technicians		Sub-titling		Aerial TV
Typical profit range	10%	up to 1000%	7–10%	10–12%	12–20%
Typical risk	Low	High	Low to medium	Medium	Medium
Key factors	Glamorous, hopeful	Cyclical, talent dependent	Technical connections	Contacts, market share	Fashion, market penetration

simplified example) is in Stage Two/Component manufacture, in the form of film making. The next best profit levels are found in Stage Five/Retail to final user. However, both stages are subject to the highest risks and most difficult factors. Stage Two is highly dependent on talent, a notoriously difficult predictive variable. The magic mix of the ingredients of a film such as choosing the director, the actors and the

Table 8.2 A simplified value chain of the physical distribution industry

	Stage One	Stage Two	Stage Three	Stage Four	Stage Five
	Finding raw materials	*Manufacture of components*	*Assembly of final product*	*Wholesale distribution*	*Retail to final user*
	Food suppliers	Office buildings	Managing live warehouses	Total warehouse and distribution companies	Offices
	Non-food suppliers	Intelligent warehouses	Road logistics management systems	Single unit operators	Internet distributors
	Trucks	Distribution software	Haulage	Multiple groups	Mail order houses
	Trailers	Traffic management systems	International logistics	Shipping specialists	Industrial distributors
	Ships	Pallets		Rail specialists	Retail shops
	Airplanes	Trained personnel		Air specialists	
	Tractor units				
	Railways				
	Warehouse buildings				
Typical profit range	12%	15%	5–7%	5%	15–50%
Typical risk	Medium	Medium			
Key factors	Someone else's problem	Little credibility without experience of Stage Three	Not a lot of benefit from size	Low barriers to entry	Dependent on understanding retail customers

story seem to be the key variables which make great or terrible films. It is highly idiosyncratic. The second stage is dependent on the previous growth and development of market share. Thus, with regard to the higher margins of Stage Five, whether you are a single cinema owner or the manager of multiplex groups, then you have to read both fashion and your local markets exceptionally sensitively. Making high profits is dependent on building sufficient market share to ensure that when a great film is available, you are not forced to share the profits with other owners.

Table 8.2, showing the value chain of the physical distribution industry, demonstrates how closely profit margins tend to be correlated with the level of risk involved. They are also closely linked to the barriers to entry, levels of technology, 'state of know-how', and levels of competition.

The best margins of profit in this value chain for the distribution industry are in setting up systems for clients (Stage Two) and final marketing to customers (Stage Five). Back in the 1980s, the National Freight Company (later NFC) was a leading distribution and logistics (Stage Four) company. It had achieved over £2 billion revenue and £150 million profits a year before tax. When its leaders undertook a strategy review, I urged them to gain a deeper understanding of Stage Five (final retail systems and marketing). This was for two reasons. The first was that there were much better margins in it. But I also felt there was a great opportunity to find new customers. As retailers expanded internationally around the world, if a distribution company understood marketing distribution, it could set up and work with new entrants to national markets. As retailers enjoy a higher margin of profits in that Stage Five activity, the efforts of the transport supplier (in this case it would have been the NFC), would mean the Stage Four business could share in the increased profits of the retailer.

Differences between value chain components

Each component in the value chain has different problems. It also affords multiple opportunities. I will examine each component in turn.

Stage One: finding raw materials

The meaning of the term **raw materials** differs between industries. Raw materials in some industries (e.g. steel making) might refer to the actual mining of the necessary metals. In others the same stage might refer to

Table 8.3 Value chain of the UK floor coverings industry

	Stage One	Stage Two	Stage Three	Stage Four	Stage Five
	Finding raw materials	Manufacture of components	Assembly of final product	Wholesale distribution	Retail to final user
	Wool manufacture	Reels of materials	Woollen carpets	National warehouse distribution	Large retail chains
	Other natural fibres manufacture	Reels of materials	Other natural fibre carpets	Regional warehouse distribution	Single retailers
	Chemical-based fibre production	Reels of materials	Man-made fibre carpets	Small whole-salers	Internet distributors
	Woods	Planks	Wooden floors	Single central national distribution	Contractors
	Plastic materials	Pallets of materials	Linoleum	Multiple national distribution	
Typical profit range	10%	20%	20–25%	7–10%	15–30%
Typical risk	Medium	Medium to high	Medium	Medium	Medium
Key factors	Tends to be large scale	Controlled by first arrivals	Fashion conscious and tends to waste investment	Low barriers to entry	Not marketing oriented

the creation of totally finished goods. For example, one of the Stage One (raw materials) for the distribution industry is the finished truck, ready for the road. If we were looking at the truck-manufacturing industry, that would be Stage Three in the value chain analysis. It also demonstrates that this analytical tool is thoroughly subjective. It should contain what is relevant to the business and industry one is examining. Consider a simple value chain – the floor coverings industry in the UK.

Table 8.3 demonstrates that the two places *not* to be in the floor coverings industry are Stage One (raw materials) and Stage Four (physical distribution). While working with a client (who was firmly entrenched in Stage Four) it became obvious that the only way to increase the value of the business and grow the wealth of the shareholders was to:

1 Create brands which would enable the business to capture 1–3 percent of the retail Stage Five's profitability (the business could not actually move into Stage Five because it had been told by the DTI that it would be considered monopolistic and leaders of the business believed it would offend their retail customers).

2 Integrate backwards into carpet manufacturing (Stage Three in the analysis) to increase the profit rate of the business.

The two strategies were calculated to increase the revenue of the business by 60 percent in two years from £350 million to £560 million per annum. The profit rate would increase by about 2 percent from 7 percent to 9 percent+. It was estimated that this would increase the stock exchange value of the company from a capitalization of £150 million to £450 million in those two years, thus trebling the value of the business for its shareholders. It would also increase employment for many in the industry. Finally it would give great opportunities to many employees who (it had been found in our strategy analysis) were ready for much bigger jobs, if only they could be created within a larger business. The client also decided that he had understood enough of the strategic points being made to him and required no more help from advisers. He did not renew the contract when invited. It was purely to help him develop his strategic understanding. He made all the decisions about which businesses to buy on his own.

In reality the leader chose to buy more businesses in Stage Four in industries in which he was already laterally involved. He bought businesses in curtaining (buying material, cutting and preparing it as curtains and distributing it). He bought other business involved in supplying aspects of floor preparation (such as fittings and emergency floor lighting). He kept to Stage Four, low-margin businesses through-out. Within a year the company's profits plummeted and failed to match stock market expectations, the share price plunged and he was sacked, perhaps.

Stage Two: manufacture of components

The manufacture of components tends to be rather specialized. It could refer to pumps (as used in cars, machines, the food industry, etc.) in which case all five stages would look at the pump industry. But if one were analyzing the automotive industry, the only reference to pumps would come as a Stage Two item. Similarly, with the industry of battery manufacture, we would examine five stages:

- Stage One – the injection moulding of plastics, assembly of lead
- Stage Two – the creation of lead grids and cases for the battery
- Stage Three – the assembly of the batteries, filling with acid, labelling, etc.
- Stage Four – delivery to manufacturers (as original components for cars) and to retailers for sale to car owners as replacements
- Stage Five – sale to customers, use by car manufacturers.

However, if we were examining the industry of (say) truck manufac-turing, then the battery would make a brief appearance only during Stage Two of the analysis.

Stage Two is often a fairly profitable stage of most industries. That is because it usually requires technological knowledge and proprietary information, which take many years to develop. Some parts may also be protected by patent registration of processes. However, this stage rarely offers substantial opportunities to move forwards or backwards to other stages of the value chain. Why? Because moving from Stage Two to Stage One usually requires excessive increases in the business's investment in capital for land, machinery and knowledge. Moving forward to Stage Three requires the assembly of exponentially more know-how, which is usually countercultural to the Stage Two form of knowledge.

A business can often grow best from Stage Two by moving upwards and downwards along its own stage, finding other products and services which are so similar to its own processes that it can easily glide into them. The business may expand by increasing revenue or profitability or both. To continue an example used earlier, pumps are used in almost any industry. However, if one already manufactured pumps, it would take an investment in hygiene within the manufacturing plant and a special study of food industry requirements to enable a business to move into the production of pumps for food industry customers. This could be done with relative ease and is a far more feasible strategic move than moving (say) into engine manufacture or food machine manufacture.

Value chain analysis is important because it focuses on where the profits are being made in an industry. Nowadays institutions, stock markets and private investors make intelligent analyses and recognize that profits not revenue are the key to value (unless the business is in a fast growth stage in a new emerging industry where market share has to be fought for to make profits later on).

Stage Three: assembly of final product

The assembly of components is more profitable with complex products like automobiles, buildings, airplanes or information management systems. The more complex the product (usually) the more profitable this stage will be, as well as less vulnerable to integration competition from suppliers. For example, car manufacturing, in the late 20th century, was very much a Stage Three-dominated industry. Few of the small parts manufacturers could dream of integrating forwards into car manufacture. The only key component manufacturer that could integrate forwards would be one supplying (say) engines, a major component of a vehicle. For this reason, all the major car manufacturers have their own engine-making facilities. In 1998, BMW managed to spoil the sale of the Rolls-Royce car-manufacturing business to VW because it supplied the engines to Rolls-Royce for the car. It could not prevent the sale of the other half of the business, that of Bentley car manufacture, because it held no contract for the supply of engines there and that part of the business was not vulnerable to BMW's influence. But merely by stating it would not supply engines after the contract date, it managed to secure the brand name of Rolls-Royce for itself and prevent its major rival, VW, from bagging both Rolls-Royce and Bentley brands.

Stage Four: distribution to retailer

This stage is notoriously unprofitable for several reasons:

1 It has few barriers to entry.
2 It usually requires a low level of profound know-how.
3 It is hard to maintain legal barriers to entry (other than hygiene for food and legal for pharmaceuticals).
4 It is easy and common for Stage Three businesses to integrate forwards to control their own distribution networks as soon as they can afford it.

Businesses are always well advised, when stuck in Stage Four, to integrate forwards or backwards. Unless they have a particular advantage against other businesses in that stage they should not just stay stuck in it. The means of integrating forwards are not always self-evident. But business leaders need to be imaginative and determined. For example, in the food distribution industry, one can integrate forwards increasingly into food packaging, offering controlled special conditions for delivery and even food layout in retail stores. Many Marks & Spencer suppliers are responsible now for not only delivering but also placing stock onto clothes racks and laying them out in the stores. This enables Marks & Spencer to concentrate on its core skill of retailing; it also offers an opportunity for increased margins for distribution businesses, which are otherwise stuck with margins of 5 percent or less.

Stage Five: retail to final user

This stage is the most likely to be subject to revolutionary change. This will be as a consequence of the increasing presence of the global internet. The effect of this could be that many goods distribution systems in current use will be sidetracked or abandoned as newcomers to the retail industry search for more convenient or less costly ways to get goods to consumers. Every sleepy or vulnerable retail business that is not managing the retail revolution for its customers will find them drifting away. There are some industries which will lend themselves to this process more easily than others. Some obvious ones that have already been successful are suppliers of books, records, compact disks, basic clothing, holidays, travel in general and computers. Once enough customers have e-mail and are on the internet, almost any business can get to them, sell them goods and find a means to deliver those goods or services physically, bypassing 20th-century methods, such as high street shops, out-of-town sheds, retail parks and catalogues. The internet facilitates product demonstration, credit control and customer address verification. The goods can be stored in any low-cost shed away from expensive sites with massive savings against the rents of high street shops. The only important condition they need is access to good delivery systems by air or road. Goods can be delivered by the lowest cost means according to customer urgency. The retailer can use the lowest cost supplier of distribution. Any modern retailer which is not currently re-examining the Stage Five (retail to final user) aspects of their business may find they their business disappearing beneath their feet over the next five or ten years.

Consider the case of the retailing of automobiles. Although they are still largely sold through retail showrooms most people could easily form a decision about which car they wish to buy by going on the internet. Indeed it is likely to be a better experience for them for they can see any number of models on the internet whereas most showrooms are specialized in one manufacturer's brands. Having chosen which vehicles interest them it should be no problem for an internet supplier to arrange for a demonstration vehicle at the potential purchaser's home. From that point of view purchases are likely to be easier than it appears to be from a car showroom.

So far the costs of creating these new retail Stage Five businesses have been high because it is new territory. Profitability will come only after vast investment enables newcomers to capture meaningful shares of targeted markets against the incumbents. A prominent example in the late 1990s was Amazon, the global retail books supplier. It has become the world's largest supplier of books to retail customers by using the internet rather than retail shops to undercut the prices of incumbent retailers such as Barnes & Noble in the USA and Dillons, Blackwells and Waterstones in the UK. These groups have been forced to compete head to head on Amazon's own, chosen territory, the global web. It will be interesting to see if the traditional retailer's knowledge of book retailing beats Amazon's lesser level of expertise but greater mastery of the new retail sales systems.

Table 8.4　A simplified value chain of the tourist industry

	Stage One	Stage Two	Stage Three	Stage Four	Stage Five
	Finding raw materials	Manufacture of components	Assembly of final product	Wholesale distribution	Retail to final user
	Planes, ships, coaches, trains, cars, bikes, etc.	Airplane schedules		Internet	Holiday organizers
	Hotels	Tourism shops		Retails shops	Group holiday companies
	Takeoff slots at airports	Internet availability		Brochures	Single holiday specialists
	Resorts	Plane and hotel deals		Advertising in newspapers	Customer segment specialists
	Cultural infra-structure	Assembly of holiday packages		Advertising on bill-boards	Holiday resort specialists
	Service-minded population	Customers' population segmentation		Database selling	Holiday management
	Willing customers	Brochures		Telephone sales	Internet sales
	Insurance	Holiday insurance		Sales at holiday venues	Holiday insurance sales
Typical profit range	15%	8%	N/A	7%	12%
Typical risk	Medium	Medium to high	N/A	High	High

	Stage One	Stage Two	Stage Three	Stage Four	Stage Five
Key factors	Capital intensive with high 'write-off' rate forcing owners to sell marginal increments at any revenue possible	Innovation is the key to finding new markets	N/A	Undisciplined oligopoly with each season's first mover grabbing the pie each year	Regular bankruptcies offer temporary relief from excess supply caused by low barriers to entry

Examination of Table 8.4 illustrates that the tourist industry appears not to have a Stage Three. One could move what I have called Stage Two to the Stage Three slot if one wishes. Typically, the higher profit possibilities in the value chain are situated at either end of the horizontal chain at Stages One and Five. Setting out the simplified value chain of the tourist industry demonstrates an inherent tendency within that industry – businesses specializing in transport (planes, ships, trains, coaches, cars, etc.) tend to move horizontally forwards along the chain to package and sell holidays as an extension of their basic transport competencies. Similarly, many Stage Five holiday specialists have integrated backwards into owning their own means of transport in the search for more profit and to achieve greater control over their final product. In many advanced nations the tourism industry periodically makes higher than average profits. However, these are subject to regular and painful downturns into losses or low profitability. This happens because businesses in the industry break the 'natural' rules of oligopolistic behaviour, i.e. that a small number of businesses should only compete in limited competition on quality and service and never on price. Tourism businesses tend to particularly disregard the recommended behaviour in times of economic slowdown or recession.

Profit margins and value chains

The pros and cons of value chain integration

There are no fixed rules about which part of the value chain will make the highest profit margins on revenue. All the usual rules of strategic analysis will apply to increase or decrease them. However, for the specific 'workout' analysis, consider the following causative variables:

1 The ease or difficulty of entry into that stage.
2 The quantity and quality of proprietary knowledge.
3 The potential for transferring favourable customer attitudes from one part of the business to another.
4 High-technology stages always make more profit than low-technology stages. One can usually increase profitability by making Stage One of the business you are involved in more technical or technological. However, such changes in the level of technology must always be customer oriented and cost effective (i.e. they should make the total package into something that is perceived to be better value for the customers of that stage).
5 The higher the share of the total market for that stage, the greater the profit level (and vice versa).
6 The more important the stage to the total value chain, the more profitable it will be.
7 The lesser the components' importance to the stage, while remaining a vital ingredient, the greater the profit.

The vertical value links

Each stage offers opportunities to move vertically up or down. If one knows how to make cars, the business could probably make small vans or trucks. If a firm can sell groceries, why should it not retail cooking utensils, newspapers and eventually banking? If an organization knows how to make shoes, why not boots? If an enterprise has to fly planes for business schedules, why not fill the empty seats with tourists? If your business is trucking goods from Ohio to Denver, why not sell the return journey of an empty truck at any price to anybody who needs goods transported in that direction? If one is making hair-brushes, why not toothbrushes? If you know how to build swimming pools for private use, why not look for local government authority opportunities – they usually require bigger ones!

Every business should be searching for growth if it is available. Even declining industries have winners and losers. To be a winner, you have to expand at the cost of the losers. There are always likely to remain some core businesses in any declining industry – a leader's job is to ensure that your business is one of the survivors. Continuously asking questions in your own business such as those just suggested should be a standard discipline. Beware those jaded members of the business who have been around for too long and who always say 'we tried that idea five years ago and it didn't work out then.' There are very few new ideas in managing a business organization. The key to success is applying the right ideas at the right time in the right way.

The horizontal value links

I have already discussed the facility with which you can move from one stage to another and the potential profit from doing so. However, there are also clear constraints and dangers awaiting those businesses that move into other stages, whether forwards or backwards, without careful planning. The questions you should ask are:

1 Are my current customers or suppliers going to be offended and withdraw business from me if I go into their business and market?
2 Does the business have the necessary know-how, core competencies and skills to move into a forwards or backwards stage?
3 Does my supplier or customer maintain its attractive profit margins from its own special, non-replicable situation or can I achieve its higher margins when I do what it does?
4 What difference will a move to a new stage, either forwards or backwards, make to the structure, management systems, information technology systems and culture of the current business?
5 Will my institutional and other investing backers react favourably to my move?
6 Will other businesses in the current stage follow the business in its move to other stages, thus causing excess supply and a general lowering of every business's profitability?

7 Are the mores and ethics governing the forwards or backwards stage different from the values of businesses in the stage your business currently occupies?

8 Almost all movements in the value chain will require organizational redesign and restructuring. There are no cases where the structure will be less complex. Are the leadership and organizational systems likely to be able to cope?

NB It is nearly always easier and wiser to move upwards or downwards in a value chain, than to move into a new stage, backwards or forwards. The skills are likely to be more relevant and the necessary changes, both technical and managerial, less onerous.

Final warning

The costs of movements up and down or along the value chain (forwards or backwards) are usually high. A business either needs to borrow the capital to buy competitors, suppliers or customers or to learn their know-how for itself. Why are the costs nearly always higher in real capital expenditure than one predicts when starting out on the process? It often takes longer to get established than one guessed in advance, particularly when compared with goods or services one already knows well. There are usually hidden costs, unforeseen expenditures and technical hitches that take longer to resolve than the time allocated. The most complex and difficult conundrums to resolve are usually problems associated with recruiting and training human resources. You should calculate whether your business will be able to cope with the almost inevitable decrease in profitability before the projected increases in revenue and profits start coming. Will your backers stay with you in the crisis? Have you prepared them for it adequately?

Further reading

G. Hamel and C. K. Prahalad, *Competing for the Future*, Harvard Business School Press, Boston, 1994

M. E. Porter, *Competitive Advantage*, Free Press, New York, 1985

M. E. Porter, *Competitive Strategy*, Free Press, New York, 1980

P. Q. Quinn, *Intelligent Enterprise*, Free Press, New York, 1992

VALUE CHAIN ANALYSIS WORKOUT

Analyze your business's current position(s) in the value chain(s) of its main products and services.

Fill in the vertical and horizontal opportunities for products and services currently being supplied by competitors.

	Stage One	Stage Two	Stage Three	Stage Four	Stage Five
	Finding raw materials	Manufacture of components	Assembly of final product	Wholesale distribution	Retail to final user
Typical profit range					
Typical risk					
Key factors					

Consider your organization's backwards and forwards integration opportunities from the point of view of each of the following:

1 Attitude of customers

2 Availability of business to purchase or capability of competitors

_____

_____

3 Profit margins

_____

_____

4 Your business's competencies and alignment with the desired strategic direction.

_____

_____

Numerical evaluation

Introduction

Every organization must keep track of the health of its business by running management and financial accounts. The management accounts tell the manager how the business is performing. The financial accounts pertain to the pure state of the finances of the business. This chapter intends to tell readers about the more important aspects of accounts and how to use them.

Probably the most important aspect of any mathematics that anybody learns at school is the skill of approximation, that is the ability to check whether a calculation is roughly right or wrong. It is a very simple process. For example, if a company is producing 2.5 million lawnmowers which are wholesaling for £73 each, revenue will be approximately £200 million. Any boss should know he will want gross operating profits of about £30 million and net profit on revenue of about 10 percent at £20 million. Any less and he should be looking at what the competition is doing in that industry. More and he should be looking over his shoulder in case a monopoly commission or department decides to investigate some time. That is what the skill of approximation should be used for.

Some of my most interesting and simple strategic evaluation jobs were based on large company operations which were literally turning over billions of pounds of revenue for almost no profits at all. Of course, the leaders and senior management were being paid large salaries for running a big company. Frequently, the non-executive directors had no idea how to demand from them a reasonable profit from a smaller revenue rather than no profit from large revenues. During all my years as a consultant, particularly in the later dot.com madness years, I was astonished how many leaders would calmly tell me that they had invested tens or hundreds of millions of pounds in the internet, while having not a jot of an idea how that investment would become commercial or whether there was any potential profit at the end of the investment period.

What all this amounts to is the simple rule that, in business, there is no substitute for the old-fashioned idea that every business has to buy or make something for less than it sells it for in order to stay in business. And the leader needs reasonably strong arithmetic skills to ensure he knows where and why the business is profitable.

This chapter aims to tell leaders and managers how to look at the important aspects of measurement in their businesses. Sometimes the figures don't exist because the accounting department has never been asked to produce them. It is a manager's or leader's duty to insist that they be produced in a form that he or she can understand.

Accounting and strategic numerate assessment

This book is not intended to be a substitute for technical books on the particular subject of accounting processes associated with the analysis and implementation of strategy. This chapter especially has to be read with that in mind. Few subjects in this book have as many specialized techniques, using arithmetic and mathematical formulae, legal and technical aspects, legal precedents and historical lessons as does accounting and finance. When the leader of an organization is considering strategic opportunities he must consider some of the detail and a lot of the broad brush aspects of accounts and finance which are covered in this chapter. Most strategies, even during periods of recession, have growth aspirations. Growing businesses must always takes into account the need for capital, finance, methods for financing potential takeovers, acquisition and merger accounting and the various sources of capital and finance. The consideration of these, technically, strategically, and with regard to the business's capacity for communicating to key stake holders, is a vital aspect of strategic analysis and the leader's capacity to both take and implement strategic decisions.

What accounts do you want?

As a manager the accounts you want should give you the information to tell whether your budget forecasts and your team's actions are synchronized. Are you being successful? As an operations manager, for example, you'll need to see whether the budget you set at the beginning of the year is evolving as you predicted. Are materials costing more or less this year than forecast? Is your machinery costing more to maintain than predicted? As a marketing manager you will want to see whether revenue is matching your budget. Are advertising costs higher or lower than planned? Are your salespeople being successful, individually and as a team? All these are aspects of ordinary management accounting. When you participate in the tactical planning which goes to make up the strategic direction that the leader of your business is implementing, you will have been asked to make these forecasts and promises for the leader of your business to ensure that the strategy is achieved.

As you rise in the organization your managerial responsibilities will increase so that you become interested in the health and condition of the whole general business. Again you will be interested in seeing how the business is performing against the forecasts which are the measure of strategic achievement. You will be looking and examining the accounts against the forecasts for both annual and triennial performance. You will be looking at whole departments such as marketing, sales, production, research and development, legal, human resources and so on. You will be scanning for trends which show particular departments or managers missing their forecasts. Some may be overachieving and others underachieving. You will need to ask why to understand whether you have to adjust the plan or the strategy.

Assessing the state of accounting

In order to judge the quality of accounts in a business, as a manager you must ask whether they give you sufficient data of the right quality and accuracy to enable you to do your job. To make this judgment consider how often you find numbers that contradict the reality of your own experience. When your numbers are reported upwards at divisional level are they still recognizable? When your division has reported its accounts to corporate centre do they then become so manipulated for tax or other purposes that neither you nor any shareholder could really tell what was going on in the business?

When do management accounts become financial accounts?

At some stage in the accounting process ordinary management accounts, which are there to help one manage the business, become financial accounts, which are there to help senior executives manage the business strategically, assist bankers to assess the risk on their loans and enable investors to make judgments about their share holdings. Financial accounting is intended to ascribe value to all the assets the business is using for trading. A manager does not usually care how much his building is worth as long as it enables him to house the staff in suitable conditions. That building's value as a building is important in the financial accounts. The two concepts meet when the cost of the building is allocated against the manager's budget, making it more or less likely that his achievements will be successful.

In most businesses the allocated cost of assets is a highly political and behavioural science. For example, if a manager has to issue estimates for storing a client's goods during a building contract, the cost of the building is chargeable within the estimate. If his competitor offers the same service but has a similar building allocated at half the nominal rent, his estimate will be uncompetitive, not because of his efficiency but because of the allocated cost of rent for the building. If that allocated rent is a result of the property manager trying to look good internally within the business rather than deliver realistically priced buildings, the problem is a political one rather than economic within the firm.

The financial accounts are intended, as we have said, to enable strategists to decide how healthy the business is and what its potential could be in terms of raising capital, its vulnerability to takeover or likelihood of survival during a recession. Unfortunately, the financial accounts of many businesses are distorted. This is a consequence, partially, of accounting conventions and, sometimes, the implicit intentions of executives of the business to mislead or render the true condition of the business obtuse. Again, it is not the purpose of this book to set out the complex ways in which financial accounts are misleading. However, it is sufficient to give one or two case studies of what goes on.

The half-billion dollar hole

One business I was advising made a $9.5 billion takeover of a competitor, giving it mastery of that industry in the USA and international domination of the sector around the world. When it went to examine its new Australian subsidiary it discovered that the due diligence team had failed to see that the Australian business was subject to a conditional agreement which could trigger off losses of up to $80 million a month! That could create a massive hole in their results.

They decided to sell off that subsidiary immediately and practically gave it away to a UK-owned rival (which later made it a successful asset). But the Australian subsidiary stood in the books at a bid and takeover value of $500 million and they did not want their debtors to see their mistake. The accounts and finance department quietly changed the allocation of the $500 million that had just been paid for the Australian business to the Far Eastern group that had been purchased in the same deal.

Of course, the corporation that had sold the businesses did not change their accounts. The only way my client could be found out would be if some clever analyst looked and compared both the sales and the purchase agreements of the documents accounting for the takeover, both totalling the same number, but allocating $500 milllion revenue to different geographical sources. Nobody was likely to and nobody did. But that is how you lose a $500 million mistake!

Public company accounting

Most companies nowadays are set up as public limited companies (PLCs). That means that their shares are quoted on one of the many stock exchanges around the world. Some of the more famous are the New York Stock Exchange (NYSE), the London Stock Exchange (LSE) and the NASDAQ, which is run from Chicago and which specializes in technology companies.

Stock exchanges exist to enable people to buy and sell shares in businesses. Their other major function is as a market for companies (both private and public) to offer new shares in their business to raise capital to expand their business. Occasionally private individuals who have successfully built up a large business want to cash in on their achievements. They want to turn their locked-in business capital into cash which is disassociated with the business. This may be for personal reasons or to raise capital to start another business.

Issuing new shares is one of the means by which private and public companies raise further cash for investment in the business or to pay for takeovers. The attractive thing about this means of making takeovers or growing a business is that most ordinary shares make no specific promises about how much dividend the company will pay each year (**preference shares** are different and usually do promise to pay a particular rate of interest – they also normally have rights to payment ahead of **ordinary shareholders**). That means that the business has a relatively low cost use of **equity** money compared to the rates at which the company can borrow from banks, finance houses, pension funds or pension fund institutions. At the least, it avoids some of the types of restrictive covenant finance that organizations would impose compared to the relatively lax conditions surrounding the issuance of shares. Of course, if the payback on the shares is too low people will sell them, their price will go down and the company may become a takeover target because its assets, represented by the shares, can be bought cheaply by a competitor.

PE ratios

The total dividend paid by the company each year, divided by the number of shares, gives its price earnings ratio (PE). That is the ratio which tells a purchaser of the shares how long it would take to get back the purchase price of the shares from receiving dividends. This is rated in terms of how many years it would take. Shares that are not highly rated usually have low price earnings ratios. That could be because they are associated with high risks or are unfashionable at that time. For example, in 2001 most shares in tobacco companies had very low, single-digit PE ratios. That was because most investors do not wish to invest in companies that sell products which damage the health of their customers. In addition there is a high risk attached to companies associated with tobacco products because of the punitive damages that are being awarded against them in courts of law in favour of customers who claim that consuming tobacco has caused them attributable health damage.

The great advantage for a publicly quoted company with a high PE ratio is that it can offer 'paper' (that is to say 'shares') rather than borrow money from other sources (which we will describe later). In some ways this can appear to create wealth for the acquiring company. When it buys the shares of a company with a low PE ratio it is buying those shares with its own high PE paper. That means it has bought a lowly rated company with highly rated paper. If investors believe that the acquisition has not reduced but has increased the potential future earnings of the acquiring company the PE ratio of the company will remain high. That appears to create wealth merely by the act of obtaining assets at a low price. That is real growth of asset wealth. However, it will only remain an increase in wealth if the acquiring business is able to create synergies in combination with the acquired company and achieve new and greater potential for the combined businesses. The evidence is that the majority of takeovers are better for the acquired company (whose shareholders take the money and run) than for the acquiring company which frequently finds itself unable to take advantage of the strategic synergies it deemed were available.

Raising capital

There are many other ways in which a company can raise cash (or capital) to grow. Growth can come from acquisition or be internally generated. A business can take loans from banks or issue bonds to merchant bankers, pension fund management institutions, institutions managing other financial funds or finance houses. The advantage of any of these is that they normally have professional investors who will give them the money against carefully agreed conditions. These conditions range from insisting that the company achieves particular ratios of performance (such as levels of cash flow to debt or ratios of revenue to assets). The certainty of the agreement is sometimes preferred by a company to the uncertainty of passing fashion in stock markets. But raising capital through these means has drawbacks. First, professional investors often expect that if they lend enough money (through bonds or loans) they will get representation on the board of the company. Even when they do not expect representation they may and often do ask for prime rights and charges over the best physical assets of the company. If the company breaches any of its covenants those assets will be the first to be seized by the debtors. That may damage the credibility of the rest of the business and accelerate a company's downfall if it gets into trouble. Those bonds and other forms of debt have another drawback. They are taken into account when the gearing (see later) of the company is assessed. When gearing is high a company may be considered to have placed itself at excess risk and become less favoured among professional investors.

Cash and assets

One of the most important assets of a business is its cash. It is an old truism in business that 'a business may make no profits for many years but it can only run out of cash once'. What does this mean? It refers to the fact that cash is the lifeblood of any business. Some years ago, in America, merchant bankers and institutional analysts began to use a concept known as EBITDA as a possible gauge of the state of health of businesses involved in new technology. These businesses would need to fight for market share for the first few years of the industry as the technology established itself. EBITDA is meant to represent the free cash flow of a business, thus giving an indication of the business's health and capacity to take on debt to grow the business. Typically, firms involved in high growth (often new technology) are measured with this analysis tool. Examples are cable television entertainment businesses, firms attacking established industries through the internet, dot.com technology organizations creating new sources of data, information or service or 'old economy' businesses intent on particularly fast growth during a strategic window of opportunity.

EBITDA

High growth businesses tend to use EBITDA as a measure rather than old-fashioned concepts like revenue, profits or debt-free assets. EBITDA stands for **E**arnings **B**efore **I**nterest, **T**axation, **D**epreciation and **A**mortization. Many traditional strategists believe that such a measure gets rid of all the important charges on the business that should be taken into account when assessing a business's important current and potential liabilities. EBITDA is really measuring the cash flow without taking account of all the potential charges on the cash. It thus gives only a partial insight into how long a company may survive. It fails to take into account changes in demand, increases in competition, changes in the variable rates of interest, changes in the economic climate or the possible rate at which the business will issue more debt and accumulate greater interest charges. Any investors looking only at EBITDA (which too many do) will fail to take into account many of these potential causes of diminished cash flow into the business.

Another aspect of strategic development evaluation is the level of **gearing** in the company. Gearing, put most simply, describes the level of debt that the company has against its assets. In other words, the value of the assets that are available to be sold for cash within the business compared to how much money it is liable to pay out if all its debt were called in at the same time. This ratio is known as the **gearing ratio**. A business with no debt obviously has zero gearing. Most businesses run themselves with some debt, often overdraft agreements with their banks, which they use as working capital. In other words, they lay out money on resources, make their product and then pay off the bank debts with the revenue. That debt would be part of their gearing. They may also get 'geared' debt by mortgaging their properties or having leases on their machines.

Some companies accumulate a lot of cash because their leaders believe in being prepared for rainy days or expect opportunities for takeover bids for other badly run businesses to become opportunities in the near future. These will have positive rather than negative gearing, i.e. they have cash rather than debt. Sometimes, institutions and merchant bankers distrust leaders who keep cash piles for too long because they believe it shows a lack of strategic imagination. However, many such leaders, in the long run, have proven to be wise managers of the long-term health of their business. (Cash piles attract the attention of merchant bankers in particular because they see them as sources of fees when they recommend takeover targets and available businesses.)

Debt

A company may have high levels of debt compared to its net assets. This means that if its debtors were in a position to insist on the debt being paid, the company would be unable to find enough assets to pay off those debts. As mentioned earlier, most debt is governed by covenant conditions which leaders only enter into because they believe they will be able to meet those conditions for the foreseeable future. However, given the classic cycle of recessions which many optimistic leaders want to believe will never happen again, conditions in the marketplace often change drastically enough for covenants, which leaders thought presented no risk, to become impeached.

The levels of debt and gearing are also important measures because the interest they engender can be charged against taxation. That may be important in profitable companies when they have to decide whether to grow by acquiring new businesses and paying for them through issuing new share equity, taking on loans or issuing bonds. Share equity does not provide the same advantage. What it does deliver is a relatively low cost and with, usually, very few promises about the levels of dividend interest they have to pay to the shareholders. Of course, that low level of promise can become a nightmare if profitability dips, market sentiment changes drastically and the company finds itself unable to match the implied promises of a minimum level of dividend payout on the shares. When that happens, the share price might decrease drastically and the business leader who sought to grow by taking over other businesses may find their business **in play**, i.e. subject to takeover by others.

Barclay Knapp and NTL

At the beginning of 2002 NTL, the leading cable business in the UK and some parts of Europe, and its leader, Barclay Knapp, were facing a meltdown in the company's standing on the NASDAQ stock market. Barclay Knapp won the leading share of the UK market when he bought the cable assets of Cable & Wireless plc. He then went on a spending spree buying shares in cable businesses around Europe. His UK business had roughly two-thirds of the UK cable market. The other third was controlled mainly by Telewest plc, which was capitalized at approximately one-third of NTL by the late 1990s. Many investors thought Barclay Knapp would have been best advised strategically to stalk and win Telewest to gain a virtual monopoly of the UK cable market. That would have enabled his business to take on the battle for viewers against Rupert Murdoch's satellite business Sky TV.

Barclay Knapp chose instead to let Telewest stew. Later he authorized some limited conjoint actions with them in cooperation against Sky TV's grip on the channels of entertainment available for screening through the cable networks. Telewest itself appeared to be going nowhere once it lost the fight to buy Cable & Wireless' assets and to become the UK number one itself. Barclay Knapp's buying spree around Europe was based, presumably, on a strategy which assumed that the Telewest assets would be available any time but the European cable opportunities had to be seized while his company had a relatively high standing and ability to borrow money from banks and issue debt and bonds. Unfortunately, his predictions about the growth of the businesses he had invested in did not materialize.

Consequently, investors began to believe that he would be unable to drag enough cash into his businesses to pay his debtors and bond holders. NTL had to ask debtors to write off up to $6 billion of debt. Those primary charge debtors will demand shares to replace the loans and bonds they forfeit. All the other shareholders had the value of their shares written down so drastically that their value was extinguished. If Barclay Knapp had only issued shares to buy the cable assets in Europe their decrease in value would be of little consequence. He was not obliged to pay dividends on the shares and NTL would have been able to ride out the downturn during the business recession. With debt and loans and promises to pay interest at fixed times a business has no choice but to make enough money to pay those charges. Once that ability goes the leadership loses all strategic control over the business. Frequently, the leader also loses his job.

ROCE

Return On Capital Employed is another valuable measure that many leaders use when assessing strategic opportunities. It looks at the capital of the business and enables the leadership to assess how well it is making the assets work. In any strategic opportunity ROCE will be carefully examined to decide whether growth is likely to lead to a better or worse ROCE. In other words, a better or worse use of the assets.

A key problem with a concept such as ROCE is that one of the most important assets of the business, the human resources, cannot really be accounted for properly. For example, if the company invests in people through a development programme the charges for that programme will go down in the books as a cost, whereas, if the development programme is effective, it is likely to lead to an increase in the human resource skills within the business and therefore a higher valuation of the people assets of the organization.

Goodwill

When one company takes over another it acquires control and ownership over all the assets of that business. If the amount of money it pays is less than the value of those assets then it has made an obvious gain in value. However, that is rarely what happens in reality. Most businesses pay a premium over the value of the real tangible assets of the acquired business. There are many valid reasons for paying this premium. First, the acquiring company is gaining control over somebody else's business. Second, they are probably gaining a greater market share which may enable them to achieve economies of scale and greater profits. Third, with greater market share they will also have increased control over the total market which might enable them to increase prices and remove duplication. Finally, many business leaders, in the heat of the fight to gain an acquisition target, get tempted to pay too much.

The premium of the money paid over the value of the net assets is called **goodwill**. In larger bid situations the sum which must be allocated to goodwill can amount to many billions of pounds or dollars. Recent changes in acquisition accounting force acquiring companies to write off the goodwill relatively soon after the acquisition. This can create a considerable dip in the quality of profitable results the combined businesses make after a successful bid. However, accountants are adept at finding ways around this problem. In America, for example, many businesses call the research and development expenditure they find in the acquired business **investment capital**. By this means the need to allocate the excess premium paid for goodwill (which should theoretically be written off) is avoided. By capitalizing everything possible and avoiding any allocations to goodwill, they can depreciate the assets over many years instead.

Inflation

It seems incredible to think that inflation seemed to have been brought under control by most governments by the beginning of the new millennium. Just 20 years ago **inflation accounting** and all its strange distortions were a vital item on every senior manager's development programme. It also had to be taken into account when judging the accounts of an organization's success or failure in its growth strategies. Inflation is defined as an increase in prices with no equivalent increase in goods. It is brought on by excessive money supply, sometimes triggered by high wage demands without equivalent increases in productivity.

How does inflation distort? It enables businesses to pretend to themselves that they are growing because the nominal value of their revenue and apparent profits is distorted by vast increases which are the consequence only of inflation in the nominal value of the business revenue. Because these figures, when inflation is rife, increase at rates up to 30 or 40 percent a year, there is much room for finance directors and chief executives to play games by leaving out important costs from one year to the next which enable the results to look good and increase shareholders' impressions of success of the business. This, in turn, increases the price of the shares and the consequent key PE ratio. Any company which plays this particular game could then go on a spending spree buying other companies which are not using the same inflation accounting tricks.

Outside periods of inflation the same game is sometimes played by a few leaders who talk up the value of their shares by creating great strategic dreams of growth and economic nirvana in a few years' time if only the bankers, institutions and shareholders would suspend their disbelief about either the facts of current poor trading or that they are fighting for market share in order to exploit a potential future monopoly or oligopolistic domination of the market.

Accounts that count for strategists

Looking at the accounts can be a fascinating insight for a strategist. In my consulting career I would always read a company's annual report before I met its chairman or chief executive. They were frequently shocked and astonished at how many secrets I was able to divine about their business from the annual report when they thought their finance director had carefully covered up the more sensitive information.

What was it I was looking for? First, I would examine the annual report to see what its texture, general layout and style were telling me, beyond what the designer intended. Is it flashy or tasteful? Is the colour photography there to help communicate or is it just excessive exuberance? Are the glossy pictures meaningful or just superficial glamour? This can be particularly subtle. For example, L'Oréal is a leading global international personal styling business selling beauty products. Its annual report frequently contains beautiful pictures of glamorous models displaying some of the results of the use of their products. In their case the annual report of this very successful company has an appropriate glamour. If exactly the same glamour were transferred to a transport business or one involved in waste management, one would have to ask 'what is being covered up here?'

The next thing I examine are the obvious storylines of the accounting year and its comparison to the previous year. What was the revenue and how much more or less than last year is it? The same for profits before and after tax compared to last year. Are the profit levels good or bad compared to the industry? (That depends on your knowledge of the industry. If you don't have it look at the annual reports of similar businesses.) I usually then look at the profits after tax to see the company's approach to taxation. If the profits are normal but the taxation rate is low I normally suspect that the company is using accounting devices to avoid taxation, possibly by reporting its best results in low-tax havens. This always makes me suspicious because if they will do that for taxation what would they do to avoid telling the truth about bad results? Furthermore, one has to ask questions about any business's ethical fibre when it doesn't pay their fair share of taxation. Taxation is needed for governments to supply national defence, national and local education and infrastructure. The business is taking advantage of all these benefits. If it does not pay its fair share of taxes then it may also cheat in other aspects of its behaviour.

Rupert Murdoch's Business Structure

The Economist of 20 March 1999 published a report on Rupert Murdoch's media empire. The parent corporation is News International which comprises almost 800 subsidiaries. Sixty are incorporated in tax havens such as the Cayman Islands, Bermuda, the Netherlands Antilles and the British Virgin Islands. During the four years ending in June 1998 News International reported consolidated pre-tax profits of A$5.4 billion. It paid only A$325 million of corporate worldwide taxes. That is a tax rate of 6 percent average over a four-year period. A typical rival, such as the Disney Corporation, paid 31 percent average over the same period.

The average corporation tax rate in the three main countries in which News International operates, Australia, America and Britain, was 36, 35 and 30 percent respectively. Thus, on average, the empire which Rupert Murdoch controls through News International pays one-fifth to one-sixth of the normal rate most tax-paying corporations expect. It would appear that Murdoch's corporation is structured to siphon the profits made in high-taxation countries and transfer them through the various tax havens mentioned.

Always read the small print

After checking the style, texture and basic accounting information I then turn to the **cash analysis** section of the accounts. Cash is usually something which cannot be manipulated or lied about because the auditors always check banking statements. Does the company have more or less cash than last year? Did it raise extra money through loans, debts, overdrafts or issuing new shares? Is there enough cash for a healthy business to run itself for a while if it had to change bankers or to manage itself through a recession or a growth spurt?

Then, I look at the accounts in general and see which figures have indices against them indicating explanations or remarks in the small print at the back of the accounts. Those small explanations usually hold all the secrets that the company would prefer investors not to know but which they are legally obliged to tell. If they practise peculiar interpretations of the accounting rules it will show here. If they made a bad purchase or are hiding business mistakes in a peculiar way they have to tell the story in the small print. If they are using different, unusual or peculiar depreciation or amortization standards the company has to tell it in this section of the accounts.

Finally, I always look to see the share holdings of the board of directors. They are legally obliged to report this as well as any share options they have on offer against the future performance of the company. Have leaders sold off their share holdings in the past year? Have they cashed in their share options? All these sales could indicate their pessimistic views about future business results, in total contrast to the obligatory cheerfulness and optimism most proffer in the opening pages of the annual report. That might be a signal to sell or at least not to invest any more in that particular business.

Summary

This chapter could just as easily been placed later in Part Two of the book, as it is here in terms of strategic analysis. Eventually, I decided it belonged in this position because deciding on growth strategies is normal and is a consequence of long-term management and leadership of the business rather than something one can do for a very brief time as a standalone activity. Furthermore, those responsible for strategy should look at and complete the workout on the following page(s) in order to assess whether, if they choose a great strategy, the business is in a state of preparedness for their activity.

Further reading

J. R. Franks and J. E. Broyles, *Modern Managerial Finance*, John Wiley, Chichester, 1979

P. C. Haspeslagh and D. B. Jemison, *Managing Acquisitions*, Free Press, New York, 1991

D. Parker, *The Strategic Finance Workout*, Financial Times Pitman, London, 1996

S. A. Ross, R. W. Westerfield and B. D. Jordan, *Fundamentals of Corporate Finance*, McGraw-Hill, New York, 2002

THE ACCOUNTS EVALUATION WORKOUT

Are your business management accounts accurate?

_____

Does the accounting service of the business help or hinder your work?

_____

How?

_____

Do you have to deliver more figures than are used by the accounting department?

_____

Name three improvements you would make to the accounting system

1 _____

2 _____

3 _____

Are your business financial accounts accurate?

_____

Does the annual report accurately report results?

_____

If not, what does it distort and why?

_____

What is your business's cash flow?

_____

How does your business's financial health compare to that of the best business in your sector?

_____

What is your company ordinary share dividend rate?

_____

How well is this covered by pre-tax earnings?

What is your business PE ratio?

_____

How does this compare to that of the best business in your sector?

_____

What is your company's ROCE?

_____

How does this compare to that of the best business in your sector?

_____

Could your business borrow enough to buy its largest competitor?

_____

Being creative about the long-term strategy

Creativity in organizations

The creativity expected from the managers and executives is not that of a poet or artist. It is creativity based on judgments about the use of the competencies and capital of the organization they lead. The best creativity in strategic thinking requires a combination of both EQ (emotional intelligence) and IQ (analytical thinking). It has become a cliché to require strategists to 'think out of the box'. But in fact very few strategic situations require lateral thinking. Most strategists have to come to their best judgment about the external market situation, assess the attitudes of the stakeholders and then take an optimal decision on behalf of everybody involved. That is the **creativity** strategy requires.

The creativity expected from the managers and executives is not that of a poet or artist.

The creativity of the organizational leader is different because it's concerned with strategic vision. They must evolve the corporate mission and maximize the potential of the corporation. They have to scan the total external environment and find the growth opportunities or intuit dangers and steer the corporate ship away from them. They also have to understand the internal strengths and culture of the firm and the best and fastest way to repair any weaknesses. They have to sense the **core competencies** of the business and know how to conjure up the additional skills necessary to achieve the strategy. Above all they have to guess the future, which is essentially unknowable. Another area of creativity needed is the skill of communicating the strategy in a way the whole organization can understand. In summary the areas which require strategic creativity are:

- the definition of the mission statement
- the human resources they select and appoint
- the development and evolution of the finance and the budget process
- the communication of the strategy to staff, customers and stakeholders
- the ways they symbolize the culture and values of the business through behaviour.

Can creativity be created?

Every employee has different qualities which make up their unique set of attributes. Few will find they lack any capacity for original thought when working out strategy. The good news is that there are not too many fresh or original ideas that could possibly work in any strategic situation. Choosing a new strategy does not require creativity but judgment. It is not *what* to do that is difficult but *how* to do it.

It is advisable, when the corporate or business team has done all the analysis, to take the team away for a session together to assess recent performance and adjust the strategy for the period ahead. During these sessions brainstorming for ideas is a well-known technique, when everybody just comes out with any wacky or straight ideas which the data have inspired. Anybody might come up with the great idea which guarantees the future. It is a classical brainstorming rule that all criticism and assessment are held in abeyance during the 'ideas creation' period. This avoids the sterility caused when criticism engenders self-awareness and inhibition which then destroys creativity.

Intuition is a source of creativity; it demands equilibrium and neutrality as a background to the ability to let ideas flow over the full range of 'scenarios' that a leader must contemplate. This allows minds to find the optimal design for the organization's future. Intuition induces the ability

to conjoin ideas that do not naturally belong together, but
conjoined, create concepts for new products or services th
tomers will appreciate and buy at profit-making prices.

Creativity can also apply to the use of numbers (in the n
businesses measure themselves and are measured by others —
cally). Most strategies need to be tested arithmetically for their impact on
the market and their value on the bottom line for the business. Numbers
can be a creative medium for people who think mathematically rather
than verbally.

Wisdom and cleverness

The behaviour that is most required in organizations is **wisdom** rather than
cleverness. Wisdom is the profound insight which comes from empathy
with people and sensitivity to the economic environment. Cleverness uses
the deductive and analytical capacity which stems straight from IQ.
Cleverness allows a leader to cope with the enormous quantities of data he
or she must ingest and understand when contemplating taking decisions
on behalf of the corporation. A classic example of a 'clever' manager was
John Birt (now Lord John Birt) while he was at the BBC. He was very clever,
but quite lacking in wisdom. He (and his consultants) analyzed the BBC in
detail and then maximized its theoretical cost effectiveness. Unfortunately,
the creative people who made the programmes that the world wanted to
view were utterly alienated as were many of the customers.

Wisdom represents the ability to have insights into multiple agendas, to
understand with the heart and the head at the same time. When it comes to
creativity, wisdom is vital, because it informs how to be both the adult and
the child, how to be objective and subjective, how to be both creative and
analytical and, ultimately, to know how to decide on the optimum solution.

Managing the creative juices

Pure creativity is often associated with younger people. It nearly always
dies down or subsides in later life. Most Nobel Prize winners in science
do their best work in the third decade of life. The person responsible for
strategy does *not* have to come up with all the best ideas – he or she

merely has to have the best judgment about all the ideas to select those most likely to succeed. Indeed, being the originator of an idea can actually get in the way of the leader's ability to decide which is the best from among several contrasting solutions to a problem. Judgment is much harder to exercise if one owns too many of the ideas from which you are choosing. The strategist has to exploit the imaginative ideas of others. High quality judgment is a much more desirable quality.

Much of the creative work necessary for strategy takes place in the subconscious while the facts and the data are being collected. I have already advised readers *not* to think ahead too much during those phases of strategy analysis. Part of the reason is that their inner mind is working away on the possibilities anyway. The creativity is taking place and they do not need and are ill-advised to try to do it consciously.

Creativity inhibitors

Angry people and a culture of cynicism and disdain are aspects of organizations which inhibit strategic creativity. This is especially true where they do not respect their customers. When British Telecom was first privatized in the early 1980s it called customers 'subs' which was an abbreviation for 'subscribers'. Unfortunately, too many managers behaved as if it was actually an abbreviation for 'sub-human'. Anger is a useless emotion that achieves little and gets in the way of judgment. It tends to intimidate people and damage their ability to think straight. The same applies to all excess tension and strain on everybody in the business.

Irrational prejudices and a lack of balance or equilibrium in an organization make it hard to make balanced judgments about strategy, as does excessive attention to detail at the stage of decision making about strategic direction. Once the team is ready to decide, it should not allow small details get in the way of taking the decision. That is often just a device to avoid the fear and pain of finality. It is terrifying when one has to decide the organization's future. Best to JDI – *just do it*.

Creatives change their mind

There appears to be a terrible prejudice among journalists and media people in general against leaders who change their minds! That is their problem. Strategists often have to change their minds because external events turn out differently from their predictions. Sometimes the human resources of the organization prove unable to implement the strategy. There are times when unpredictable trauma and events change the data. Who could have predicted what happened in America on 11 September 2001 when terrorists destroyed the World Trade Center using airplanes as missiles? Sometimes competitors behave unpredictably and have to be reacted to. Other events which just cannot be predicted might be political interference; unpredictable action(s) from regulators; even excessively hot or cold weather.

When perspectives change for the organization, judgment is needed on whether the strategic situation is so affected that the strategy has to be changed. Do it too often and it will destroy all forward momentum; too rarely and the organization will hit the buffers one day and the crash will injure it fatally.

Creativity and people

The choice of quality subordinates requires imagination and creativity. Too often the zany and witty employee is frowned on and frightened away from the business. They are doubted as 'lacking suitable seriousness' and perhaps 'not quite the right style'. This is dangerous. So many entrepreneurs and people who manage highly successful lives but fail to rise in the corporate setting say that

The choice of quality subordinates requires imagination and creativity.

'they were intimidated out of larger businesses by people's attitudes of disapproval'. I urge all who inhabit strategy departments to conserve and value the zanies and the creatives – they may be the eventual salvation of the organization.

Differences between corporate and business strategies

In the previous chapter it was pointed out that at some stage in a manager or leader's career he or she would have to pay more attention to the financial accounts than to the management accounts. In some ways this applies to the difference between corporate and business strategy. The corporation is the larger entity, the overarching body, that might include many different businesses. Each business will need a strategy for survival, success and potential growth in terms of the industry it belongs to. The corporation will have an overarching corporate strategy which encapsulates all the strategies of each of the businesses it comprises. That strategy should stand over and above them all conceptually. But it also must be able to stand alone on behalf of the corporation. If it becomes impossible to devise such a strategy then the corporation probably needs to be broken up into parts where an overall corporate strategy can be developed. As a strategist I am firmly against those businesses which see a valid corporate mission statement as saying 'we will be the best business possible in the following three industries . . .'.

What that means for users of this book is that they have to reflect on which level of strategy they have to design. Is it the business level or the corporate level? This can be a critical problem for the executives working within a large corporation. This is the point at which strategic aspiration and planning can become hazardously inharmonious. The rational or preferred strategic line for their business might not easily be fitted to the overarching strategic future of the corporation as a whole. Under these circumstances a leader is pushed back to finding resources within his own reserves to facilitate his plans or to accepting a suboptimal strategic line on behalf of the corporation but disfavouring his business. This is where reality and aspiration meet and frequently clash. Leaders who expect to stay at the level of business strategy only will probably push harder for the business's strategic line. For those who have aspirations to work at the corporate level it would be wiser and more likely that they learn to think at the level or paradigm of the corporation.

There is not a lot of choice

If one completes all the analytical processes described in previous chapters, deciding what the long-term strategy of the business ought to be is relatively easy. By now you will have examined and reflected on the most profitable parts of your business. You should have analyzed where most of your competitors make their profits in the industry and begun to focus on where you wish to concentrate. You will also have examined carefully the strengths, neutrals and weaknesses of your own business and, finally, you will have studied the culture of your organization. (Once you have defined the long-term strategy, you will be able to decide whether you need to change any parts of your culture.) You have examined the accounting and financial condition of the business and you know how ambitious the business could afford to be financially in terms of growth or how much retrenchment it needs to 'save its soul'.

Defining the long-term strategy

Now that it's time to decide what the long-term strategy should be, surprisingly, it is really rather simple because the analysis will have informed you what the range of possibilities are. There is little real choice to do anything completely new. Completely new ventures are almost always unrealistic. Most businesses do not have the flexibility, range of skills, technical capacity, wealth, management know-how or leadership ability to do most of the strategies that they might prefer. They usually have just simple choices within the range of businesses and industries they know. Most corporations are not enough of a learning organization to do anything else.

In broad terms the options are:

- make the business grow
- keep it stable
- decrease its size (possibly leading to liquidation).

This is the logical range of strategic decisions one can take in regard to the overall corporation. Of course, if the corporation is involved in several businesses (and possibly several industries), it may be possible to increase the size of some, keep others stable and sell or liquidate others. However, at the corporate organization level the choice of growth, stabilization or decrease in size is all there is.

Growth can come from internal growth or acquisition or a combination of both. Your value chain will indicate what parts of the industry it would be opportune to grow towards. The first choice is between vertical or horizontal integration, i.e. do more of what you know intimately, or move backwards or forwards and learn new tricks. You might decide to concentrate on growing your current market share from your current portfolio. Whether you decide to grow vertically or horizontally, you will certainly manage faster growth if you combine acquisition (for the larger part) with growth from internal resources.

Going for growth

In practical terms, there are not many choices about how to increase the size of the business. You can grow it organically (taking market share from your current direct competitors) or you can grow faster by buying one or more competing enterprises. You could buy indirect competitors who make products which are not exactly the same as yours but which compete with your products because they can be used as substitutes for them.

You may decide you prefer the profit levels further back along the value chain and grow the business by integrating backwards and buying organizations which supply products or components to your business. Alternatively, you can choose to grow by integrating forwards and taking over your current customers.

The choice of growing, whether vertically or horizontally, forwards or backwards, is always a real one within the limits of what national and supranational regulators will permit. Competition regulators are becoming increasingly ferocious about excessive domination of markets, especially for final consumers. They are less strict about companies that gain domination by organic growth rather than by takeover or merger. Those are the points at which one's business or corporation is likely to attract their attention and put the company in a position of being regulated. For many businesses takeovers or mergers are not a real choice: they cannot afford it and they do not know how to do it. Furthermore, acquisitions or mergers are only appropriate when one has a rapidly growing market and it is likely that only a few suppliers will survive in the long run. Under these circumstances it is vital that the corporation achieves enough market share to ensure it is one of the survivors.

You may also need to consider growing your organization by buying firms which contain useful core competencies relevant to your business and which may have some synergy with your company's skills. For example, if you are in mining, you might buy another mining company, because it has a core skill in drilling technology which is missing from your own operations.

Conglomerates

Another way of growing the business is by becoming a conglomerate and buying any businesses in the marketplace you think are cheap, even if they do not necessarily have any strategic fit with your own, other than enabling you to apply your management skills to a larger business. Conglomerates have become unfashionable since the 1980s. Most firms now try to 'stick to the knitting'. This means that, unless you have some inside knowledge or core competence which is useful to the industry or business which you are buying, then it is probably wiser not to extend your business too widely.

Conglomerates are, basically, organizations which rely on their pure management skills to achieve higher levels of efficiency from their unrelated businesses than others expect to deliver. They are out of favour, currently, because they seem to lack strategic logic. Some of the largest in the world, such as Hanson Industries, have been broken up into constituent, more closely related parts. Another well-known diversified conglomerate in the UK, Tomkins plc, has also announced it is to break up into constituent, related parts and float off each part with a separate quotation. This follows years of the chairman and chief executive, Greg Hutchings, attempting to persuade the City that his conglomerate was a better bet than any single strategically integrated business. They just did not believe him. They forced him to resign in 2000 and towards the end of 2001 he was still arguing about his departure package.

Acquisitions and mergers

In a sister publication to this book, David Parker (1996) summarizes the issues a leader must take into account as potential effects of an acquisition. In large measure the same issues may also be used to summarize what must be taken into account when evolving a growth strategy for a business:

- the market values of both the acquirer and the target company's shares during the **takeover** process
- the effect of the takeover on the **earnings per share** (**EPS**) and the **PE ratio** of the acquiring company
- the effect of the acquisition on the **gearing** of the acquiring company
- the effect of the acquisition on the **risk profile** of the business after the takeover battle.

An acquisition or merger where one expects to be the dominant partner should take account of the following questions:

1 Are the combined companies attractive?
2 Is there true synergy between the two businesses?
3 Does the culture of the acquisition company fit your own?
4 Can the integration process be managed?

5 Can all the stakeholders be persuaded to back the deal?
6 Can the financial numbers be made to make sense?
7 Can all the other stakeholders be persuaded?
8 Do all the acquired company's geographical locations fit?
9 Can the two companies combined find enough management and leadership to cope with the larger scale business?
10 Can the leaders settle down after the acquisition, lose the adrenaline kick and get back to the plain old job of running a business?
11 Due diligence (any nasties in the pre-purchase audit?).

Each of these needs a brief explanation.

Attractiveness of the combined companies

Too frequently when leaders set a strong growth strategy they get carried away and make one bid too many. It is not always obvious why stakeholders firm up against any particular takeover bid. However, once it has been mishandled it is very hard to persuade the influencers to allow a bid to take place. The classic example is when Saatchi & Saatchi bid for the Midland Bank. Saatchi & Saatchi had become the biggest advertising company in the world. But their competence to run a bank had no credibility. Their bid made them look so ridiculous that they lost their premium share price in the stock market. This meant they could make no more bids using their share paper. Eventually they became a target themselves.

Synergy between the businesses

Synergy must be one of the most abused words in the world of merchant banking or consultancy. Whenever anybody recommends a deal they always suggest that there would be business logic and synergy

> **Synergy must be one of the most abused words in the world of merchant banking or consultancy.**

between the acquirer and the acquired. It is rare that such synergy actually transpires. Why? Because too many leaders believe that the takeover process itself will deliver the synergy. This is never true. The synergy can only be delivered with a sustained effort from all leading executives over a long period in order to make the merger work after the acquisition has been made. This requires careful planning of the process of cultural adaptation, conversion of the acquired company's people to a new culture, removal of surplus production capacity, elimination of duplicate sales outlets and exploitation of all new growth opportunities.

Creation of a combined culture

The acquiring company should review its entire strategy after it has made a successful takeover bid when it finally sees exactly what it has bought. The acquired business is rarely as good or as bad as presupposed. That is also true of the acquiring company. What the leadership must do is reassess the combination of the two companies as one and review the whole business with its new opportunities and dangers, strengths and weaknesses. They must develop a new culture which fits the combination of the two businesses. They must also reassess their whole strategy in the reality of the new, enlarged business. They have to realize that the larger business is not just their old business with a few pieces added.

Management of the integration process

Much of the strategic analysis outlined in this book testifies to the uniqueness of every business. Unless an acquiring company has a specific, detailed, intelligent and empathetic plan to manage the process of integrating the combined businesses after a successful bid any potential synergies will *never* be delivered. In some companies this becomes an increasing problem when the leadership has been in an acquisitive growth mode for many years. The market sees all the activity and assumes that growth is real and that integration is taking place successfully behind the acquisition headlines. When the growth frenzy eventually slows down, as in every industry it always must, it becomes possible to see clearly whether the combined business has been truly melding into one greater and potentially more successful business. The evidence is that around 70 percent fail in this endeavour.

Stakeholders backing of the deal

Most people know the old truism that if you need to ask a favour you should go to an old friend and not a new one. It is a pity that many leaders fail to adhere to the wisdom underlying this adage when they run their businesses. Whether it concerns strategic growth and acquisition programmes or when defending one's business against a competitor's acquisitiveness, one should be asking old friends to help. That implies that leaders of businesses should be in continuous discussion with all the key stakeholders in the business on a regular basis. It doesn't do to just turn up when you need them to help oppose some aggressor's intended action. Jack Welch, the retiring leader of the world's biggest company, General Electric, decided to make one last $42 billion bid for Honeywell Corporation just as he was retiring as leader. Honeywell had big interests in Europe which meant that with General Electric's interests, there could an excessive domination of some European markets. Jack Welch had created no special relationship with the European commissioners in Brussels. They had not seemed to be important enough to him, the leader of America's and the world's biggest company, safely ensconced in the USA. Mario Monte, the EU Commissioner for Competition, said 'no' to the bid's ramifications in Europe. That removed the industrial logic of the deal. Jack Welch's last bid failed.

Rationale of the financial numbers

When the leadership asks this question it requires a special level of rationality. An honest accountant or finance director would admit that almost any proposition can be made to look rational, feasible and attractive when dressed up properly with the correct assumptions. What leaders have to ask themselves is whether the assumptions are valid and what is the degree of risk of their achievement. Above all, they must ask themselves whether the numbers are good enough to do what the next section covers, 'can they persuade all the stakeholders to agree to the deal?'.

Persuasion of all the stakeholders

Consider the case of Vodafone. Sir Christopher got the backing of his major shareholders because he spoke to them every six months for ten years – not just when he needed their backing. Persuading the stakeholders to agree to a deal is dependent on the state of the relationship with each and every one of the stakeholders. Sir Iain Vallance, ex-chairman of leading UK telecommunications company, BT, used to have his personal office staff check his diary every three months to measure whether he had allocated his working time according to a carefully drawn-up assessment of the importance of the whole range of stakeholders in his corporation. That is probably a good habit for any leader. It should also be done against a context of five to ten years rather than the next few months. It is the rainy day or the glorious rainbow that one is seeking to insure for, not the day-to-day running of the business.

Fit of the acquired company's geographical locations

One of the most obvious and most frequently neglected strategic preparations for acquisition and mergers is a simple physical check of the locations of the business to be acquired. Do their locations duplicate or fill in the acquiring corporation's own geography? Does their culture match or contradict your own? Above all, do their IT systems fit those of the company taking over? Are they big enough to use for the whole business? Or would one of the most important synergies be lost because of the cost of acquiring a new IT system for the larger combined business?

Competence of managers and leaders to cope with the larger business

The question of assessing the competence of the leader, his or her immediate team and the rest of the top echelons of both the acquiring and the target company, is probably the most difficult and yet most important question to be asked. The leader has first to make a judgment about himself. Will he be competent enough to run the larger business? On this matter, it is appropriate that the chairman and board of directors play a major role. It could be that the leader of the target company might be the better choice as chief executive. Few leaders contemplate such a radical self-immolation. The human resources director is probably the most important person to consult. He must be able to make an assessment of whether the current leadership of both companies combined will be able to grow and manage a larger and more complex combined business. It is not an easy calculation.

Calm after the acquisition

One of the most rarely considered and most dangerous aspects of fast growth periods, whether by takeover or internally generated growth, is the enormous adrenaline kick that surrounds the leading executives of the growing company. They have to work most intensively during such periods. They have to spend money fast and loosely as they employ corporate lawyers and top merchant bankers, exploit the best consultants, take big decisions about large sums of money and continuously indulge in corporate warfare. Winning the battle may also mean one has won the corporate war for domination of the industry. During such a period the adrenaline flow and the excitement of battle can be exhilarating. When it is over there is a natural period of calm and sometimes depression. Some leaders set off on the next takeover bid without realizing it is not the next business they need but the adrenaline kick. The real interests of all the stakeholders should be that the leadership and management run the business properly and competently day to day. Sometimes leaders who have been on a vast growth spree will find it impossible to settle down to ordinary day-to-day business again. In this event, it is sometimes better for the owners of the business to force the leaders to leave the company before their adrenaline deprivation drives them to make an acquisition that is the mistake that breaks the corporation's back.

Due diligence

Due diligence is the process which takes place just before an acquisition or merger is consummated. The process is very similar to that involved in buying a house in the UK. The businesses will have signed a conditional contract which is dependent on a detailed and close examination of all aspects of its accounts and the running of the business. When due diligence is over the contract completion can take place. The due diligence period is when the acquiring company's auditors, accountants and executives crawl all over the business and its books to see if there are any hidden timebombs or catastrophes which could be said to change the valuation they have placed on the business. It is absolutely vital that businesses use the due diligence period wisely. Many mistakes have been made because the chairman of the buying organization ordered his people not to find anything wrong during due diligence. Executives should always be brave enough to tell the truth. If they find a problem they must report it. If they find a problem big enough or important enough to stop the acquisition, they must be permitted to advise against going forward with the deal, no matter how much their leader wants to do it.

Selling the strategic dream in acquisition mode

The question always arises 'how much care will each stakeholder need?' The various courses of action need to be individually fashioned for each person or institution. Their requirements will also change over time, prevailing economic conditions and fashion.

Consider first the institutional managers who manage pension funds. Usually these institutions expect the chief executive and finance director to make private and confidential presentations to them. These are often cloaked in the appearance of secrecy. In reality, if plc leaders actually gave them secret and private information they would be both acting illegally and breaking stock exchange rules of treating some shareholders differently from others. Thus, the corporate presenters may imply that they are sharing confidential secrets that are not being revealed to the other stakeholders. In reality, it had better be untrue. These large shareholders need the private shows. The same applies to any individuals who happen to hold very large stakes. Sometimes these large shareholders may be entrepreneurs whose businesses the corporation has taken over in the past and who accepted a large number of shares in the acquiring company as payment for their business.

Roadshows are the appropriate medium for most of the relevant stakeholders such as those smaller fund holders who may be asked to take subordinate parts of the loan stock and debt; small pension fund managers and other small financial institutions and; unit trust and other fund holders. The roadshow should be designed for any other groups wherever the company can find an audience.

Bankers are one of a number of special stakeholders who require careful treatment. Again, private presentations are certainly most appropriate. Usually, however, the bankers will be closely associated with any major acquisitions. They will already have interests which have to be protected against the issue of any new loans, debts or shares which might affect the quality of the covenants that have already been agreed with the bankers for past facilities. Almost certainly they will be involved in one way or another with the current deal. Unless they are associated on a daily and hourly basis with everything that is taking place they are likely to become hostile and vote against any agreement or deal that is being discussed. Essentially bankers should not be left to find out the facts from the media. They should be told everything in person directly and early. The bankers should be allowed generous fees for the provision of any necessarily temporary facilities to tide the acquiring company over while the details of the loans, debts and share issues are put in place. This is usually enough to keep the bankers happy.

Auditors and accountants

Auditors and accountants are another breed of stakeholder again. They have this strange relationship of being an impartial judge about the condition of the business and yet are entirely dependent on the recipient of their judgment for renewal of the contract to repeat the business next year. This dubious relationship has led in the past to many failures of the necessary impartiality which investors expect of the auditors of a company. Consequently the auditing profession has its problems. In 2001 the Securities and Exchange Commission, which oversees the behaviour of everything associated with public companies and stock exchanges in the USA, conducted a special review of PricewaterhouseCoopers, one of the Big Five global auditing firms. That review uncovered more than 8,000 violations of auditor independence rules governing investments by auditors and their relatives in the securities of the companies they audit. The problem of independence is further exacerbated because the auditing firms all have consulting branches which are selling additional services to their audit clients. This makes it even harder for them to give independent advice. Consequently many of the Big Five are splitting off their consulting businesses. Arthur Andersen has split consulting off as Accenture. Ernst & Young sold its consulting branch to Cap Gemini. KPMG took its consulting arm public to make it more independent and PricewaterhouseCoopers is considering a split (reported in *Forbes Global* article, 19 March 2001).

Andersens, the global accounting and auditing giant, disintegrated in 2002 when it was alleged that it had encouraged many dubious practices allowing misleading accounts of their client, Enron, to be published and certified safe. Enron, a global energy giant, became bankrupt.

The key to managing the auditor and accounting stakeholder relationship is probably to give them a large part of the investigation, due diligence and consultancy services necessary before, during and after any takeover activity. Offering some parts of this to both the audit supplier and its consultancy sister will usually ensure that the relationship is under control.

Managing the bidder's staff and important employees is vital. Their loyalty is important and can prove to be crucial if a bid is seriously contested. Even more important is to target specific key employees of the company being acquired. As far as it is legally permissible to do so, specific key people should be offered share options and bonuses for staying on to run the company for the long term. Some companies involved in takeovers have been known to go beyond what is legally acceptable and make these offers prematurely in order to obtain insider information. If one is successful in the takeover one then has to worry whether such employees who were vulnerable to unethical approaches against their employers are likely to behave in the same way in the future.

The public sector

Government ministers and civil servants form another set of key stakeholders who can make or break a takeover. One has to be extremely
careful and judicious in the way one manages these relationships during
takeover activity even if one has carefully and
correctly maintained them over the long term.
One also has to differentiate between politi-

Politics and politicians are fickle.

cians and officials. Politicians are always liable to take a short-term
attitude towards any takeover or merger activity depending on their local
political needs for votes or popularity. Politics and politicians are fickle.

Civil servants and government officials are usually more circumspect
and long term in their attitudes towards business and the problems of
competition and survival. Strategically, it is wise to put any new business
conglomerate resulting from the takeover into a world or regional context which could then justify any possible local failures in competitive
activity. In terms of persuasion, officials normally like to be assured of the
company's cooperation in the future application and implementation of
new legislation. They sometimes find that cooperation in planning and
the company's willingness to make available spare resources for the general public's use are attractive offers. They often respond to unsolicited
plaudits which help their career and earn praise from ministers.

In this regard one may need to adopt original and unusual tactics. For
example, Cable & Wireless (C&W) managed to pull off a takeover of a
Japanese company, International Digital Communication Incorporated
(IDC). They did this against an incumbent Japanese company, NTT,
which had great influence on the directors of IDC and on the other stakeholders of the business. C&W used publicity in newspapers to shame the
various stakeholders into allowing them to bid until the best price for the
shareholders was achieved. They also arranged for a British minister to
telephone his Japanese counterpart to suggest that perhaps Japan was
once again not playing by the same rules of takeover fairness for British
companies in Japan as there were for a Japanese company in England.
C&W won control of IDC against all the odds.

Supranational bodies are the stakeholders that need mentioning in
regard to takeover activity. Both in Europe and America there are people
who hold sometimes apparently unimportant titles and roles but who are
major figures in terms of intelligence, influence or ego. Sometimes they

are using their positions in these organizations as a preliminary to returning to national politics or as an outlet for otherwise frustrated ambition. Neil Kinnock, the ex-leader of the British Labour party, is an example. Mario Monte, the European Union Commissioner for Competition, is another who has made a heavy mark in several takeovers, much to the surprise of some American business leaders who thought that Europe would be a pushover during their takeover bids.

Stability strategy

If you decide merely to try and keep your organization stable and neither grow nor contract, you have a different selection of strategic actions available to you. You could just do nothing and keep things ticking over. Another choice is to focus on profit and try to maximize it. Again, some firms choose, when stabilizing, to segment the business. This ensures that all the sub-markets are looked after individually. An added advantage of this strategy is that if a particular market goes wrong it will not contaminate the others.

It is difficult to hold a business in a stable condition. Invariably, there will be some parts of your business which are in growth markets and others in diminishing markets. If you still want to keep the business stable because the problem businesses prevent you from growing or demand so much cash that you cannot invest in the growth potential, you might choose selective investment. This will mean developing, relatively slowly, those parts with growth potential and counterbalancing that growth against those other businesses which are likely to diminish.

Retrenchment or liquidation strategy

If the organization is in danger because it has been trading at a loss or its market has been diminishing, there is a choice of response methodologies.

The first of these is to conduct a classic turnaround strategy. The tactics of turnaround are to reverse the normal time horizons of the business. That is to say, instead of looking at the long-term strategy and then, afterwards, deciding the short-term tactics, you have to implement immediate short-term tactics to give the firm a chance of having the luxury of a long-term strategy.

Turnarounds

In a turnaround situation the rules are very simple. First, you have to recognize that you have a profound problem. Nowadays that role often falls to the non-executive directors. It is hard for the executive chairman or the chief executive officer to face up to deep-seated problems. They are probably a root cause of the problem and step one usually requires them to be removed from leadership. Only the board can do that and that requires the non-executive directors to act in concert. Unfortunately, most non-executive directors are appointees of the failing boss. Too frequently they are his cronies and friends and they are rarely disposed to throw out the person who appointed them. Sadly, in the vast majority of cases, the non-executives only rouse themselves to decisive action to remove a leader when it is far too late for any successor to do anything useful to turn the failing business around.

The removal of leaders who have caused the problems is invariably the key starting point for most successful turnarounds. Unless the leaders, who are necessarily part of the problem, are forced out or resign, then the turnaround is unlikely to begin. As Stuart Slatter (1984) puts it: 'Most, but not all, turn-round situations require new chief executives, since inadequate top management is the single most important factor leading to decline and stagnation' (p. 79).

The second, usually vital, step in a turnaround is to centralize, as far as possible, all financial and budgeting controls to enable the financial director of the organization and the chief executive to be totally aware of everything that is going on, even if it is only bad news.

The next stage in the process of turnaround is to decentralize as many business operations as possible. Every manager, down to the lowest possible level, should be asked to state a target budget and keep to it. The budget should be profitable or cost effective and ensure the return of the firm to profitability in the shortest possible time. The new leaders need to be utterly ruthless and say: 'Now we have centralized control it is vital that you, the managers, give us the profits the business needs to survive. We now have control over the accounts so we can measure the survival of each business as it becomes profitable. We must give you a fixed time limit to return your part of the business to profitability. If you make it we will all survive and thrive. If you cannot deliver profitability in your part of the business, you must understand that your section, at least, will be closed down.' If more leaders were able to deliver simple messages like this (and ensure the financial controls allow them to do so), many more businesses would succeed in returning to profitability.

Divestment

A second retrenchment strategy is divestment. That means selling off all parts of the organization which do not have strategic synergy with the core business in order to raise cash to become a healthier organization. One variant of this strategy is to become a 'captive company'. That usually means saying to one's most important customer, 'We will supply solely to you, if you will guarantee us enough orders (even with low profitability) to be able to survive as your "captive supply company".' Basically, this means that the organization becomes a single internal supplier. Unfortunately for them, many of Marks & Spencer's suppliers have become 'captive companies', with just Marks & Spencer as the key customer. This means that when Marks & Spencer sneezes, they catch pneumonia. Marks & Spencer sneezed in 1998. It will be interesting to see how many of its suppliers survive the contagion. By 2001, several had already closed their doors or gone bankrupt.

Finally, of course, a business has the choice of liquidating its assets to try to return some of their capital to the creditors, shareholders or owners. It is always drastic and painful to face up to the hard reality of liquidation. However, it is sometimes the best thing to do rather than to go on trading into an even sadder and worse situation.

Business-level strategies

At the level of the individual business (which may be a subset of the corporation), another set of strategies is available to the organization.

Cost leadership strategies

You can try to achieve overall cost leadership of the industry in which you are involved. Your objective under this strategy is to achieve the lowest possible cost curve compared to your competitors, enabling you

to compete on price against any firm in your indus
achieve the lowest cost you can also sell at the lowest p
fore be more sure of achieving the percentage market
aiming for, matching and seeing off competitors for price i
place, or maximizing profits when competition is at a low ι

Differentiation strategies

Another business-level strategy option is 'differentiation'. This means trying to create some degree of difference between the products you supply to the market and those with which your products directly compete. The traditional way to achieve this is to ensure that your product's brand is appreciated, respected and valued by consumers. This can also deliver higher prices, even when there are no basic differences between your products and those of your competitors. Contrariwise, you can try to create real differences between your product and those of the competitors.

However you choose to differentiate your product or service, the differences should be related to marketing information whereby customers have told you they value the differences you are offering. Differentiating on qualities which are irrelevant is a pointless and expensive blunder.

In the USA, Wal-Mart guarantees lower prices on a large range of branded and non-branded commodity goods. It has established itself in local markets throughout the USA. It creates stores which attract customers from widespread sets of communities because it offers such a large range that it becomes worthwhile for the customer to drive many miles to shop there. Above all, it guarantees lower prices on everything it sells. This guarantee creates the psychological security of mind for its customers to know they will certainly save money by shopping there – and they do not need to shop around in other stores in case something is cheaper elsewhere. Wal-Mart made its name by being the cheapest for everything.

John Lewis, a retail trader in the UK, guarantees to sell at lower prices than any local competing retailer. If a customer finds a product being sold more cheaply elsewhere, the store will refund the difference. Its famous motto is: 'Never knowingly undersold.'

International Harvester, an international supplier of farming equipment, guarantees to supply spare parts within 24 hours if your equipment breaks down. SAS, the Scandinavian airline, tries to guarantee getting you to your destination 'on time'. All businesses need something to differentiate them from their competitors. The more individual and the less easy to copy a product is, the more the 'unique differentiator' will lock in customers and profits.

Focus strategies

You can decide to focus your business on a few key products or services which your analysis and research have demonstrated will guarantee a decent level of profitability. When the UK had just one, sole car manufacturer, it decided to focus on one brand, the 'Rover', and a small range of cars carrying that brand. Trust House Forte, an international hotel group, decided to focus on just a few classes of hotel: premier hotels, executive hotels for the business traveller and cheap hotels for budget business and family use. The management intended to sell off all its hotels which did not fit one of its key categories. Unfortunately, the management took too long to implement the strategy and the company was snatched up by Granada, a competitor in the entertainment and leisure industry.

Time horizons

One of the key considerations when deciding on your long-term strategy is to decide how far forwards you want to focus your vision for the business. The key variables in this regard are the size of the business and the type of industry in which it competes. Thus, if you are in the oil industry and you are one of the leading four or five firms in the world, you will need to have very long-term plans with regard to exploration, refining and trends in international demand for different types of fuel and uses for energy sources. An appropriate time horizon for the longest term strategies may well be 15, 20 or even 30 years.

By contrast, if you are in the fashion clothing industry, an appropriate time horizon for your business may be between one and three years, depending on how large the business is. That may be the maximum period in which you can organize the acquisition or close-down of buildings, the purchase of materials and machinery and the training of staff.

It is important to define the time horizon of your strategy because of the subsequent need to divide the constituent parts of the strategy into smaller time frames for your subordinates down the hierarchy. Research has shown that in the best organizations, the longest or most appropriate time horizons are normally those of the leaders. The managers below them should have shorter time horizons. For example, in a medium-size chemical production business a five-year time horizon might be appropriate. This may be influenced by the research, development and the technological time spans of the industry. However, the leaders of other divisions may be working at two- to three-year time horizons. Leaders will need to subdivide the five-year strategy into three-year subparts for the subordinates at the next level down. Their subordinates in turn may well have to further subdivide their strategic objectives into shorter one-year targets for their respective subordinates.

Eventually, the large-scale strategic objectives will be reduced to one-week or 24-hour jobs and tasks for the workers on the shop floor. When you complete the workout audit sheet at the end of this chapter you will see this time horizon concept in very simple form. It asks you to define what the appropriate time horizon should be. If it is ten years or more, then fill in that column. If it is five years, then complete that column only. Then break that five-year strategy up into its constituent three-year and two-year parts. (See also Figure 10.1.)

Integration and differentiation

Two researchers at Harvard, Paul Lawrence and Jay Lorsch (1967), researched the time horizons of people with different functions in a number of organizations. They discovered there is a 'functional effect' on the time horizon of senior and other managers. For example, a senior manager responsible for research tends to think a long time ahead on behalf of the organization. Marketing managers also tend to have long time horizons. In contrast, sales managers tend to be rather shortsighted in their time horizons, usually because they are tasked with sales targets to be achieved in the near term (see Figure 10.2).

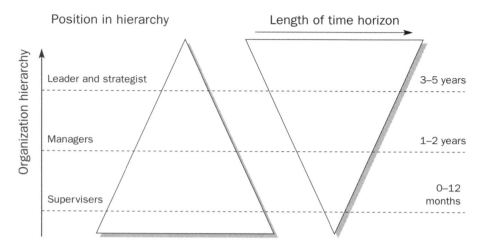

Position in hierarchy   Length of time horizon →

Organization hierarchy

Leader and strategist   3–5 years

Managers   1–2 years

Supervisers   0–12 months

The higher up the organization, the longer the time horizon
Different jobs have their own time horizon associated with the job
The most efficient businesses have leaders wth the longest time
horizons and their subordinates having ever decreasing time
horizons at each succeeding lower level in the hierarchy

Figure 10.1 Time horizons and hierarchy

Most organizations appoint one person to be the marketing and sales manager or director. Given the time horizon difference between the long-term marketing role and the short-term sales role, he or she will be faced with a natural conflict in the time horizons of the two contrasting functions. Usually the shorter will take precedence over the longer and the organization will become increasingly short term and neglect the long-term marketing development of the organization.

My research (published as a PhD thesis *Managerial Time Horizons and Decision Making and their Effects on Organizational Performance*, London Business School, 1984) showed that when leaders ask senior managers to think carefully about the whole organization's strategic time horizon, the differences between the functional time spans can disappear. In other words, when managers are careful to ask their people to think in organizational terms rather than functional terms, they are capable of thinking and behaving rationally in the best long-term interests of the whole organization, rather than pursuing their narrow role interests. I also found that in

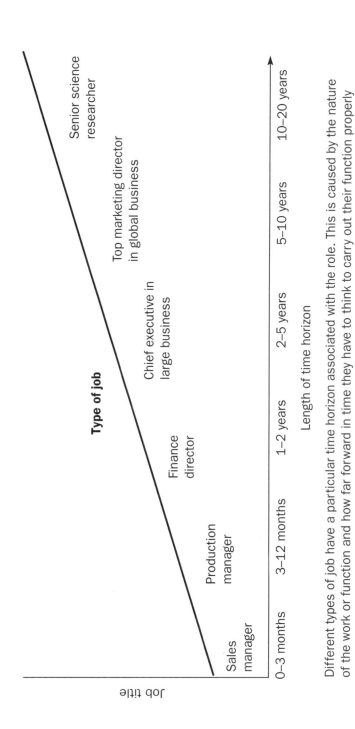

Different types of job have a particular time horizon associated with the role. This is caused by the nature of the work or function and how far forward in time they have to think to carry out their function properly

Figure 10.2 Roles and associated time horizons

inappropriately appointing people with a short time horizon to senior positions in the organization can knock the organization's time horizon alignment out of kilter and have a catastrophic effect on the resulting profits. The common sense of this is often experienced. How many readers have described their strategies for the year or two ahead and their boss consistently responds with questions about this week's results! That is a short time horizon boss confronting a subordinate who is seeing further in the future than he can. The subordinate becomes frustrated and angry. The boss gets frightened and intimidated. The solution is to find some way to ensure the organization adopts the right strategy in spite of your boss' shortcomings (see Figure 10.3).

Time horizon-aligned organizations are more profitable than those which are not time horizon aligned.

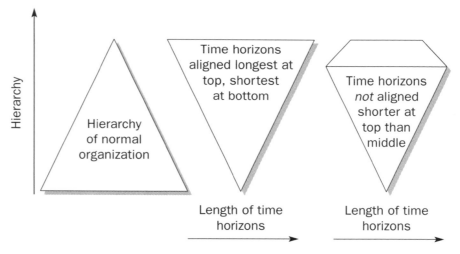

The first triangle represents a normal organization hierarchy. The second, inverted triangle represents an appropriate time horizon alignment with the longest at the top and reducing sequentially downwards. The third figure represents an organization where the time horizons have become distorted with people in the middle of the organization having longer time horizons than their bosses. That organization will have a frightened top management and a frustrated middle one

Figure 10.3 Time horizons and hierarchy distortions

Strategies to avoid

A prime rule in strategy is to avoid 'following the leader' in the in[...] Normally, the leader will have adopted their particular strategy be[...] it has special competencies. You are unlikely to be able to imitate and beat them. You will thus always offer a second class service or product if you merely follow what the leader does.

You should also avoid trying to repeat successful formulae that worked in the past. In other words, if the firm's first breakthrough in the marketplace was with a new type of refrigerator or a new engine for an automobile, it may well be that your next innovation should be a new way of streamlining an automobile. Your real skill is probably in innovation, not new engines. It is difficult to repeat the same success twice, whereas you can use the same competence many times over. Consider Swatch, which created a world leadership position in wristwatches, using a natural advantage of their domestic Swiss reputation for quality watch making. They followed this with a new design for a small fashion motor vehicle which captured a following all over Europe.

It is also sensible to avoid direct confrontation with your competitors. It is almost always invidious. By and large your competitors will specialize in what they do. For example, if the competitor uses the lowest cost strategy as just described, confronting that competitor on his own low-cost territory is only likely to lead to a fiasco and a defeat for your organization.

It is also recommended not to try to do everything that everybody in your industry does. It is impossible to be the cheapest and the best segmented, the most differentiated *and* to offer the highest quality on every aspect of your product or service. If you try to be everything to all customers, you are likely to be the fastest to disappear completely from the market.

It is also wise to avoid 'throwing good money after bad'. If you have been investing a lot of capital into a new venture or a new service and after a long and sustained effort it is not working, then stop. Frequently executives think that if they just put another million or two in, it is bound to come right. After all, they say, 'We couldn't have wasted £50 million, could we?' Unfortunately, the answer is: 'Oh yes, you could and did. It was a waste – and another million or two will not put it right.' Classically, the best motto is: 'If you are in a hole and digging does not seem to help, stop digging.'

Consulting firms also screw up

Recently one of the largest auditing and consulting firms in the world decided it had to improve its billing and control system. It sank £30 million into a new accounting system which was intended to allow the consultants and auditors to keep a computerized record of their chargeable time and also to act (in theory) as an invoicing system. The installation of the IT system had been initiated by one of the most senior leaders in the firm. The system took much longer to design and install than was anticipated and did not begin to meet the specifications and promises made for it.

Consequently, in this highly political organization, nobody in the business was prepared to take on the task of telling the boss that he had led the firm into an appalling and expensive mistake. As the business was run as a partnership, it meant that every single partner had actually invested and lost £100,000 of his personal income. Every new person that came in to help the firm was asked to do 'another special study' to see exactly how much money had to be spent to make the system work properly. It was a standard joke within the partnership that 'every partner could have had a new Maserati instead of the non-functioning accounting system we are stuck with'.

Of course, it was impossible to tell the boss the undisguised truth that the whole thing had been a terrible mistake. He was too autocratic and inflexible. He really needed to be told: 'You have wasted the millions you have put in. Try and find another system and start the whole project from scratch.' Because the chairman's ego would not allow that truth to be uttered, they continued, fearfully, to try and make a ridiculously inappropriate and poor quality system work. Even today this prestigious consulting and accounting firm may still be sending out wrongly calculated invoices and continuing to have little idea of what the true state of their business is. It is lucky that, as a partnership, nobody is auditing the auditors!

Summary

Strategy formulation does not require great creative genius. It requires a diligent assembly of all the important and relevant facts. That is what these workout audits are getting readers to do. If you do that part thoroughly, the answers will be obvious and glaring. Take those conspicuous routes and lose your fear that you may be missing some subtle, creative route. Most of the great companies have been built by leaders just making the obvious strategic choices, simply and effectively. Others may conclude you are a subtle genius. That is their choice. It is implementation which is hard. That is the reason others have not tried the obvious route – often, they didn't know how!

Further reading

J. R. Franks and J. E. Broyles, *Modern Managerial Finance*, John Wiley, Chichester, 1979

G. Hamel and C. K. Prahalad, *Competing for the Future*, Harvard Business School Press, Boston, 1994

P. C. Haspeslagh and D. B. Jemison, *Managing Acquisitions*, Free Press, New York, 1991

E. Jacques, *Measurement of Responsibility*, Tavistock, London, 1956

E. Jacques, *Time Span Handbook*, Heinemann, London, 1964

P. Lawrence and J. Lorsch, *Managing Differentiation and Integration*, Harvard University Press, Boston, 1967

C. J. Levicki, *Developing Leadership Genius*, McGraw-Hill, Maidenhead, 2002

D. Parker, *The Strategic Finance Workout*, Financial Times Pitman, London, 1996

S. A. Ross, R. W. Westerfield and B. D. Jordan, *Fundamentals of Corporate Finance*, McGraw-Hill, New York, 2002

S. Slatter, *Corporate Recovery*, Penguin, Harmondsworth, 1984

LONG-TERM STRATEGY WORKOUT

Consider each of the following stakeholders and give each a mark of level of importance in your strategic thinking, with 1 for low to 10 for high influence.

Share-holders	Bond-holders	Merchant banks	Pension funds	Institutions
1 2 3 4 5 6 7 8 9 10	1 2 3 4 5 6 7 8 9 10	1 2 3 4 5 6 7 8 9 10	1 2 3 4 5 6 7 8 9 10	1 2 3 4 5 6 7 8 9 10
Staff	Pensioners	Unions	Central government	Local government
1 2 3 4 5 6 7 8 9 10	1 2 3 4 5 6 7 8 9 10	1 2 3 4 5 6 7 8 9 10	1 2 3 4 5 6 7 8 9 10	1 2 3 4 5 6 7 8 9 10
Auditors	Senior executives	Bankers	Regional bodies (EU, ASEAN, SEATO)	
1 2 3 4 5 6 7 8 9 10	1 2 3 4 5 6 7 8 9 10	1 2 3 4 5 6 7 8 9 10	1 2 3 4 5 6 7 8 9 10	

What competing products and/or services would you like in your own business's portfolio?

_____

Are there any competitors you might like to take over that are available or buyable? Name them.

_____

Are there any suppliers making profit margins superior to those of your own business? Could you effectively take over and successfully manage them? Name them.

_____

Are there any customers making profit margins superior to those of your own business? Could you effectively take over and successfully manage them? Name them.

_____

Should the firm grow, remain stable or diminish in size?

_____

Which parts of the business should:

Focus?   Differentiate?   Be an industry cost leader?

_____

What will be the organization's three key achievements at the end of the next five years?

_____

What will be the level of revenue in five years' time?

_____

What will be the level of profit in five years' time?

_____

What will be the main three industry areas of interest in five years' time?

1 _____

2 _____

3 _____

Will your corporation have a local, national, regional or international reputation in five years' time? For what?

How much of your budget needs to be devoted without exception to people development to achieve the strategic vision?

Organizational structure

Definition

The structure or design of an organization is the system of reporting lines and job titles that set out the way the organization runs itself. Structures evolve both naturally and by artificial design. I believe that natural structures are almost always superior to those created to suit a theory or a strategy for the future of the organization. Sometimes the structure of the organization can get in the way of the business. On those occasions it is necessary to try and adjust the system to fit the organization's needs. A typical problem may be when a business has grown by acquisition. For example, Unilever, the global manufacturer and wholesale supplier of cleansing products to retailers, has grown by acquiring many different brands and types of product. That means that, on any one day, a wholesaler may receive visits from several representatives of different divisions of the company. That is wasteful of resources for Unilever but also expensive to the buyer who really does not have time to see so many people. Under circumstances such as these one could change the structure of the business to ensure that each salesperson manages a rational portfolio which minimizes the cost per visit to the customer and the use of the customers' time.

Theory versus what happens in practice

Some academic theories of organizational design recommend that structure should be designed after the leaders have decided the long-term strategy. I believe, from my long experience working with leaders who had to design working structures for real businesses, that it is wiser to make as little change as possible in structure terms. Why? Because it is hard to get it right, so likely to go wrong and thoroughly destabilizing to the people in the business. It is not worth the bother and it rarely makes a vital difference to the business.

Theoretically, the advice to develop your long-term strategy and then design the structure of the business that will get you there is sound. Obviously, one should only decide which vehicle (the structure) to use for a journey after one has decided where the journey (strategic future aims) are intended to take the traveller (the organization). You do not get on a bus and then decide to go to India. Usually, most people decide to go to India and then decide an airplane might be the best mode of transport in preference to, say, getting on a bus.

> **You do not get on a bus and then decide to go to India.**

In practice, most executives behave differently and try to sort out structure and design problems soon after they are appointed to a new position. I have reflected on this discrepancy between theory and practice for many years and concluded that there are clear and valid reasons why real-world practices contrast so strongly with the recommended theory.

First of all, structure and design change in organizations makes for very high levels of political instability, demotivation and a loss of work impetus among the workforce. Maslow (1970) demonstrated that one of the most basic human needs is for structure and stability. This is in contrast to arguments of some modern theorists (and some executives) who assert that it is advisable continuously to change structure to adapt to the external fast changing environment which prevails in the business world. My observations are that frequent change only causes instability and chaos which is never useful when trying to manage an organization or business for long-term profitability.

Classic strategy theory (Chandler 1962) suggested that leaders should develop their entire strategy for the long term and only then design a structure to enable that strategy to be achieved. Unfortunately, the real world is rarely as straightforward as that. First, organization structures, even those designed to fit the longer term, have to continuously react and adjust to external realities. Second, people working within organizations often find their own solutions to customers' problems or to improve operational inefficiencies which are based on their realities. Their solutions are nearly always superior to anything designed in the human resource department, divorced from the practicalities of the problems. Third, organizational structure is never stable. It may be based on a few formal rules and design set by the leaders but in reality it is adjusted by the normal process of people relating to people who are trying to do their jobs efficiently and effectively within the limits of their ability. Formal structures rarely take these realities into account sufficiently.

Most managers do it

This does not answer the intrinsic puzzle of why so many managers, when they first arrive in a new post, tend to restructure the department or business first and only afterwards get down to analyzing their strategic purpose or create a plan. Why do so many do that against the theoretical advice? The reasons are related mainly to human nature and common sense.

Most managers tend to form opinions fast about the people they work with. They rarely change their mind even though there may be evidence showing that their initial opinion was wrong. They thus tend to build the structure of their department, division or business around their impressions of their people rather than the strategic needs of the corporation. Second, most managers prefer to restructure and remove people before they develop emotional attachments or relationships with them. After a few months most managers will have developed relationships with their team members and will find it much harder to get rid of them when they will have begun to like them and form reciprocal relationships. That may explain why they like to do it early before those emotional attachments are formed.

Some managers make a habit of 'taking their favourite sons with them' when they go to new appointments. These are people whom they trust. However, they often need to remove a few people from their new department to make space for their favourites. Great leaders and managers do not need to do this. The best managers are people who make optimum use of the human resources they find when they arrive, rather than trying to shape the team to fit their own needs. Unfortunately, there are far too few great leaders around (see Levicki 2002).

Purposes of organizational structure

Structure facilitates strategy implementation

The structure of the organization is designed to help achieve the strategy. For example, if an organization makes just a few products in one central factory but needs to have a national distribution system it may decide, strategically, to remain centralized for its operations but farm out its distribution to a supplier of that service which already has a national setup. This solves the problem at lowest possible cost at the price of a small forfeit of autonomy and control. Alternatively, if the company has many products, it may design the organization around the different products and the markets it serves. It would, therefore, have managers reporting along product lines rather than geographical or functional ones. Very large organizations, where each subdivision is equivalent to a corporation in its own right, often divide themselves along functional lines. For instance, in automobile manufacture, there could be an information technology director, a director in charge of operations and, possibly, another in charge of marketing.

Structure allocates tasks and responsibility

The organization structure helps people to understand what their tasks and responsibilities are. If the organization is functionally based, then it tells people which part of the function they work for and what their priorities are. In the last example, if you work on the assembly line of an automobile company, you know that assembly of the vehicle is the dominant function of your part of the business. You will almost certainly be responsible for one particular part of assembly, perhaps fixing the doors or controlling quality or ensuring that parts are delivered by a subcontractor to be available on time on the assembly line. The structure is there to always remind you what you, individually, and, as part of the team, do to work for the corporation overall.

This also points to one of the problems of this kind of structure. If something goes wrong in the engine-manufacturing plant, even though with experience you could solve the problem, the structure tends to prevent you from helping even if you want to. You will not know the right person in the other plant to whom to report the problem. Furthermore, it may be politically incorrect to cause problems for people in other departments. You never know when they might reciprocate or retaliate. You might, therefore, ignore a problem, even though you could resolve it.

Structure establishes formal reporting relationships

The design of the organization also designates who shall report to whom and what position people have in the organization's hierarchy. Ultimately, every organization needs its people to accept that they report to another person and are responsible to that person. That relationship designates what they can and cannot do and what they should expect from the person above them, as well as what they must expect from the people below them in the formal structure. It formalizes the system and indicates exactly how the organization is intended to work and who is, nominally, in charge of anybody else.

Structure groups employees efficiently

There are many theories about what is an efficient number of people to work together. There are various concepts about suitable group size for maximum efficiency. Whichever school of thought one belongs to, the need to group people into teams to enable them to be effective when working together is real. IBM, the leading world computing business, believes groups of more than 250 people cannot be effective as a working unit. Whenever they grow above this number they find a reason for subdividing the business into another working unit. Many people believe that fairly small units are more effective in business than large ones. Keeping to relatively low numbers ensures efficiency.

Organizational structure designates authority, discretion and control

Every organization needs to authorize each person's level of responsibility in terms of budget, revenue or power. The organizational structure formalizes that authority and describes who will control people below them and from whom they accept control.

Similarly, structure facilitates the monitoring and evaluation of all the human resources of the organization by allowing management to see clearly what each person and group is meant to do.

Structure facilitates communication

The formal structural design indicates who needs to give information to whom. If an organization is structured as a matrix it is easy for different departments to forget to tell others who will need to know what they are doing with customers. In matrix organizations, it is frequently the case that several project teams have different relationships with the same customer. If they do not keep each other informed, it could lead to the undesirable consequence that the customer becomes the proxy manager of the supplier's matrix organization.

Even within the business, the formal structure indicates which department must talk to which and when they must do so, to make sure that everybody has enough information to do his or her job effectively.

Structure maximizes motivation

We mentioned earlier that design and structure organizes people into groups which are efficient and effective. The grouping into units serves a further purpose because it is also motivational. The formal structure tells people what the senior, middle and junior jobs are. It also tells them where the job opportunities exist in the organization. It enables them to see a path for their careers and how they can measure their success.

The 1980s and 1990s saw a growing trend in re-engineering, downsizing, right sizing and restructuring. These have reduced enormously the scope for middle and senior managers to move up ladders of promotion. However, once this misguided fashion has run its course, normal promotional systems will continue for the majority of people. People also like to know that they are not moving backwards in the organizational structure; they will accept different responsibilities, even if the job change represents a sideways movement rather than upwards, in order to expand their experience.

Different bases of structural design

Simple business startup structure

Most business startups use the energy of the founder and one or two associates to build momentum and some reserves to grow the business further. Consequently, the founding owner and his associates often have to use family and friends to provide finance and labour. This means that they all tend to be both generalists and specialists in the business.

The owner often has to conduct his own marketing research (possibly because he cannot afford to buy it); he tends to do the selling himself (and, therefore, manage the customer relationships); he often also helps in production and sometimes even does the accounts himself (usually when the owner is meant to be having a break from work at the weekend). The essential feature, therefore, of the small business structure is that it is composed of generalists doing many various specialist jobs (see Figure 11.1).

Boss, owner, general manager				
Duties	Wife	Old friend	Security	Driver
	People handling	*Accounts and general labour*	*Admin and databases*	*Packaging and distribution*

Figure 11.1 Conceptual structure of a small business

Functional structures

Functional structures divide the organization around the skills that are needed within the business. They usually include marketing, sales, research and development, production, operations, accounting, finance, treasury, general management and corporate services.

The advantages of functional structures are that they can foster a sense of professional identity among employees of similar skills. Such groups are easier to supervise by similarly skilled functional employees. They also give opportunities for specialization in particular skills and provide specialized information and knowledge to other departments of the organization.

Functional structures can cause disharmony between departments as professional groups make stereotypical appraisals and conclusions. For example, marketing people too easily think that production standards are not good enough. Production people often conclude that marketing wants too many varieties. And both believe the manager does not understand reality! The allocation of cost and responsibility for performance become difficult and subjective as accountants attempt to distribute real costs fairly but appropriately to each function. Did engineering fail to deliver a product on time because it is inefficient or because the salespeople changed the customer's specification? Who can really say how much heating a department consumed or what would be a fair share of the cost of the management overhead?

Finally, and importantly, functional structures tend to inhibit the development of well-rounded senior managers. If the functional structure is relatively rigid, then it will be used right to the top of the organization. That means that the senior managers from whom the general management appointments are usually made will have gained experience of only one functional skill area while rising to the top of the organization. Consequently, one finds that the choices for chairman or chief executive (i.e. general leadership roles requiring an understanding of all the functions of the organization) must be made from a selection of people who only understand a single aspect of the organization. Inevitably, these people can have tunnel visioned and lack balance when exercising overall judgment skills (see Figure 11.2).

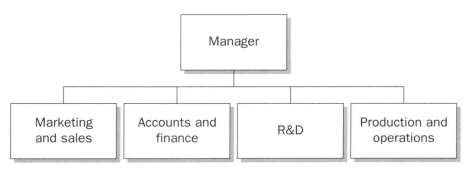

Figure 11.2 Conceptual functional organization structure

One often finds that organizations which are rigidly functional in their promotional and structural systems have to appoint people from outside the organization when they are looking for new chairmen or chief executives. The problem then is that these people have to spend the first few months in their new appointment getting to know the business – rather than running it.

Product structures

If an organization has a wide range of products it may be advisable to structure the business around those product lines. This may be particularly appropriate if the products cross different industries and marketplaces.

This is particularly important if a corporation has a large range of products each of which is at different stages of development in each of the markets where it is sold. For example, Procter & Gamble, the global hygiene products business, sells the same toothpaste with variations in taste, colour, flavour and packaging in each of its many markets across continents and countries. It is wise to gather together all the expertise on that product so that it can be applied at the appropriate time in developing the product for each market.

One advantage of a product structure is that it allows for easy accounting practices facilitating focus on costs, profitability and possible losses throughout an organization. A further advantage of this structural form is that decision making can be allocated specifically where problems arise. For example, a conglomerate such as Tomkins plc (a UK-based international diversified conglomerate) does not really want a divisional person in charge of gun manufacture in the USA making decisions about bread making in the UK.

A disadvantage of product structures is that they can duplicate resources. For example, each product will need general management, accountancy and, probably, marketing and sales functions. They may also necessitate separate buildings, headquarters and general staff. This can be an expensive addition to the cost structure of the organization.

Product structures can also miss out on the advantage which functional structures have, whereby specialized occupational skills are developed. People tend to be generalists within their product area and may have less knowledge about particular functions than their counterparts in functional organizations. Thus, a person may become brilliant at understanding every market preference in flavours and taste in biscuits but understand nothing about how to calculate the viability of the market or how to depreciate the cost of buildings and trucks.

Another consequence of product structures is that they encourage competitiveness between divisions. This can be counterproductive if the divisions have similar products to sell to the same customers. This problem can be exacerbated in organizations which use the same brand name. Clients get an impression of wastefulness when they see three salespersons from the same corporate parent. The client will not necessarily appreciate that this is efficient for the supplier (and, therefore, for the customer) because they are selling different products within a rational and optimal structure (see Figure 11.3).

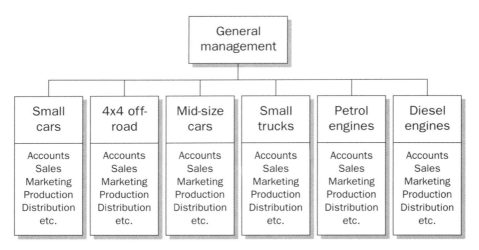

Figure 11.3 Conceptual example of a product structure

Structure based on geography

Where a business is manufacturing or supplying bulky or weighty items or where a major cost factor is transportation, it is advisable to structure the business along geographical lines. Similarly, if the market is highly segmented at the local level, whether subnational, national or continental, it is often convenient to structure the organization along geographical lines.

Most of the advantages and disadvantages described for product structures apply equally to geographical structures. An additional problem with geographical structures, especially international ones, is that they can build up heavy travelling costs, in the form of both actual costs of travel and wasted executive time. In these structures it is normally necessary to restrict international coordination to a few leaders at the top. The subsequent advantage is that these managers become extremely knowledgeable. The disadvantage is almost nobody else does (see Figure 11.4).

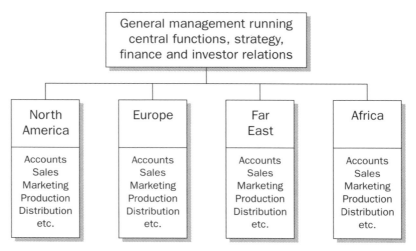

Figure 11.4 Conceptual example of geographical structure

Matrix structures

Matrix structures were conceived around the idea of people having more than one separate line of responsibility. These may be any mix of function, product, geography or organization.

The definition should also indicate how complex and difficult matrix structures can be for employees, customers and suppliers. Earlier in the chapter it was explained that one of the purposes of structure is to clarify role and responsibility within the organization. Matrix structures blur and obfuscate those clear lines of demarcation and responsibility. They do this because people are never quite sure what power or authority anybody has within the matrix organization. For example, in matrix organizations it is quite common to put the person with the most knowledge about a particular subject in charge of delivering that project, no matter what level of power they have within the organization. Consequently, people in the team are never quite sure, when they have a conflict of demands on their time, who they really must deliver to first and foremost. In theory, it should be to the most important client or project – in practice it is rarely that simple as people, ultimately, pull authority and rank to get their needs dealt with while others consequently fail to deliver their promises on time because the team did not consider their requests carried enough weight.

Misery and misunderstanding

In a logistics business I knew, each functional leader was allocated a geographical country to manage. Thus, the finance director was also chairman of the Spanish subsidiary. The human resource director was the chairman of the Belgian subsidiary and the managing director in charge of grocery marketing and sales was also the chairman of the German subsidiary. Most did not know the language and customs of their areas of responsibility. For them each trip was a joyride and a nightmare as they each confronted, in loneliness, the hopelessness of their ignorance and their isolated responsibility. There was no centre of expertise they could turn to for help. Eventually the business found a Belgian human resources director who had worked for an international company in Belgium. They were so ignorant of what mattered they thought that made him an expert in developing an international business. They had to sack him a year later, a broken man leaving behind another set of busted flushes.

The advantage of a matrix organization is that it encourages interdepartmental ideas and sharing of knowledge. It can also increase flexibility in the use of human resources as people work some of their time for a geographical area and another time in a functional role. It tends to maximize the effort that people put into the organization. Overall, it can develop well-rounded managers.

Matrix structures can develop serious disadvantages which make it difficult to manage them comfortably or to deliver satisfaction to a boss within. There are a few types of industry which use them effectively, such as project-based businesses which need to form teams for relatively short-lived projects such as business consultancy IT service installation. Other businesses which find them useful are those which use several different types of expertise for each project, such as large building projects or architects' practices.

Would you let your best friend have one?

Why are matrix structures so difficult to manage? First, they tend to maximize employees' feelings of insecurity because staff members are often not sure which boss they should be reporting to at any given time. Staff can get caught up in power struggles between different leaders for the use of resources. That forces employees into making difficult judgments about the relative power of their different leaders. For example, a person may report, in a matrix organization, to both a product and a geographical leader. He could please one enormously and displease the other – and damage his career prospects as a result because he pleased the lesser boss in terms of who could affect his career most. Matrix structures can put enormous stress on managers as they try to balance their multiple roles, trying to judge which form of success will aid their careers.

Finally, matrix organizations are infamous for leading to conflict because the lines of authority and responsibility get blurred and lack clarity.

Matrix organization is recommended, cautiously, in firms which require the constant creation of project teams to resolve particular problems on behalf of clients. However, it is only normally successful with a well-educated and highly intelligent workforce which is trained specifically in team skills and where mutual respect is based on expertise, rather than on positional power (see Figure 11.5).

	Manager manufacturing	Manager sales	Manager accounting	Manager human resources	Manager business reputation
General manager in an information technology consultancy					
Project 1 led by main board director	Mainframes	Industrial apps	Financial	Personnel	Media PR
Project 2 led by supervisor from the accounting department	PCs	Wholesale market	Management	Industrial relations	Risk management
Project 3 led by a research scientist from R&D	Chip technology	Retail market	Treasury	Pensions	Corporate charity
Project 4 led by a middle-ranking sales person	Hard drives	Mail order	Regulatory	People development	Corporate ethics

Figure 11.5 Matrix structure

So, what structures work if they all have weaknesses?

Much of this chapter has focused more on why each structure does not work rather than what is best for each need. The reader must be feeling bewildered. The problem is that no structure or design is ever perfect. The best structures are those that have evolved over a long period and answer real business and customer needs. They are usually a mix of product, geography, functional and even matrix aspects. Few can be defended in terms of academic purity, simplicity or elegance – but many do work. A good example of a company which uses a mixed model is L'Oréal. There one comes across a mixture of functional design, with accounting, marketing, sales, human resources and production clearly delineated; but in other parts of the business they exploit a geographical structure, with each country having its own HQ and corporate structure; they use matrix structures when necessary, for example when taking particular initiatives in new product development. Then they would put together many executives from various countries to take part in project teams managed from the centralized global HQ in Paris.

Informal structures

The strongest structure in any organization is usually the informal structure, rather than the laid-out design of the organization. The 'informal structure' refers to the way people actually make things happen in an organization. Sometimes this mirrors the formal structure fairly accurately but usually it cuts across the way the formal structure says the business is meant to work.

Most people in organizations like to cooperate and help each other. People do not go to work to do a bad job. If they see where they can help others do things more effectively or efficiently they usually will join in and help, even if the formal structure does not indicate that it is their responsibility or ask them to actually do it. Friendships get formed as people move around the organization. When their careers move in different directions, possibly with one person accelerating ahead of the other in the formal structure, they will still retain

Top telco – 'the grapevine'

Many years ago I was working on strategy development with the senior managers of a telecom company, a leading international telecommunications business. It was a highly formalized bureaucracy in those days. It had stretched bureaucracy and hierarchy to the extreme, with anything up to 30 different grades of manager. Of course, it could be argued that this was not too many for an enterprise which, in those days, had over 200,000 employees.

However, in order to demonstrate the differences between the formal and informal structure, I always used the following episode with new teams when they first came for strategy instruction.

I would mention two people who had recently been promoted to exactly the same grade and the same title of 'director'. Both people had received the same monetary reward and each would get a Jaguar to signify his new status and importance. However, because the business, in those days, never liked to make people redundant or to dismiss them for other reasons it would frequently promote them to a job which could sideline them and get them out of the way of the efficient running of the organization. One could always choose examples of two people where one had received a genuine promotion and the other had received a promotion which was intended to sideline that individual.

I would test the audience with a question such as: 'How many of you wrote a letter of congratulation to A?' (where A was the person who was really being sidelined). All hands would stay down. I would then ask: 'And who wrote a letter of congratulation to B?' Most hands in the room would go up – it was a very polite organization and letters of congratulation were normal behaviour in those days. I would then ask: 'How did you know that the first person was being sidelined and the second was really being promoted?' Most people would laugh and say: 'We just know these things.'

That is how the informal structure and grapevine works. People know where power and authority lie, even if the formal design of the organization does not show it. That is why wise managers frequently wait to find out where the informal power structure lies before they start redesigning their organization.

affection, friendship or trust which will encourage them to retain contact and help each other, even when the formal structure could not explain the relationship at all.

The informal structure is also the way that information passes around the organization most effectively. Try keeping secret an affair between two senior managers or the boss and her chauffeur!

Practical approaches to organizational design

Spans of control

Some managers can manage up to ten subordinates, although most are more comfortable with between five and eight. This is a good guide as to how to organize the management and supervisory layers of the business. If one applies these numbers as a guideline to the typical IBM core group of about 240 people, it could be devised thus:

- 240 people divided into groups of eight = 30 groups.
- 30 groups could have one of the eight appointed as a supervisor.
- The 30 groups could be divided into six sets of groups of five each.
- Each of the six sets would need a manager in charge.
- Finally, the set of managers would need a leader or manager who will be responsible for the overall work of the whole department which is now 252 people strong.

Thus, to get 240 people working, we need 30 of them to dedicate some of their time to supervising rather than working. The supervisors will also need managing. The managers will need managing, too. Finally, we need a leader to coordinate everything. This simple example shows how soon and how easily the cost of management and the potential for things to go wrong evolves – just because the system needs structure and management (see Figure 11.6).

Rationality

Obviously, the spans of control rule is meant to be a guide. If the level of supervision required is low, a manager might manage up to 12 people. Anything over this number becomes somewhat inflexible. I have met

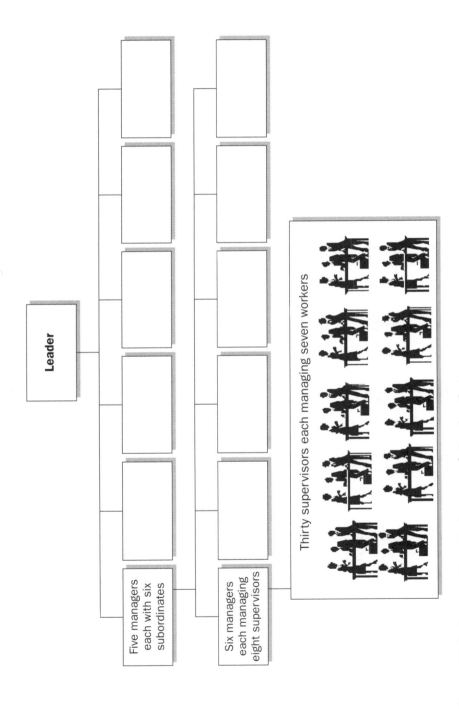

Leader

Five managers each with six subordinates

Six managers each managing eight supervisors

Thirty supervisors each managing seven workers

Figure 11.6 A span of control approach to structure

many managers who have larger spans of control. Although they assured me they were managing effectively, one often discovered their subordinates were unhappy and felt neglected.

Rationality also applies to the design of the structure. Some simple rules apply:

1 Keep relevant groups physically together. For instance, I recently worked with a business where the CEO and the FD (finance director) worked together in one building in Northampton while the chairman, the MD of one (of its three) divisions and his deputy worked in Birmingham (about 60 miles away). I was not in the least surprised when my client's opening statement when we met was, 'We don't seem to have a strategy.' A short while later he did not have a job either!
2 Ensure that groups, or group leaders who are physically dispersed, have reasons to meet regularly to maintain the business relationships that are vital if the business is to run smoothly.
3 If the business is divided geographically, ensure that there are enough people leading geographical divisions who speak to each other and carry corporate strategy along as well as guarantee that the business does not miss opportunities.

Communications

If you are an unemployed executive or under employed consultant, you could always start a 'corporate communications consultancy'. To make it a surefire success offer the clients a free communications audit of a sample of the employees. You will always find that some or all of the employees feel their bosses do not communicate sufficiently with them or that important information is being withheld from them. This represents a defining aspect of the human condition of mind.

The underlying serious point about communication is that it is the leader's job, when designing the organizational structure, to ensure that the structure facilitates communications, both laterally and vertically. The culture must encourage communications as strongly as the organizational design is meant to facilitate them. I remember working with a global pharmaceutical business which seemed to render its people paranoid as well as force them to work excessive hours. In one ten-storey building the company had put easy chairs, coffee tables and coffee machines on each floor, next to each elevator. They were there, theoretically, to encourage people to relax and talk to each other. Those seats were always empty because people were so scared about being thought lazy that they didn't dare to be seen relaxing in an easy chair in full view of any manager who might use the elevator.

The leader and the leading strategic team

The team leading the corporation, especially at a time of strategic growth, develops as a team by sharing offices together. If a team consists of functional leaders who, necessarily, need offices near the production units or near the sales outlets, there should also be a headquarters building which enables them to spend time together (a day or two each week, perhaps) where they have the opportunity to discuss problems and opportunities and to ameliorate or maintain their relationships. This apparent waste of building resource will more than adequately pay for itself in improved effectiveness and cooperation.

Conclusion

A great deal of time and effort goes into the design of structure. One chief executive I worked with used to spend almost half a day of every week thinking up different ways he could organize the firm. Ultimately, it was all futile as he did not know how to manage the business.

The final advice, therefore, is to be imaginative and unconstrained in organizational structure design. If it appears to be working, leave it alone or tinker at the edges only. Remember that people like stability. Even when the organization has to be radically changed, it should be done quickly and then left alone. The evidence is that continuous change is anathema to most staff and executives and catastrophic to the organization.

Please note: The workout for this chapter is a set of questions to help you to focus on the important aspects you should consider before setting out the structure of your organization on a clean sheet of paper. Think about what you would design if you were designing the structure just to achieve the pure business purposes of the organization. Think how much you could change from the actual form to the pure form that the organization probably really needs. Then, do just a little of what you think you should!

Further reading

T. Burns and G. M. Stalker, *The Management of Innovation*, Tavistock, London, 1961

A. P. Chandler, *Strategy and Structure*, MIT Press, Boston, 1962

R. M. Grant, *Contemporary Strategic Analysis*, Blackwell, Oxford, 1995

C. J. Levicki, *The Leadership Gene*, Financial Times Pitman, London, 1998

C. J. Levicki, *Developing Leadership Genius*, McGraw-Hill, Maidenhead, 2002

A. Maslow, *Motivation and Personality*, Harper & Row, New York, 1970

D. Pugh (ed.), *Organization Theory*, Penguin, Harmondsworth, 1971

D. S. Pugh and D. J. Hickson, *Organizational Structure in its Context*, Saxon House/Lexington Books, D. E. Heath Ltd, Farnborough, 1976

O. Williamson, *Markets and Hierarchies*, Free Press, New York, 1975

ORGANIZATIONAL STRUCTURE WORKOUT

What is the size of the organization?_____

People? _____ Revenue? _____ Profits? _____

What geographical area does it cover?

Local? _____ Regional? _____ Country? _____ International? _____

Does the organization provide many or a few services or products? _____

Which is better known? The company name? _____ The brand names of the products? _____

Is the organization currently centralized? _____ Or decentralized? _____

Are there lots of rules? _____ Or very few rules? _____

What is the average proportion of managers to workers? _____

How do you communicate? Verbally? _____ Written messages? _____ Electronic mail? _____

Does the organization offer the same service all the time? _____

Does almost every order require a different process? _____

How is the organization structured now?

Functional ☐   Geographical ☐   Product ☐   Matrix ☐   Mixed ☐

What is the average span of control (span of control = the number of people managed by each manager) at each level in the hierarchy of the business?

Are there rational reasons for the differences between levels in the hierarchy?   Yes   No

Why or why not?_____

How many direct supports does the leader have? _____

Does the culture encourage communications? _____

What is the total number of employees? _____

What is the total number of operators, meaning people with direct 'doing' jobs? _____

What is the total number of supervisors and managers? _____

Could you design any structure which decreases the number of managers?

(Use a spare blank sheet.)

What are the major advantages of your design? _____

What are the major disadvantages of your design? _____

Short-term tactics to build the long-term strategy

Introduction

I always carefully distinguish between the use of the words **strategy**, **planning** and **tactics**. I use strategy to mean the overall long-term set of objectives of the company, its mission and vision. Planning is a word I try to avoid completely because too many practitioners use it as a halfway house with a meaning lodged between strategy and tactics. I carefully reserve the use of the word tactics as a definition of short-term plans which are calculated to add together to fulfil the long-term strategy. Three to five years of successful delivery of appropriate short-term tactics each year should absolutely and assuredly deliver the long-term strategy.

Definition of tactics

If strategy is about the long-term objectives and destiny of the business or corporation, then year by year the company has to build, brick by brick, the essential foundations to develop and achieve the strategy. Tactics are the bricks of the organization's strategic building. Tactics need to be formulated and implemented on the basis of their contribution towards achievement of the long-term strategy, the overall integrated set of aims. If any tactic does not do that it is not a tactic, it is just a deviation from strategic achievement. If the organization fails on one or two tactics in any one year then it has to adjust its strategy to take account of that failure. Either that tactic is compensated for by another of equal value and contribution or the overall strategy will need to be adjusted.

The order of things

The key principle of strategy analysis and implementation is that the long-term strategy has to be developed first. Then the structure should be designed, bearing in mind the strictures about organization design we described earlier. Only then should tactics (the shorter term priorities) be formulated. Each of the short term tactics must form one of the key blocks to create the long-term 'building'. Sam Walton, founder of Wal-Mart, used to ask, 'How did we ever get to be the largest retailer in the world? ... We figured out a way to grow, and stay profitable, and there was no logical place to stop.' However, he'd always intended to become a very large retailer. That was his long-term strategy.

The rule for setting short-term tactics

Short-term tactics are intended to achieve the overall long-term strategic objectives when each of the individual tactical priorities is integrated. Each tactical priority should make a contribution toward the total strategy of the organization. The advice is that the long-term strategy be created first, then the structure should be adjusted; only then should tactics (the shorter term priorities) be formulated. They should always be subsidiary to the strategy because one should not try to grow the business from tactics into strategy – only the other way round. Many organizations I have come across work almost entirely on the short term, believing that if they get through this year or next year successfully, the long term will evolve out of the short-term tactical gains. I believe this explains why so many organizations go from crisis to crisis, rather than achievement to larger achievement. To repeat, for emphasis: **the short-term tactics must flow from the long-term objectives and never vice versa**.

To demonstrate this concept consider the simplest example or metaphor to prove the point. Consider the construction of a new building. Before everything else the architect must design the whole building, specify the materials and type of construction and what the building is going to be used for. Only then could anyone begin ordering building materials or the construction equipment or start to assemble the necessary and suitable workers. Nobody says, 'I have this large digging machine – let's dig a deep foundation.' The corporate strategist and/or leader is the architect of the business.

It is also worth noting that 'short term' does not mean 'shortsighted'. Tactics should be part of the growth plan and not based on just achieving this year's budget. All middle and senior managers should know how to achieve short-term results if they need to. It is easy to achieve a budget target by shortsighted behaviour. For example, failing to develop and train staff, failing to repair and maintain property as it deteriorates, using lower specification on product manufacture or reducing the long-term promotion and advertising budgets are all methods used by some managers to deliver budgets without responsibility. Many careers have been built on such shortsighted budgetary achievements. It is essential to develop tactics which achieve the short-term budgetary considerations but do not sell the organization's long-term future down the river.

Fluffy cushion syndrome

Chloride Batteries was a supplier of batteries to both the second-hand automobile and car-manufacturing industries, back in the 1980s. They thought, at first, they had a sales problem. That year the factory had produced 1.5 million batteries, but had only sold 1.4 million. Consequently the business was carrying 100,000 surplus to demand battery stock for six months – and it was costing too much.

The following year the business again made 1.5 million batteries. This time they had devised a new sales campaign and got orders for 1.5 million. Unfortunately, the distribution system let the team down. They lacked the capacity to deliver 100,000 of the batteries and annoyed the customers.

The following year the managing director redesigned the distribution capacity. He ensured that the distribution system could deliver the 1.5 million when needed, in the middle of the winter. Unfortunately, he then discovered the factory had insufficient 'refreshing' machinery. Batteries that have been in store more than a few months need recharging before delivery or they arrive flat. Once again, 100,000 customers failed to get the Chloride battery they wanted because they could not get them charged and delivered on time in the winter when they were needed.

The following year the battery-refreshing problem was solved. But something went wrong with sales and the sales force only sold 1.4 million of the potential 1.5 million that were being made. So, once again, they were stuck with 100,000 batteries.

That looked exactly like the sales problem we started with, three years earlier. We were back to square one.

After three years of this assignment it was 'fluffy cushion syndrome'.

Why? When you have a really luxurious fluffy cushion made of the best duck down, whenever you try to fluff it out to make it look nice, wherever you hit it to smooth it out, it just fluffs out on the other side. You can never get it completely smooth all round.

Bad tactical decisions in organizations are like that. If they are ill-chosen, they just cause another problem the following year. Usually the same problem crops up, again and again, in badly managed organizations. Good tactical choices always make a permanent contribution to the long term and leave no short-term hostages to fortune.

Tactics must be measurable and unambiguous

It is advisable to choose not more than two to four tactical objectives for subordinates to achieve. They should always be measurable in arithmetical or numerical terms. Thus, 'beating last year's result' is an inappropriate target. 'Beating last year's budget of $25 million profit by 10 percent to deliver exactly $27.5 million in profits by the end of the year, March 31' *is* an accurate and measurable target. All short-term tactics should be set in a measurable form like that.

You should also ensure that the tactical priorities are compatible with each other. For example, to ask your sales manager to achieve customer awareness of the product but decrease his budget on promotional expenditure by 10 percent is clearly counterproductive. When you do your review with him at the end of the year, you might find a reduction in customer awareness from 27 percent to 25 percent. If you wish to use that to withhold his bonus, the manager may legitimately respond by reminding you that he was asked to reduce the advertising and promotional budgets by 10 percent. Indeed, he may have overachieved by reducing budgets by 12 percent. He can legitimately claim his bonus. If managers set ambiguous or incompatible targets, they should not be surprised if they are eventually obliged to pay bonuses for inadequate performance at the end of the year.

All objectives can be reduced to measurable numbers. For example, customer satisfaction can be measured by the number of telephoned and written complaints. Production quality can be measured by the number of claims made on warranty or the cost of reworking products which fail factory tests before dispatch. Management efficiency can be measured by production numbers, profitability, budget accuracy and staff turnover.

Almost all tactical measuring instruments and targets can cause some deviation in behaviour. They are not always easy to devise and should be adjusted or changed relatively frequently. But without them a manager has nothing to measure the effectiveness of a team's performance. Consider the problem the British government has trying to improve the National Health Service as demand increases because more people live longer. The Minister of Health decided that length of waiting lists would be a measure of the efficiency of hospitals. The government set reducing waiting lists as the target for every hospital in the United Kingdom. One should not be surprised that managers of hospitals focused excessively on their waiting lists. They were induced to manipulate the way they compose their waiting lists to try to beat the waiting list reduction target. Some, for example, began to avoid putting people on the list in the first place. Others took to removing people from a list if they missed any appointment for any reason. Another group took to making two lists, one when the patient was referred and another when the patient was finally allocated a place on the waiting list for a specific doctor. The managers cannot be blamed. Rather we should be blaming a misguided government which set foolish targets which were not designed to solve the problem properly. The real issue was that people needed faster medical treatment. That should have been the target. Using the waiting list as a proxy for the truly desired objective was a mistake.

Budgets and tasks

A short-term tactic should *always* have a budget number attached to it. The budget should be couched in terms of how much revenue must be achieved or what maximum costs are permitted for a given quantity of output or sales. Tactics, being a subpart of the overall strategy, should be determined by the needs of the long-term strategy. If it is possible to benchmark them against competitive standards, particularly competitors who are beating your organization in the market, then so much the better.

Criteria for short-term objectives

Increasing or decreasing manufacturing capacity

If the overall strategy of the organization is to move out of one sector and into another, it may be appropriate to decrease manufacturing capacity in one part of the business as it transfers resources to another. Other reasons for increasing or decreasing manufacturing capacity will be to try to achieve product cost leadership in a sector or to become a more sales and less manufacturing-oriented organization. An organization may discover that it can buy in its products more economically than manufacturing them in-house. This should lead to a decrease in manufacturing capacity to cut expenditure and release resources for other parts of the budget such as marketing.

Improved technology

The improvement of technology is a difficult short-term tactic because technology is complex and cannot easily be improved in the short run. Technology can only be improved at the same rate as the human resources that run the technology can upgrade their skills. That type of training requires development programmes which rarely show results in the one-year time spans that are relevant to short-term tactics. However, it could form part of a two-year strategic objective.

Increasing or decreasing the workforce

This particular tactic was prevalent during the 1990s and has dominated the tactical planning of many organizations. Whether re-engineering, downsizing, or right sizing, decreasing the workforce is rarely the panacea that it is claimed to be by the re-engineering consultants who specialize in these techniques.

Given the social and legal constraints that prevail in many advanced industrial nations, the costs of decreasing workforces are high. In recessionary periods, the workforce is reluctant to leave and it becomes difficult to select the members of the workforce who should be removed because they are the less effective workers. One often finds that the best human resources go and the worst stay. In addition, organizations which have undergone re-engineering frequently find that they have overdone it and have to buy in fresh human resources – usually people who have neither the skills nor the accumulated know-how of the people who have recently been discarded. In many organizations, the easiest target group for immediate cost savings without commensurate damage is the marketing department. In these circumstances, re-engineering becomes a short-term gain which replaces the long-term future – which marketing exists to capture.

Increasing the workforce is also a difficult short-term tactic. Accumulating new quantities of personnel is easy. Finding the right personnel with the appropriate skills and inducting them into the cultural value system of the organization often takes longer than one or two years.

Improving quality

Improving quality, like the workforce considerations just examined, can only be *started* as a short-term tactic. Quality should always be improved on a continuous basis. Making quality improvement a tactical objective is a useful tool when standards have fallen so low that the organization is in danger of losing all consumer confidence in the product or services provided. In those circumstances, attention must be unequivocally focused on improving quality to convince the customers that the company has a right to exist. But it should be done as the start of a process that will never end – not as a one-off, short-term fix.

Maximize profits

There are two circumstances when maximizing profits is an appropriate tactic. The first is when long-term strategy is inapplicable because the firm is in a turnaround situation. Under these circumstances all normal rules are put aside. Unless the stricken firm accumulates some short-term cash, it is unlikely to survive for any long run. The rule that long-term strategy precedes short-term tactics should be reversed. The objective is to maximize cash flow or profitability in the short run to ensure the survival of the organization.

The second circumstance when profit maximization is advisable as a short-term tactic is when the organization has had a series of short-term tactical successes over some years. These might be aimed at achieving a targeted share of the market, the lowest manufacturing cost profile or a particular level of development of its human resources. If the organization is close to achieving its long-term strategy and mission, it may be appropriate to concentrate on maximization of profit as a short-term tactic. However, most organizations which had achieved so much would probably find a larger scale mission and an even longer term strategy to aim for, rather than merely try to maximize profits.

APV – refusing to make profit

APV was a multinational food machinery engineering company with an annual revenue of $1,500 million. It made a paltry profit of about $20 million a year. It had been established for over 100 years and had a long track record of supplying quality machines to the farming and food-processing industries around the world. It even kept design records for every machine as long as it remained in operation, sometimes 80 years after it was supplied.

The chairman asked consultants to undertake a worldwide tour to understand why the business was making so little profit. Could the consultants find a fast-track idea to bring in short-term profits to prevent a takeover bid?

The scrutiny found that the firm made almost no sales after the installation of its beautiful machines, either to service its installed machines or to sell spare parts. This was caused by the obsession of the senior managers with innovation and installation. They loved installing bright gleaming stainless steel apparatus and solving unusual and difficult customer problems. They were entirely uninterested in the nitty gritty of making profits. The consultants estimated there were up to $25 billion of installed equipment, all being serviced by competitors or small local businesses. The annual turnover in spare parts could be, at least, $500 million, at net profit levels of 30 percent.

They recommended that a new division be created to take advantage of the servicing and spare parts business which was being grabbed by small local suppliers wherever their equipment was installed. They advised it should be done through a new division with newly appointed managers and workmen from outside the body of the business, because the established managers were uninterested.

The chairman accepted all the advice except the bit about investing in new personnel. He felt unable to go that extra step when profits were already so low. He gave the new division to one of the established divisional leaders who tried to implement the idea halfheartedly. The new division never took off. The firm continued to make appallingly low profits. It was finally taken over in 1998 and most of the firm was dismembered.

Improved productivity

Productivity is the measure of the organization's effectiveness in producing its goods or services for its customers. This can be subdivided into human resources, the use of capital resources, speed and effective distribution. There has been an important increase in the amount of information available in the public arena which enables organizations to benchmark their standards of productivity against their competitors, both in their own industries and associated or non-aligned industries.

Benchmarking data is a useful means of setting standards and clear tactical objectives. Again, it is appropriate to emphasize that benchmark targets should be unambiguous and compatible with the other tactical objectives.

Create strategic business units

Strategic business units refer to identifiable businesses which can stand alone as a unit serving a specific segment in a market. For example, a general hair and beauty organization, such as L'Oréal, could break its businesses up into strategic business units concerned with face or hair products. These could be further broken up into the strategic business units of hair colourings, hair treatment and shampoos. The advantage of breaking the business into strategic business units is that it is easier to judge each one's success or failure and discard the poor performers.

Marketing

Once again, although this is presented as a potential short-term tactical target area, marketing should usually be regarded as a long-term, continuous effort. The essential features of marketing are market research, market information collection, product pricing, market segmentation, product differentiation and the combination of all these into the promotional aspect of selling, advertising and PR. Almost all these are long-term strategies that should be maintained continuously for an organization to be marketing oriented. This does not preclude the possibility of using particular aspects of marketing as short-term tactics. The key ones are increases in sales, or increased use of advertising or promotion.

Financial objectives

Financial objectives are highly suitable as short-term objectives. They are specially relevant when aiming for profit maximization, decreases in costs or an improvement in productivity (see earlier). Other financial objectives that are unambiguous and useful as tactical standards are increases in cash collection speed, decreases in credit availability to customers, decrease in credit days, increase in speed of invoicing, increase in agreements with customers for direct debiting or increase in agreements from customers for cash flow invoicing rather than invoicing after the total service or product has been delivered – indeed, anything which improves a business's terms of trade.

Other financial objectives may be improvements in standards of budgeting or management accounting. These are most useful in turn-around situations when part of the problem is that the information flows are inadequate.

It is worth noting that this area is often missed in short-term tactics. Accountants are skilled at telling everybody how the accounting function will measure every department's performance. They rarely bother to measure their own. The boss often forgets (and accountants don't remind them) that the accountants should have tough targets, too.

Workforce training

People development, in general, should be a continuous long-term strategic policy. Nevertheless, training the workforce may also be used as a tactical objective. When used as a tactic rather than as part of a long-term strategic programme, it should involve the following:

- correcting areas where specific people skill weaknesses have been revealed
- recruiting and developing personnel in new core competencies
- as a factor in the long-term strategic development plan with clear objectives developing supervisory, management and operational skills.

A further example would be placing a short-term tactical emphasis on telephone skills in an organization where the overall objective is to increase the sales skills of all customer-facing members of staff.

Summary

The list of short-term tactical objectives can be much longer than the suggestions listed here. It should be as long and varied as you wish it to be. The criteria must always be clear parameters, no contradictions or ambiguities and absolute measurability. Above all, if the organization wishes to use bonuses or reward systems to motivate the whole or parts of the workforce to deliver short-term targets, then the bonus systems must be carefully and precisely aligned with the achievement of given targets. Failing to tailor a reward or bonus system to fit the target is one of the most sure ways of failing to reach your short-term tactical objectives.

Further reading

K. Blanchard and S. Johnson, *The One Minute Manager*, William Collins, Glasgow, 1990

A. Campbell, M. Devine and D. Young, *A Sense of Mission*, Hutchinson, London, 1990

T. E. Deal and A. A. Kennedy, *Corporate Cultures*, Addison-Wesley, Reading, Massachusetts, 1982

G. Hamel and C. K. Prahalad, *Competing for the Future*, Harvard Business School Press, Boston, 1994

C. Handy, *Understanding Organizations* (4th edn), Penguin, Harmondsworth, 1993

J. Hunt, *Managing People at Work*, Pan, London, 1981

SHORT-TERM TACTICS WORKOUT

Part One: The tactics

Remind yourself here of the three key long-term strategic aims.

1	2	3

Choose three from the following areas of appropriate tactical objectives that you should focus on this year to contribute to the achievement of the long-term aims:

- product improvement
- quality improvement
- market share increase
- profit rate improvement
- distribution change
- marketing
- operations productivity improvement
- human resource development

Name precisely this year's numbers and statistics relating to the three you have chosen:

1	2	3

Has your business ever attempted to put right or improve any of these areas before?   **Yes**   **No**

If yes, what went wrong last time necessitating making them a priority again this year?

_____

What is different about this year's approach which obviates whatever went wrong last time you tried to improve each one?

1

2

3

Part Two: The accounts

To get your tactics into context

Corporation/business/department's total revenue $/£m   ———

Operating profits $/£m   ———

Profits before tax $/£m   ———

This year's profit as percentage of net revenue   %   ———

Cash flow $/m   ———

Assets $/m   ———

Budget for your department

(Complete the lines that are relevant to you.)

Total expenditure $/£ ———

Total costs $/£ ———

Total sales $/£ ———

Budgeted profit/loss $/£ ———

Total number of subordinates in the department at beginning of year

Total number of subordinates in the department at end of year

Total bonus for department $/£ ———

Targets against which the bonus is set $/£ ———

International considerations

Introduction

In the 21st century many businesses, even small ones, become international at a young stage in their evolution. That was not always the case. Until about 1980 it was perfectly possible for a business to grow large, even becoming one of the top 100 in their domestic economy, without bothering to do business abroad. But the world has truly become a global village and even young entrepreneurs in an early phase of their business growth would consider it totally normal to begin looking at markets halfway around the world long before they would have saturated the domestic market or the regional or continental. It is appropriate to put in some of the more important considerations of international strategy for the do-it-yourself workout strategist.

Strategic considerations

Others parts of this book explain more to readers the delicate balance between strategy, leadership and management, three concepts that are sometimes carelessly and misguidedly intermingled. The failure to clarify and distinguish these individual components into their separate meanings has important consequences in demonstrating muddled thinking by both theorists and leaders. Each has distinct areas of skill which differentiate them from each other. Too frequently, when boards of directors are selecting leaders they fail to realize that good managers sometimes make bad leaders and vice versa. Sometimes, they fail to see that success in the national business arena may not indicate proficiency in either international management or leadership. A clear example of this easy misapprehension was Bob Horton, the ex-leader of BP Amoco. He had had a stupendous success turning around Sohio, the American subsidiary of BP which had gone badly wrong. Bob Horton sorted this problem out brilliantly in this special 'American business situation' and made his reputation with the board of BP. They subsequently considered him a shove-in for the leadership of the whole international corporation when the vacancy became available. Horton failed to shine as a global corporate leader. The subsequent failures of Railtrack, where he eventually surfaced after being thrown out of BP following a boardroom coup, show that he lacked some necessary leadership skills when he moved up to overall total organization responsibility as sole leader of a large enterprise. He seemed to me to lack long-term circumspection. He was reputed to be brusque and tough. Those qualities may have masked a lack of empathy which was his undoing and the cause of his strategic visionary failures.

Leadership and management

Recent industrial changes in the natural rate of business progression have made it necessary for leaders to take decisions earlier about taking the business into the international arena. In turn, this forces them to think clearly about how much of the international business strategy should be managed by leadership behaviours (vision, strategy, doing the big deals, chairing the key resource expenditure decisions, setting the tone for the business style) compared to management (setting up the accounting systems, selecting teams to implement the strategy, finding locations, meeting new customers, choosing the distribution system etc.). Why do leaders decide to take the business international? Reasons include the following:

- growth opportunities
- market internationalizes
- domestic market is saturated
- foreign competitors are growing fast
- leader wants a grander business life.

Growth opportunities abroad

The usual and most common reason for international growth strategy is growth opportunities abroad. This could be because the product or service has limited applications in the home market and the business has to seek fresh markets abroad. Or the market may be saturated with no growth opportunities existing in the home market.

Simple business economics offers a number of impetuses to go abroad. Many businesses can achieve economies of scale by increasing their production capacity. Selling the surplus abroad may be the only way to find markets for the extra products being manufactured. This can sometimes prove a false economy. Diseconomies of scale rapidly set in. These may be diseconomies of distribution, marketing, sales, management skill or leadership. They may encounter a specific problem on the international scene. Many disasters begin when a business first becomes international. As we look at some of the difficulties that businesses have to encompass when they become international it will also become evident why so many fail at the stepping off stage.

Market internationalizes

The onset of computerization, the internet and the global web has been exciting in enabling young and moderately sized businesses to fairly easily achieve an international presence early in the process of growth. Strategically, it makes sense to occupy the international space in any marketplace early, especially if the business is being run as a virtual company from a relatively low-cost domestic base. Consider a supplier to the automobile industry which has rapidly become global over the past decade. If supplying a business parts, logistics or software services isn't international it probably has little chance of matching car manufacturers' needs – they are nearly all run as global businesses.

It has become easier to develop into an international business nowadays. There are so many opportunities for international physical and telephonic communication at low prices that international business costs little more to support than the supply of domestic services. Tariff barriers and import duties have also diminished as many countries reach trade agreements to decrease or remove trade barriers. One of the larger complexities of export in the past has been the management of currency exchange rates. With the creation of the euro in Europe and the dollar already a fully international global currency many of these dangers are removed. A business can become international at a much younger stage in its evolution.

Domestic market is saturated

Every market has its saturation point. Some reach it early in limited markets such as executive jet airplanes or haute couture. Other markets are enormous but still have a point where growth is limited and impetus stunted. For example, the conference organization industry or consultancy. A young business or one with continued growth impetus will push to keep moving forward. Often the only markets left to grow are those abroad.

Every market has its saturation point.

Modern markets seem to have changed in their growth rates from those that prevailed in bygone days. The development curves of businesses take place in months or years rather than decades and centuries. Businesses spring up and grow to large size in a few years. This is partially the result of the vast amounts of growth capital that are available from financial institutions but also because the techniques of business development and growth, management, leadership, accountancy, acquisition and strategy are taught in business schools throughout the world. When relatively simple good ideas have demonstrated they can create customer demand then the capacity to grow them fast is available more easily than ever before in industrial or commercial history.

Consider a simple example of the coffee booths that are springing up at so many railway stations throughout the United Kingdom. This simple idea probably began as a one-off experiment. The relatively small portable booths can occupy a tiny footprint of physical space in any busy thoroughfare. They offer high quality coffee and small accompanying eatables such as croissants or a piece of fresh fruit. This simple idea appears to have grown into a major large revenue business in just a few short years. In earlier times such growth might have taken 20 years. Had the creator of this idea waited that long, almost certainly some other entrepreneur would have copied the concept and snatched his growth opportunities from under his nose. It could even be that this simple idea should be considered for internationalizing now rather than take the risk that some bright entrepreneur will notice the concept on his or her travels in the UK and copy it in their domestic market. At heart, there are no 'domestic' or 'international' markets – there are just **markets**.

Foreign competitors are growing fast

The process just described which happens in every domestic market continuously is the same impetus for those businesses to internationalize their operations sooner rather than later. There is an increasing tendency for young entrepreneurs and business people in general to form clubs and societies where they mingle and meet their counterparts throughout the world. Sometimes these events are the consequence of the normal intercourse of socialization as they holiday in similar places or meet at international conferences. Some join young presidents' clubs or are influenced through the intervention of their merchant bankers or other backers. These people are all very aware of the increased rate of fast business growth. Some of it is due to their direct intervention, encouragement and pressure for fast and high levels of growth and profit. The pressure to 'go international' bears down early on every successful business in the modern era.

Leader wants a grander life

Another reason that many businesses become international which is neglected in some textbooks is the sheer glamour and fun of the international dimension in business. International travel, meeting foreign suppliers and customers and, often, the advantage of adding a tax-subsidized brief holiday to a trip is a major inducement for a small business person to take the business international much earlier than the business rationale might demand. We mentioned earlier the adrenaline kick of international mergers and takeovers and the occasional failure of leaders to remember that the business is about the dull, day-to-day management which makes the year-to-year profits that the owners, the shareholders, want to rely upon.

How?

There are many ways of beginning to trade internationally. A classical line of progression is as follows:

- exporting
- agency
- licensing
- wholly owned new startup
- strategic alliance
- acquisition
- merger.

With the easy availability of internet facilities a business no longer needs to go through the agency or licensing hierarchy of progression to becoming international. Although many will still begin by exporting, once they have proven there is a real market for their service or goods abroad they will go straight to either a wholly owned startup or a strategic alliance in a relatively short time. If it proves that there is a solid and large market to be developed, with the preponderance of availability of merchant banks and venture capitalists keen to create wealth at a fast rate, there will be no shortage of people marching to their door with acquisition and merger opportunities for which capital is available.

It is worth clarifying the differences between strategic alliances, acquisitions and mergers. Strategic alliances are intended to be temporary arrangements to run a business in which both parties are interested, although not always in a third country. Each brings different skills to the alliance which is why each needs the other. Some strategic alliances are set up to last for just a few months. However, most are created to enable the partners in the alliance to penetrate a mutually desired market together. Often the strategic alliance agreement does not have a time span attached to it. This is usually the beginning of the problems that can go wrong with strategic alliances. A strategic alliance should be treated like a marriage. Everybody gets married with the intention that it will last for life. However, the evidence is that 50 percent of marriages do not. The evidence for strategic alliances is closer to 70 percent failure rate. Most good marriages would be helped if people thought about what they might do if anything went wrong. A strategic alliance with a divorce arrangement worked out is more likely to survive than the one which begins in impossible dreams and ends with ugly nightmares.

A merger is sometimes used by business which have almost equal capital and equity values. Sometimes it is preferred over a takeover because the leadership egos cannot handle the necessary subordination of one to the other after the takeover. Sometime it is done because the share structures do not fit takeover rules or one or other of the corporations has 'poison pill clauses' which are calculated to obviate an acquisition. Sometimes it may just be inappropriate at that time in the capital or debt situation of one or other party (e.g. one has taken on debt with certain bank guarantees which would be breached if the two merged their conjoint debt or loans). Sometimes it is not the right time for some of the stakeholders. It is frequently the case, when a strategic alliance is set up, that one or both parties conceives the long-term possibility that one will eventually make a full bid for the whole strategic alliance business or, possibly, for the whole of the strategic ally's business.

When

As I have said earlier, taking the business international happens nowadays much sooner than it used to in classical business development. However, the familiar reasons for going international still apply. A primary reason is when one's domestic market is saturated. It is always much easier to grow abroad where the market may still be developing than to enter a ferocious fight for market share in a mature and difficult domestic market. The parallel to taking your business abroad is when international competition arrives in your domestic market. That does not always mean going into the market where your new international competitor has come from. It is usually wiser to go looking for a younger, fresher market which your new competitor and others have not yet discovered.

One of the signals that the market abroad has become suitable is when its vital economic indicators show that the country has enriched itself enough to become suitable for one's products and services. Choosing the moment might then depend on opportunism – finding the right site, winning a few lucky sales or the classically simple and time-tried method of following one's clients abroad. To understand better the nature of inter-nationalism in modern business consider Table 13.1, which shows the UK's largest companies at the beginning of 2001. The largest firm listed in the table is Vodafone which on its own was equivalent to 10 percent of the whole of the FTSE 100 in the UK at the end of 2001. That business did not exist 20 years earlier. It started up with a small radio telephony licence in 1983 and was devoted entirely to the UK cellular telephone market until the late 1980s. Then it dipped its toe tentatively into the international market by getting one or two licences abroad. Ten years later it is the world's largest mobile telephone company and is installed in every important region in the world.

Compare that record to the second and fourth businesses listed, BP Amoco and Shell. They have been international companies almost from the birth of the business. Why? Because the world resources for oil are concentrated mainly in one geographical sector while demand for the product comes from most markets around the world.

If one considers the two pharmaceutical companies represented in the list both operated as local and then national suppliers of pharmaceutical products to national markets in single countries for many years from their foundation by their originators. It is only in the last 20 years that the pharmaceutical industry has become global and their most successful corporations became installed in most markets in the world.

Table 13.1 UK's largest companies			
Company	Sector	Market capital (£bn)	FTSE 100 weighting
Vodaphone	Telecoms	145.9	10.1%
BP Amoco	Oil	122.5	8.49%
GlaxoSmithKline	Pharmaceuticals	116.7	8.09%
HSBC	Banking	90.3	6.26%
Astra Zeneca	Pharmaceuticals	60.5	4.19%
Shell	Oil	54.6	3.79%

International evolution

Businesses become international in a series of stages indicated by the following:

- multi-domestic
- multinational
- international
- transnational.

If we follow the development of Vodafone over its brief history we can see it followed exactly this line of development. First, it got a domestic licence for the UK. Three or four years later it achieved its next two licences abroad in Europe. It went international to protect its domestic competitiveness. Within a year or two its leaders had seen the trends of the market in mobile telephony and realized that this was a new global industry which was repeating the same market growth and technological pattern across continents and regions. They realized that if they did not join in and win the competition for market share throughout the world, later, they would be taken over by a business which was being more successful than theirs. They decided to compete and ended up with the winning ticket at the great lottery called the global mobile telephony industry.

International trends

One of the most important trends in the growth of internationalism is the process of regionalization. This refers to the polarization of large groups of countries into regions which offer their partners preferred levels of duty or no import duties at all, easy bureaucracy and administration and a common currency to facilitate mutual exchange rates and ease of transaction. The most visible centres are China and the Far East, North America and South America and the European Union. Africa has not yet managed to create a similar union although its geography and interests seem to indicate it should. Another anomaly is India which has not really fully joined in the SEATO (South-East Asia Treaty Organization) group. However, India is such a large and autonomous market of its own that it may not need to join any other.

Risks

Going international raises and increases the risk profile of a business. These risks are associated with the increased complexity that an international rather than a domestic business engenders and because it increases the amount of knowledge needed (and thus raises the relative level of ignorance of the organization). People within the organization need to know matters related to the political sphere, the way the economy works, different aspects of the national cultures they are encountering, the law and legal ramifications, the need for different management skills and the increased level of leadership skills that are required within the firm. Sometimes they don't know what they don't know!

That is why it is often easier to grow a business internationally by means of international acquisition or merger. When a business takes over an already established business in its target country or region, it simultaneously acquires the know-how and some of the geographical market spread. This may be at lower costs than would be incurred by overcoming the business's ignorance of a region in terms of development, contacts, distribution and market patterns and, of course, the element of time. Time is probably the most important and, in real terms, costly. New markets, production facilities, services and technologies evolve very fast. It may be, for example, that mobile telephony has gone from being a developing market into a mature one in the course of one year, that year being 2001. That market will now require a totally different form of strategic leadership than has been appropriate over the past five years when it wasn't one of the most rapidly developing industries in the world. The leaders of corporations in this industry will have to come to terms with that and change entirely their strategy, style of leadership and approach to the market in a matter of months. In previous years they would have been able to reflect for a year or two while assessing whether the nature of the market had changed substantially and installing a new management team to cope with the changed circumstances.

From the supply side problems arise with the need to check out new clients' creditworthiness. It is in suppliers' best interests to be there internationally and manage the risks, for example, by offering tough conditional contracts to overcome the risk of delivery of services and goods without equivalent guarantees of payment or finance.

International culture

The concepts of international culture are different to those described in the earlier chapters of this book where the reader is taken through the means of analyzing the culture of the business. The culture of a firm is just one of the many aspects of international culture which must be taken into account. The full list includes:

- the culture of your firm (covering its history, leaders, technology, stories, anecdotes, myths and legends)
- your personal culture (you and your antecedents' personal culture?)
- your national culture
- the culture of the target business (covering its history, leaders, technology, stories, anecdotes, myths and legends)
- the culture of the client's industry (does the industry have its own national culture and way of seeing the world or does it have a global culture? E.g. farmers in many parts of Europe are highly addicted to governmental subsidies)
- the culture of the country (or countries) the target company operates from.

When you consider the target country (or countries) you want to grow into, you need to consider the prime defining characteristics. Is the country, in general, rich or poor? Is its political system democratic or oligarchic? Is its legal system based on French Napoleonic principles or those of English common law systems? Does the public sector predenominate over the private sector or vice versa? Is the economy strong or weak? Which, if any religious denomination prevails, Catholic, Protestant, Muslim, Jewish or none? Is the physical country a large or small landmass? Are there long traditions of civil tolerance or intolerance? Finally, is the ambience of the country cosmopolitan or local? Or does this differ in different regions requiring a varied management style?

Personal qualities suited to internationalism

The people aspects of becoming an international company are also important and difficult. The following qualities are those that should be looked for when choosing executives from the domestic company to represent the business in its foreign subsidiaries:

- tolerance of ambiguity
- interest in other cultures
- capacity for non-aggressive feedback
- open attitude
- good communication skills
- skilled at constructive criticism
- knowing how to express feelings
- capacity for fostering trust.

Most of these need no further explanation. The summary of this list is that one has to choose a culturally cosmopolitan, people-oriented empathetic community that is good at communication. Usually, if one has any people like this one needs them at home running the domestic business.

Business qualities suited to internationalism

The style, culture and fabric of an international business has to be fashioned and moulded to fit international needs. That often means fundamentally changing the culture and management style of the business. Consider momentarily a well-known international company such as General Motors, the leading American car manufacturer, or Shell Petroleum, the Anglo-Dutch oil giant. These companies think globally in their approach to business. People are developed and trained to be fit for service at home or abroad. The company has personnel management systems which take automatic account of the need for a stint abroad. When people are sent to a foreign subsidiary they are fully briefed in the language and the local customs. They never put people abroad and then let the human resources department forget them. There is always a job ready for them when they have completed their tour of duty. Everybody who is hoping to serve at the senior levels of the organization will have had to serve at least some of his or her time in another country in order to be considered ready and fit to work at the top of an international business.

The following list summarizes the qualities that are widely important and must be taken into account when devolving the culture of an international corporation:

- team atmosphere
- clear roles
- shared leadership
- high standards
- population used to international travel.

The list needs little comment other than noting that it is easier to make the list than to implement the qualities and standards the list indicates. Team atmosphere is necessary because executives working abroad often feel cut off from the main business. Roles within the business need to be clear because the leader abroad has to take so many decisions that could otherwise lead to confusion and misguided strategy.

The leadership has to be shared because, necessarily, the leader of the corporation or whoever is responsible for the foreign subsidiaries cannot physically be there all the time. Sharing the leadership merely defines the only way one can manage internationally. High standards are always necessary but more so in the international arena because international businesses are automatically and necessarily more complex and difficult to manage than exactly the same business in a domestic market.

> *Travel is neither glamorous nor fun, contrary to popular conception.*

Finally, the simple concept of using people habituated to international travel is important. Travel is neither glamorous nor fun, contrary to popular conception. It actually inflicts immense wear and tear on the executives who have to do it. Using a company population used to it is advisable.

Causes of difficulty between HQ and foreign subsidiaries

Many businesses experience friction between the subsidiary and the parent company. These problems are frequently exacerbated when growth abroad has been created uniquely through acquisition. Most causes of friction are based on differences in the respective views of the future of the industry, company histories, evolution of leading executives to their current position, the uniqueness of their starting point in business life and possibly different levels of commitment to success.

Becoming international may have serious effects on the domestic business because the international part of the business may be where the glamour resides. The international chaps jet around the world, earn increased salaries through subsidized housing and attract the attention of the senior executive body. Companies that are only learning how to be international often exaggerate the importance of the foreign subsidiaries over the domestic business which is providing the income, wealth and capital to enable foreign growth to take place. Eventually the best domestic executives leave because they are being disfavoured against lesser managers abroad in what they consider to be a costly part of the business. That is another reason why it is essential to install exactly the right employment conditions for ex-pats and domestic employees.

Summary

Business is becoming international much sooner than it used to in normal corporate evolution. Understanding the subtleties of international culture, complex management and the different and high standards of multinationalism is an important part of becoming an international company. When one considers those companies which have been global for many years the difference between being multinational as a normal behaviour and going international as a new adventure becomes clear. Getting the human resource policies right is probably the first and most important key. After that, the business should be careful about who they do business with abroad. They need to ask, strategically, whether they should be there at all before setting out on the adventure.

INTERNATIONAL STRATEGY WORKOUT

If you are considering becoming international answer the following questions to assure yourself it is the right move:

Are you already exporting to any countries and should they be your first target destinations?

Which of the following seem to be the right way forward and why?

Wholly owned new startup ☐ Strategic alliance ☐ Acquisition ☐ Merger ☐

Why?

What changes will be necessitated in the domestic business and why?

Strategy?   Why?

Culture?   Why?

Complexity?   Why?

Management?   Why?

Leadership?   Why?

Accountancy?   Why?

Financing?   Why?

What aspects of the target country's (or countries') culture is most potentially dangerous to this project?

What are you doing about it?

What are the key features of the culture of the target *business* from among the following?

- history
- leaders
- technology
- stories
- anecdotes
- myths
- legends

Is specific action required to deal with any potential problems this feature raises? If yes, what action?

_____

What are the key features of the culture of the target _country_ from among the following?

Is specific action required to deal with any potential problems this feature raises? If yes, what action?

_____

Have you identified staff with the following qualities which are vital in executives working in foreign subsidiaries?

- tolerance of ambiguity
- interest in other cultures
- capacity for non-aggressive feedback
- open attitude
- good at communication
- skilled at constructive criticism
- know how to express feelings
- capacity for fostering trust

If you have insufficient people of this type of temperament, what search programmes are being put in place to seek them out?

_____

Implementation through leadership and management

Up to this point in the book the reader has been taken through all the steps necessary to conduct a strategic analysis. It began with the formation of a mission statement. The reader was accompanied on a voyage around the world outside the company. You were then brought inside the business to look in detail at the strengths, neutrals and weaknesses of the business as well as the intricacies of its culture and behaviour. By then you would have understood enough to form a set of long-term strategic objectives. Following that key point you considered adjusting the way the organization works (the structure) to make sure that no parts could prevent the achievement of the targets. The reader then decided which tactics, year on year, would ensure that the long-term objectives would eventually be achieved. Finally, youconsidered taking the business into the international arena.

Chapter 13 was deliberately transitional. It is the point where the internal strategy meets the external environment and symbolically encapsulates the essential conundrum of how the internally engendered strategy of the business meets and begins to adapt to the external world.

In Part Two we go further inside the company and yet still remain outside. The two ingredients that are absolutely vital for the strategy to succeed are the **leadership** and **management** of the enterprise. In Chapter 14 we look at leadership and in Chapter 15 at management.

Leadership is important because it is always the leader's responsibility to analyze the strategic situation of the organization, form the long-term vision and strategic objectives for the future and then create the will and conditions within the organization to ensure that future is achieved. That, essentially, is what the leader does.

Chapter 15 analyzes what the strategic team around the leader should do to play their part in achieving the strategic future of the organization.

It is worth noting at this stage that this book is *not* a text on leadership or management. Those deserve books in their own right. Indeed, I have written a much more detailed text on leadership to which you are referred if you are interested. However, these two chapters are offered to help the reader understand the essential basics of how leaders succeed or fail in their duty to analyze and implement the organization's strategy and how managers are best advised to go about that particular part of their responsibility of delivering the strategic objectives and tactics to their leader.

14

Leadership

Introduction

The prime duty of a leader is to deliver and implement a rational and deliverable strategy for the business. He must convince his board, the owners and the investors it is right. Then he must convince the employees of the business. If they do not believe in the strategy, they will not achieve it. First, we should ask how the leader can get the strategy wrong. There are three key ways:

1 Strategists fail to judge the organizational situation objectively.
2 They fail to balance the interests of stakeholders properly.
3 They have poor objectivity about weaknesses (both theirs and the organization's).

The second primary duty of a leader is to implement the strategy once he or she and the strategy team have done the necessary analysis and decided on an appropriate strategy. Implementation fails because:

1 Leaders and managers do not know when to stop analysis and start implementation.
2 They do not understand how to be strategic leaders (rather than company managers).
3 Most organizations and managers are too firmly locked into short-term behaviour.

The beginnings of strategic failure

In theory, when an organization has an elegant strategy, implementation should follow and success be assured. It is rarely that simple. Problems arise from three main causes:

1 People select the wrong strategy.
2 They implement the chosen strategy poorly.
3 The leaders ignore the strategy to concentrate on tactics.

All three problems must be attributed to the leadership. Only the leader is responsible for strategy, therefore only the leader can choose the wrong strategy. Second, strategy implementation begins with communication. Leaders, in general, can only implement through the communication of their values, vision and behaviour. It is the task of leadership to make it happen. The leader has to set stretching, but achievable budgets; he or she has to ensure that everybody accepts the standards of quality for customers that will capture market share and ensure the best use of corporate resources; above all, they must inspire everybody with a belief in the 'achievability' of the strategy.

> **Only the leader is responsible for strategy, therefore only the leader can choose the wrong strategy.**

Too frequently leaders get involved in detail and get sidetracked. They concentrate on the short-term tactics and side issues and fail to keep their vision focused on the long-term strategy. Sometimes they just lack courage – particularly when they have to tackle the people problems. But all these are grievous faults. They are, in fact, issues of ultimate and utter leadership failure. A leader who cannot design and focus and deliver the strategy of the business is unfit to remain leader for a day, let alone a year. He is unfit for purpose. He or she is the very negation of what a leader must be because if he cannot deliver the strategy then he is not a leader.

Stakeholder concepts

Stakeholders are the various groups of people who have an interest or stake in the enterprise. They range from bankers and other financial institutions to shareholders, debenture holders, stockholders, trade unions, employees, customers and suppliers. In short, everybody or

every group which must be taken into account when deciding what to achieve, when and how much.

The key aspect of stakeholder theory is that the different stakeholders' requirements often conflict with each other and those of the organization. For example, the employees want the highest possible levels of remuneration, whereas the shareholders might want lower levels of wages to ensure higher profits and dividends. The organization's financial backers may prefer a low-risk approach to achieving the organization's objectives, whereas senior managers, who may be on high levels of bonus for short-term achievement, might want to take greater risks to achieve the objectives earlier. Should the corporation pay higher dividends to underpin the share price or higher wages to attract the best employees? If managers believe that raw materials supply is a key to the future of their industry, they might manage negotiations with suppliers in a conciliatory manner. However, if they pay more to suppliers, should they keep wages low, prices high or dividends low?

Stakeholder theory demonstrates that managers and leaders are always making tradeoffs between conflicting demands on resources. This requires fine judgment which, ultimately, is what they are paid for.

What goes wrong?

Leadership and management are intrinsically different

Why do so many executives get it wrong when they land strategy-leading positions in organizations? The two prime reasons are related to the type of person who is driven to reach senior posts in organizations and because the process of reaching the leading job can affect people in harmful ways and render them unfit for the role by the time they get it. Many people appointed to leadership positions were only ever fit to be managers, not leaders. Those responsible for their promotion did not distinguish between the two (see Levicki 2002).

Many more leaders fail than succeed if one measures success by whether they make a difference to the organization. It may be the nature of leadership in the modern era that causes failure. Teamwork is a key concept of management yet **leadership** implies the opposite of teamwork or management. People have to be effective managers to reach the top of the organization. But as they move up the hierarchy of the organization, more leadership skills and fewer management skills are needed.

Management is not the same as leadership. It requires different qualities. We will discuss that in the next chapter. Managers organize people to deliver organizational objectives. Leaders have to decide what the objectives should be. Managers (apart from making inputs themselves) receive strategic direction from others who are making the really difficult judgments about the balance between the different stakeholders' requirements.

It is leaders who have to make major, strategic decisions at the top of the organization, on behalf of all the stakeholders.

Leaders forget to stop being managers

One of the hardest things for managers to do when they become leaders is to stop managing. Classically, this often happens to engineers. In engineering businesses engineers take charge of increasingly large projects as their careers develop. At the higher echelons there will be more management than engineering input into those business decisions. At the top of the company, although the leader might need some understanding of engineering he or she doesn't need any actual engineering skills at all. The leadership role requires the leader to give strategic direction. They implement by selecting the most appropriate team members to deliver the strategy. If a leader, who has been promoted on the basis of his engineering judgments, cannot stop being an engineer and become a pure leader, they will fail to make the necessary breakthrough on behalf of the organization. The same problem will apply to any functional specialist, be it sales, marketing or accounting, if they fail to let go of their functional specialism and become purely a leader.

One of the hardest things for managers to do when they become leaders is to stop managing.

The common problem is that people often rise to the top of the firm by displaying excellence in just one function, whether it be engineering, sales, accounting or personnel. None of these, on its own, can possibly develop the capacity to handle the wide range of stakeholders that leaders have to cope with. Furthermore, these skills can never be fully tested or proved in advance of getting the top job. This explains why the 'Peter Principle' (that everybody, eventually, gets promoted to a job above his or her level of competence) applies most forcibly to those who reach the top jobs.

Everybody has difficulty coping with promotion. New jobs are difficult and each one has its own learning curve. It is only in the top leadership position that the learning curve affects the whole organization. It is also the only learning curve which demands comprehensive judgment about all the stakeholders' interests. That is why it is hard to predict success and even harder to be successful.

Leaders begin to believe their own mythology

There is an inevitable process which happens to successful people. It begins as they start to rise up the organizational ladder. They are often singled out for success. By the time they get near the senior echelons of the organization, they have developed a belief that they are more successful than others by some divine providence. This process takes place naturally and applies to good as well as poor leaders. However, the good ones will have reflected on what it is they do, subconsciously or consciously, to ensure that people are led to success by conscious and careful leadership. Poor leaders will not have gone through this conscious thought process and will still be managing in a style which reflects their innate belief in their accidental good fortune or contrivances in moving up the hierarchy.

The leader must know his own weaknesses

By definition, everyone makes mistakes; only teams can avoid them. Most management systems encourage people to avoid responsibility for mistakes or to avoid taking risks. By the time a manager becomes a leader he may have become totally risk averse. At the top of the organization one has much more to lose than when climbing the ladder.

A further consequence of hierarchical organization systems and the avoidance of mistakes is that when leaders arrive at the top they tend to think they need no further training or personal development. They would never fail to make sure that their company automobile gets a regular maintenance check. But they willingly and foolishly neglect themselves by failing to go for further training at the point in their careers when the company needs them to learn and to know more than ever. A lack of humility in leaders is a flaw that can eventually prove fatal.

I observed this in a major international corporation which had been highly successful and was regarded as likely to become a world beater. The chairman, chief executive and human resources director struggled to persuade the executive operations directors that they needed to close the gaps in their knowledge base, especially on accounting, quality and IT matters. The executives always avoided the further training they were offered on the basis that they were too busy to divert their attention from the business just to attend development programmes. Eventually that $3 billion corporation lost its way under the leadership of those executives. They all lost their jobs and were replaced by younger, more highly trained managers. However, the organization also lost out. All their experience, knowledge of the industry and their contacts with customers were lost. When they joined new organizations, of course, they all had to undergo the training they had avoided so studiously earlier.

Failure to grow into the job

Some managers arrive at the top of their organizations with an unrealistic view of their own limitations and a tendency to see mistakes as something which other people commit but which they must correct. Too often the leader arrives at the top with an inadequate understanding of his own weaknesses. When he starts to assemble a team, or make adjustments to the team he inherits, he will often fail to ensure that it covers his worst weaknesses. He may even select people who resemble him in behaviour, thus exacerbating any dangerous aspects of the strengths he may have and failing to cover his weaknesses.

Fear of excellence

A number of behaviours indicate leaders' discomfort when they are encountering difficulties adjusting to their job. Although the behaviours come in many guises, the main ones to look for are:

1 failure to use the best people for fear of looking bad themselves
2 a massive increase in political behaviour
3 rapid turnover of senior executives, particularly those close to the leader
4 excessive use of external consultants

5 creation of new corporate headquarters, usually away from the more competent members of the organization

6 continuously asking for more data whenever their subordinates push them to make decisions

7 stopping consulting their best friends about their problems because they are afraid to confront possible evidence of failure.

A simple case of 'analysis paralysis'

I was asked to meet the managing director of a large food company. It took several months to arrange the lunch as he cancelled several meetings at short notice.

When we finally got together he arrived about 45 minutes late. He pointed out that he knew every theory that I knew (he had a reputable MBA) and that his judgment had to be at least as good as mine because he was being paid a lot of money to do the job. Unless I could come up with something original instantly he could not see what use I could be.

I had to agree with his infallible logic. Without being allowed time to learn about the company, I could make no observations, original or otherwise. But, with impeccable logic from his point of view, without a valid contribution why should he commit any time to me? We agreed to go no further.

He had employed the same impeccable logic with all his employees (of whom there were at least 3,000). Later, I learned that he had not made a decision for over three years. During that time his office and the corridors around his office had become mired in paper from the computer room. He had been building ever larger databases to prepare himself to take a decision. He never took it.

Ultimately, his subordinates went to the chief executive to ask him to relieve them of their appalling situation. For three years they had been trying to get agreement on various courses of action they had proposed; the MD always asked for more information and avoided making a decision.

His departure became their solution. Within a few months the results of that division leaped forward and it became the best performing division in the corporation.

Fear of failure

Most people who achieve the level of leader of a large or important organization have a nagging fear of failure. Holding supreme responsibility brings to some people the harsh realization that 'the buck really stops here'. Being in charge is, by definition, a lonely job. Many leaders feel insecure because the role of leader is always overlaid with political and organizational connotations. Most things a leader says or does are imbued with a special meaning by those around him. Anything or everything may be taken by some subordinates as a signal that somebody is in or out of favour. Whatever they do differently from previous bosses may be adopted as 'the new way we do things around here'. Anything can give a wrong impression or lead the firm in the wrong direction. Having the confidence to be the boss takes inner belief. If they don't get it (or later lose it) it is time to go.

Occasionally the problem may be linked to overdeveloped ego problems. Leaders of large organizations, by definition, should be concerned with long-term achievements. A difficult aspect of chairing any organization is judging the balance between short-, medium- and long-term investment requirements. Most jobs the boss will have had before the appointment as leader will have required shorter time horizons than the top position in the organization. There is always a temptation in the senior job to chalk up 'easy wins'. This is human but unfortunate. It also gets in the way of thinking about the longer term needs of the strategy.

Some leaders just never grow into the role. Symptoms of this failure may be that they concentrate on too many short-term objectives or too much on the long-term interests of the organization. Sometimes the latter is accompanied by the assertion that: 'The board just does not think far enough ahead to understand where I want to take the organization.' Comments like this usually mean that they have missed the balance of judgment between long-, medium- and short-term considerations that must be achieved if the organization is to be successful and thrive.

Nobody can predict with total certainty whether a person will succeed when promoted to any level in the firm. The least predictable promotion of all is at the level of the role of leader because that job calls for skills that were never previously needed. The key skill, that of comprehensively balancing all the stakeholders' interests inside and outside the organization, is a level of judgment that will never have been tested before because by definition only the leader has this responsibility. The job also carries a need for political (with a small 'p') skills which may also not have been needed before. This is why promotion to the top is the hardest to predict.

Most managers dream that at some time in their careers they will be promoted to a job where they start with a completely clean slate. They fancy they will have, at last, a clear set of objectives and be able to select a totally new team. This choice, they believe, will assure a total success. The dream can never happen. There are always some people in the team one would never choose to work with and some objectives one would not choose for oneself.

Why leaders love laggards

Sometimes one observes the leader retaining people around them who appear to lack the skills for the job. Why do leaders retain people who seem to lack the necessary skills? There are usually good reasons why these relationships are sustained. Sometimes that person has the skills for the job but the observer cannot see the problems confronting them and is therefore making a poor judgment on insufficient criteria. Occasionally the subordinate is somebody with a strong **political** grip on the post and the chairman chooses not to pick a fight at that time. The leader and subordinate may owe each other favours which observers will not be aware of. They may have a strong emotional commitment to each other which they consider more important than the performance failures. These emotional ties are strong and difficult to break. Leaders need people around them they can trust.

Who does what?

Another way leaders fail is by forgetting to agree the parameters of the different roles at the top of the organization. For example, the chief executive and the chairman often assume each knows what the other is meant to do. They, therefore, never make clear to each other, or to their subordinates, the different roles or tasks which they think each is responsible for. This can create confusion for them and those around them, especially if they issue contradictory instructions and policies. The problem can continue for a long time because most subordinates will be reluctant to act as go-betweens for their leaders. This tends to be one of those situations when it is relatively easy to be the 'messenger who gets shot.'

The 'overendowed' intellectual

I worked for many years with a bright and extremely intellectual leader. We first became acquainted when I was his tutor in strategy on a managing directors' programme that he was attending.

We had evidence that this man had a large capacity for intellectual analysis of most business problems, but he did not seem to relate at a human level to his subordinates at work. This doubt was recorded and explained why his promotion to managing director status came several years later than expected.

When he had been in the post about a year he telephoned to tell me his board of directors were not really knitting together as a team. Could I help? By the time he called me in, he had already changed most members of his team. He had a new marketing director, a new information technology director and was about to appoint a fresh finance director.

I asked him what criteria he had used to compose his team. He responded: 'They are a thoroughly intellectual group of people. Every one of them has a high IQ.' I pointed out that he, as MD, had enough brain power and IQ for any team. What he needed from his people was empathy and emotional insight into the feelings of the company and its customers. He agreed – but it was too late; the new people were in position.

A year later he and his board decided to change the company's technology. It was an intellectually daring and exciting challenge. The change went catastrophically wrong when the workers in the company proved unable to change their work habits. The company started to lose money at the rate of 10 percent of total revenue. He and his board were all asked to leave the company.

As managers climb higher in an organization, they need to become increasingly conceptual in their thinking and leadership style. The problems they have to solve are less technical and more conceptual. They are employed to make judgments and select solutions from many different ways of achieving the purposes of the organization. The solutions are never simply 'right' or 'wrong'. Solutions are made successful by the determination shown by leaders in making them work.

Leaders have to make choices from equally valid, largely incomparable solutions. Their leadership skills are tested when they have to turn their personal belief into a practical solution that everybody in the organization believes in. That is when the leader needs a certain level of 'character' to ensure effectiveness. Character must be used to convince subordinates that policies, strategies and solutions will work. A leader needs to convince people the solutions they believe in are right for the organization's future.

The team around the boss

There is a special tension attached to the role of executives reporting to the leader. Usually at least one of those reporting is a 'director of finance'. This role carries the added burden of a legal responsibility to report the finances and accounts of the organization in a manner which conforms to legislation. This can be used to exercise power but it may also be a source of stress when it is necessary to enforce rules against the wishes of the person who is nominally in charge.

Further considerations apply to others reporting to the leader. Often the board includes the managing directors of important divisions of the business and leaders of key functions such as marketing, human resources or operations. These executives are running their own show in substantial parts of the business where they are perceived as the supreme boss. Often they also want to retain maximum independence of action. However, for the boss, their key role is to deliver their promises about budgets, plans and profits. Any senior executive who fails to commit to those promises cannot be allowed to remain at a senior level for long. Although a senior executive deserves and needs time to adapt to his position, he also needs the ability to 'hit the ground running', i.e. to deliver results even while he is learning the job.

When executives complain that they cannot be judged on one year's performance when the investment decisions they take have two or three-year payoff periods the leader needs to remind them that the right to have two and three-year investments comes from delivery of the one-year targets!

Every organization depends on loyalty

There is one absolute rule for all organizational life. Behaviour in organizations must be based on loyalty to the organization and one's colleagues. It is always shocking when managers, who invariably demand absolute loyalty from their subordinates, so often fail to give it to their own boss. Any display

> *Any display of disloyalty will always be instantly picked up by a team.*

of disloyalty will always be instantly picked up by a team. Subordinates always notice any odd disparaging or disloyal phrase from their manager about his leader. Even if it is only a passing angry moment it will not pass unnoticed. Once a manager sows the organizational seed of disloyalty, it will grow to haunt him and may well destroy him when he most needs loyalty from his own subordinates.

Being loyal does not mean that one never criticizes aspects of the firm's way of conducting its business. Neither does it mean accepting blindly and without question the boss's plans. It means that, when criticism is necessary, it is constructive. It should be heard respectfully. But if it is rejected the debate is over. If the issue is big enough to be worth a resignation, get out. If it is not, whether the manager has won or lost, loyalty means one accepts the decision, stands by it and loyally communicates it to one's team, without any damaging or disparaging comments.

Whistleblowing

Being loyal to the organization cannot preclude 'whistleblowing'. If your organization has committed unethical or immoral acts, whether in its sales methods, the quality of its products, the way it handles after-sales service or the way it treats its employees, there is always a higher level of loyalty to oneself, one's own ethical standards and to society as a whole. But that does not mean one can easily assume that the organization is wrong because it has transgressed one's personal standards or mores. One has to consider carefully whether the organization is breaking objective important social moral standards. If the answer is positive then one has to place the public interest before that of the organization and reveal the truth.

It is difficult for those that stay in an organization that 'has been whistleblown'. Often the leader (if they are responsible for what is wrong) continues to insist that they are right and the whistleblower wrong. The people around them get asked to support vindictive, irrational behaviour against the whistleblower. It is at times like these that your moral fibre will be tested to the maximum.

Dead mouse syndrome

We keep a cat at our home in the country. It is necessary as vermin seasonally invade our house. I noticed our cat has a habit, when it catches a mouse, of bringing it to my wife, expecting admiration for its success in protecting us. My wife is utterly dismayed by the presentation of these triumphs by our beloved cat. The fact that it is distressing her has passed completely by the notice of our cat. It just carries on bringing them home. I call this 'dead mouse syndrome'.

I believe I have seen the same syndrome in many of the executives I have counselled. There is a similar pattern in their childhood backgrounds. I noticed that many were brought up by highly aspirational parents who give tough conditional love to their children. When they came home from school having scored perhaps 49 out of 50 in a test these parents would give a short 'congratulations' but immediately go on to ask 'how did you lose that other mark?' This continuous pattern of tough love given for excellent results in childhood seems to induce in many people an adult version of 'dead mouse syndrome'. These leaders are still bringing home 'results' for their parents to admire. Sometimes those parents are long since passed on – that does not stop the leader with 'dead mouse syndrome' from continuing to bring home 'dead mice'. It is truly rather sad.

How can you become a great leader?

Although many assume leaders are 'born', some aspects of leadership can be learned. A first guideline to becoming a great leader is to be ruthlessly honest with yourself, particularly as you reach the higher echelons of the organization. Have you become one of those vainglorious and arrogant people you used to disdain when you were seeking promotion in the organization? Do you mainly talk at, rather than to, people? Do you talk more than you listen? Do you enjoy visiting different parts of the organization or do you run your role from a desk in an ivory tower with just accounts and rumours as your decision tools? Are you investing in yourself to learn how to become more charismatic? Are you persuading people that your strategic purposes are rational and well thought through? Have you convinced them that the very best thing for the organization and for their personal futures is your strategy? Or do you just tell them what to do and expect it to happen?

Many leaders find it useful to have a mentor. It is strange that, although one finds many leaders subscribe to the concept of acting as mentors to their subordinates, they have not realized that mentors for leaders are equally valuable! The idea of mentoring within organizations is to ensure that particularly promising people have somebody at a senior level in the organization guiding their careers, to ensure they get chances to develop those careers. It is especially useful for women, who frequently meet male chauvinism which blocks their career progression. Mentors can also sometimes protect individuals from the enemies that successful people accumulate because they threaten less talented managers who consider themselves equally deserving. It is strange that few leaders realize that if you need mentors as you go up the ladder, you just as surely need them when you are at the top. The loneliest jobs in the world are those of chairman, president, chief executive, chief operating officer or managing director in any small, medium or large organization. You cannot talk to subordinates about your fears and inhibitions. It is not easy to trust people around you because when you admit your weakness to them you may also be removing their belief in and enthusiasm for your leadership. You may well need a mentor outside the organization. It is highly advisable that you find a friend whom you can trust. By the way, although a husband or wife is often thought of as being the best mentor, it is equally important to find a business friend who can offer more insight and business understanding than the pure sympathy of a listening ear.

Continuous improvement

Many leaders get to the top of the organization with a belief that they have learned everything and are now employed only to apply their skills. Evidence shows you can never know everything and you should never stop learning. It is vital to continue to train oneself and remember that new skills and understanding are required every day. Ask young graduate employees, who have just obtained their university degrees, what the latest developments in technology, biology or computer science are. Go to research laboratories and find out what new research is taking place. (You may also find out that they do not understand your strategic purpose. How can they conduct research for the organization if they do not know about its strategic future?) Investigate the latest hopes and enthusiasms of youth. Young people are the tomorrow the organization is working for.

Take time out to go on personal development programmes at the best business schools. Find out there, from people with similar jobs, how they are approaching it. They probably share the same doubts and concerns as yourself. You can learn from their ideas about how to become a better leader with your particular skills, personality, intelligence and strategic insight. The objective always is to make yourself a better quality individual who can make strategy happen for your organization.

Stay in touch with all your stakeholders

Many potentially great leaders fail to deliver their vision when they reach the top of the organization because they have not understood the need to stay in touch with all the stakeholders. It is especially important to retain the ability to carry the board to back their necessary decisions.

Another exceptionally gifted executive I worked with for many years was predicted to become the executive vice-president of his corporation. I always used to tell him to invest in spending more time with the non-executive officers of his business. He responded that he believed his business record would speak for itself and he was more interested in making profits for the corporation than developing political skills and techniques. Unfortunately, he only realized why he should have invested in building relationships with those important stakeholders when he did not get the top job that he had spent 25 years trying to achieve. The incumbent chairman did not like him and brought in an outsider above him, a person who had none of his business skills. That person eventually halved the value of the shareholders' stock. Sadly though, it was too late for the other leader.

Communications

Once you have decided on the strategic direction of your organization, you must communicate it. The larger the organization, the more time you need to devote to communicating with everybody in it. You can never communicate too much. That does not mean you have the right to be boring because that will defeat your purposes. You will have to think continuously of new ways to communicate the same messages about the standards, rules, values, behaviour and tasks to your people all the time.

When you visit a company site, they will notice if you speak to a secretary or pick up a piece of scrap paper from the floor because you care about the site being tidy. If you pass one of your operating teams digging a hole in the road and stop to talk to them about the job they are doing and also tell them about your hopes for the company and for their future, it will travel along the informal grapevine of the organization in hours, with a rapidity that is beyond belief. Everything a great leader does gets translated into 'the way we do things around here'. This also places a burden on you. Every time you have a violent argument with a subordinate, he will 'learn' that bad temper and rudeness is permissible. Whenever you deal harshly or unjustly with somebody who has to leave the organization, it will be seen as a less caring place.

Alternatively, whenever you act kindly to somebody whose wife is sick in hospital or whose husband has had an accident at his place of employment, the unfortunate person's colleagues will know that your organization is merciful, gentle and kind. It is possible that in your private life you believe that good deeds are done silently. This may well not apply in terms of good deeds in the organization. There is an organizational rationale to this. If you are spending organizational resources to carry out your act of kindness, then the organization has a right to benefit from it. This is particularly so if you are behaving kindly because it is also meant to demonstrate a value system about people and that this is the value you wish to instil in them. When spending organizational resources you have no right to false modesty. You are obliged to use it or allow it to be known that the kind act is an exemplification of the company's belief in kindness.

The value of stability

It is important not to change standards and beliefs frequently. One should never change rules relating to honesty and ethics, unless you have discovered a weakness and want to improve the standards. I particularly want to emphasize the word ethics as we begin to close this book. It is vital that you take the trouble to understand what you truly believe. Those beliefs should be based, as far as possible, on eternal standards, values and moral concepts. In my experience, if you do not do it consciously, your behaviour will still be seen in ethical terms – but the effect will be a series of accidents.

Over the years I have learned that all people have a right to take their ethics to work with them. I have met many religious, devout and pious people who thought they had to leave their moral precepts and the values which dominate their private lives at home. I have always asserted and, hopefully, frequently persuaded many of them that this is a wrong approach. If you are leading a high quality, moral, personal life you have both a right and a duty to take those morals and values to work with you. If those values work in your private life, there is no reason to believe that they will not be equally efficacious at work.

I do not intend here to suggest that leaders have a right to force their personal moral codes on their employees. They have to couch their value systems in terms that persuade people they are right for the business. People must be happy to behave in the moral way their leaders want when they are working for the organization. If the leader's or the organization's 'way of doing things' conflicts too strongly with the personal views of too many employees, they will soon find they have no staff to do the work.

People around you deserve and need the inspiration of the high values with which you live your private life. You will inspire them to manage and create a better quality organization.

Under most circumstances, profits can be achieved while also behaving properly and decently. In this new millennium it is vital that people take the moral high ground and enact high quality beliefs in their private and public lives. What I am offering here is an entirely personal view. There is always the risk that some of you reading this book are thoroughly immoral and unethical people. If you are, the only comment one could possibly make is that one hopes that you fail – and as soon

> *Most organizations do not exist to do good but to make profits.*

as possible. The danger of unethical people leading organizations is that they taint the organization itself and every human being in it. Most organizations do not exist to do good but to make profits (this may not apply to some charitable institutions). Nevertheless, profits should never be achieved at the cost of doing harm to society or individuals. Under most circumstances, profits can be achieved while also behaving properly and decently.

It is also appropriate to say that there may be some businesses which cannot possibly do good. I speak here of organizations which exist to sell drugs or addiction-inducing products. I sincerely believe that in the fullness of civilized time such organizations will self-destruct or public opinion will no longer allow them to exist.

Doubts and fears

As the strategic leader of your organization, you should have doubts and fears. If you do not, then you are probably a menace. Doubt and fear are the tools which give you the adrenaline to overcome your problems and succeed. You should understand that people around you, while often appearing confident, are also fearful, intimidated and frightened by the enormity of the tasks they have to deliver. They are frightened by the difficult budgets imposed by their leaders and by the complexity of an external environment that is turbulent and difficult. Do not be shy of using your own fear. It is important to understand that it is shared by many people who often give no hint that they are also fearful.

Abnormal psychology and senior leaders

Leaders are people who have climbed to the top of the hierarchy of their organizations. That takes a certain type of character. The types of people who do it seem to share some similarities and values. For many years I used psychometric tests to help me understand the clients I was working with. My preferred test is the FIRO–B which stands for Fundamental Interpersonal Relations, Orientations–Behaviour. It measures several aspects of a manager's behaviour. They are social skills, needs for and acceptance of control, affection levels and tendencies to anger. My findings on the behaviour of senior managers are startling. Frequently leaders seem able to express inclusion but don't really desire it. In other words, they indicate inclusiveness through their language and behaviour to their subordinates but do not actually enjoy people contact. This makes their behaviour appear hypocritical to their subordinates. It could be characterized as 'always ensuring themselves an invitation to the Christmas party but never turning up'.

There is a similar pattern in their leadership control needs. Most senior executives taking this test like to control others but do not easily accept being controlled by others. These incompatible behaviours seem to be part of an inner drive which explains as much about these people's rise to the top of organizations as does any business skill or talent.

The findings from these psychometric tests are important. They demonstrate that senior executives may have attitudes about inclusion and control which differ from normal populations. This, in turn, causes distortions in their leadership style. These abnormal behaviours later become the exemplars for the managers who are learning from them.

These results show there may be built-in resistances from senior executives toward concepts of teamwork. When so many senior executives prefer to control others and avoid being controlled themselves, there is a real problem for the organization's capacity for teamwork. Complex organizations need people to be capable of both giving and receiving control at every level in the organization. Managers who need to control and cannot accept control are intrinsically and psychologically unsuited to the teamwork required in many modern corporations' complex structures.

Getting strategy implementation right

The formula for success

Strategy implementation can be reduced to the following thesis which covers every successful strategy enactment I have studied. It is easy to write down but hard to do.

Successful strategy implementation requires: great leadership which is defined by vision, focus, communication skills and profound determination – all reinforced by moral fibre. The leader has to ensure there is synergy between the core competencies of the organization, its strategy and structure, the desires of the stakeholders – and then a little luck. It also requires a loyal and high quality management team. That will be considered in the next chapter.

The practicalities of strategy implementation

Communicating the mission and the strategy

This workout has shown how to ensure that one includes all the vital stages of analysis which must be taken into account before deciding the long-term mission and strategy for your organization. Previous chapters have described how many leaders get it wrong. Here I want to tell you what I have learned about how to get strategy implementation right.

Communication and dissemination of the strategy to every part of the organization is the prime requirement. This really does mean everybody. The way your frontline people treat your customers is probably a key factor in how your customers form impressions about your business. If your company is in the hotel industry, your doorman and then the reception staff are in the frontline of customer perception management. Do they know the values you espouse? Do you keep loading your staff with extra tasks which means they are never quite ready to look after customers when they arrive, hot and flustered, from whatever journey they have just completed? If you manufacture car components, does your mission tell your employees the business must be a 'fault-free zone'? If you are in a food business, does the strategy proclaim hygiene in every sentence?

The mission and the strategy of your business should tell everybody the key values directly. Otherwise your employees can only rely on the accidental signals around them. By the way, if you do not guide employees on the purposes of the organization, it should come as no surprise when entirely extraneous incidents change their attitudes, e.g. your hotel doorman frowns when it snows and smiles when the sun shines.

Subdividing the mission and vision

The most difficult task for a leader is to subdivide the total strategic direction into manageable parts for each of the executives, managers and other employees to implement. The leadership may have a vision of what the business will look like in ten years' time; they might want the business to go from national to international; from low technology to high technology with the installation of computers and standard services to clients (e.g. banks and similar financial institutions over the past 10 to 20 years); from being a specific supplier of a particular food to a supplier of a general menu (e.g. McDonald's used to sell only hamburgers, now it sells chicken, pizza and fish products).

How should the leader subdivide the strategic vision of what the changed organization will look like in ten years' time? One cannot expect subordinates to know what action to take to implement that vision. It is the responsibility of strategic leadership to allocate tasks to each executive, manager and staff member to ensure that they understand what has to be done to make the mission and strategic objectives happen. That does not mean that the leader writes the job description for every person in the firm. But he must allocate all aspects of the mission and strategy to each of his subordinates to ensure that they understand what they must do. It is the subordinate's role, if competent, to further break it into smaller tasks for his own team members and so on throughout the business.

For example, if it is the mission of Boeing, the US aircraft manufacturer, to achieve a 50 percent share of all civil aircraft supply to airlines throughout the world within (say) 15 years, then the executive president might divide that task up among his senior vice-presidents for finance, operations, research and development (R&D), human resources, marketing and production. To the operations officer he may say: 'I will judge you over the next five years if you manage to capture 30 percent of the world market, because that gives me hope that we can achieve the 50 percent within 15 years.' He may say to his marketing manager: 'I will judge you within three years if you have achieved an order book which shows the potential for 23 percent of world sales because that gives us a chance of delivering my 30 percent to the president in five years and the 50 percent he wants in 15 years.' To his research and development senior vice-president he will probably say: 'I want drawings and plans for three civil aircraft that can capture the long-haul, short-hop and private fleet markets that carry more passengers per mile at a cheaper rate by a margin of 15 percent than any other competing aircraft available from any of our competitors in the world. I expect those plans to be so exciting that our order book, at least on tentative orders, will show a potential of 45 percent and a probability, after cancellation, of 25 percent within three years.' To his senior vice-president for production he might say: 'I want to see working drawings on those planes that make it look probable that at least two of the three can be built in the timeframe envisaged and meet exactly the specification and promises our marketing department is making to the customers.'

The point of this example is that no particular subordinate is responsible for achieving the overall strategy. That is the leader's role. The achievement by each subordinate of his part of the strategy will deliver the overall strategy in the timeframe envisaged.

Examine and test your team

A further point about the example is that the leader's role in subdividing the strategic objectives is effected when each subordinate is given a set of tasks that he or she feels capable of achieving. The reason he or she feels capable of achieving it will be based partly on that individual's own self-beliefs. It will be equally based on the leader's skills in communicating to the individual his belief that he or she can do it and that the leader, with the subordinate, fully intends to achieve the objectives. Inspiring people with the belief that things can be done is a key skill of leadership. The underlying psychological skill is to understand how the mind of each of your subordinates works. Leaders need to know when subordinates are fearful and how to make them feel courageous. What kind of task can they accomplish easily? When do they need special, motivating reinforcement to make them believe they can do it? Your belief in them is part of their belief in themselves. They must perceive it as unfaltering, unwavering and absolute. It should never be the leader's demotivating lack of belief in somebody that causes the person to fail.

You also have the duty of regularly examining the basis for your belief in each individual in your team. One has continuously to consider whether the team members are working beyond the limits of their skills. Just when do they become strained because they do not have the conceptual power or intelligence to carry out the next difficult task or role? If you recognize that anybody is reaching that point, you may need to share your feelings with that person. This is the moment when your greatest wisdom as a leader can manifest itself. How? The person who is not performing at this level spent many years getting to this position and has probably given sterling value to the organization and has made profits for it. It is not a good idea for such a person to leave the organization. A wise leader will find another job within the organization that he or she can accept with dignity and which uses all his or her accumulated know-how and experience for the continued good of the organization. It might also be wise to check one's own decision and be sure that it is not the decision which is at fault, rather than the executive.

Conclusions

It is difficult to be a leader. Sometimes this is because leaders forget how difficult it is to be a follower. Few people who get to the top did not do it by design. That does not mean they are gifted people. It certainly means they also had the good judgment, sense and competence to avoid the wide range of catastrophes waiting along the road of everybody's career.

This chapter has tried to offer warning signals to leaders about the potential traps along the path to the top. Formulating strategy at the highest level of conceptual power has to be carried out at the top of an organization. There are many structural reasons why leaders get it wrong. However, some of the dangers can be avoided if they have both the talent and humility to heed the warning signals. Leadership is a vitally important role in society and commerce. Dealing with the symptoms when things are going wrong as well as constantly trying to learn from the mistakes of the past are the minimum safeguards that should be heeded to try and get it right.

Further reading

M. Belbin, *Management Teams – Why They Succeed or Fail*, Butterworth-Heinemann, Oxford, 1991

G. Hamel and C. K. Prahalad, *Competing for the Future*, Harvard Business School Press, Boston, 1994

C. Levicki, *Developing Leadership Genius*, McGraw-Hill, Maidenhead, 2002

S. Slatter, *Corporate Recovery*, Penguin, Harmondsworth, 1984

Strategic management

Translating strategy into tactics

As we said in Part One the tactics for the year-to-year budget or plan are engendered from the overall long-term strategy of the business. The beginning of that task is the responsibility of the leader as he or she allocates responsibility to the team of managers around them. The manager must then further subdivide and translate the strategy into achievable pieces for the next layers downwards. This is the first point of danger in strategy implementation. If the managers responsible for delivering the year-to-year tactics do not understand the overall strategic picture or find it too hard to translate it into practical action then the strategy will not be implemented. Where leaders have the special talent to visualize the strategic potential of the future, managers need the supreme political skills to turn that into practical action.

Table 15.1 describes some of the differences in qualities between leaders and managers.

Before gangs of leaders or managers send bags of protests to the publisher let me assure readers that the list is not intended to assert, for example, that a manager cannot be visionary. Neither is the use of the word 'plebeian' meant to be pejorative. The list is intended to give deliberately contrasted insights into particular qualities used while doing the job of either **leader** or **manager**. Managers tend to be 'plebeian' when they think about the short-term

Table 15.1 Some role variations

Leaders	Managers
Visionary	Plebeian
Strategic	Tactical
Inspirational	Motivator
Communicator	Messenger
Good with people	Enabler of people
Corporate	Business oriented
Organizational	Political
Moral fibre	Passive ethics
Equilibrium	Hierarchical
Transformational	Transactional

delivery of a plan or a budget. It is not their role to be visionary and, most of the time, it would be inappropriate for their subordinates who mainly want straightforward instructions, advice and deadlines.

Similarly, it is not asserted that managers are never inspirational or that leaders never need to be motivational. But, in general, it is the inspirational part of the leader's role that is important to their effectiveness. When managers are doing their job properly they need to motivate their people to get the job done efficiently and effectively, rather than be inspirational. Inspirational behaviour can overwhelm the middle manager who really needs advice more about how to get the job done than to be inspired to want to do it.

Once again, where leaders need to communicate, managers merely carry those communications as messengers. Communicating the vision and strategic objectives is a key role in strategic implementation that the leader must deliver.

Below that we suggest that the manager has to be an enabler compared to the leader's 'good with people'. That means they have to help people who may be frightened or intimidated by difficult tasks to achieve them better and more effectively. It is not suggested that leaders never do this, merely that, in this guise, they only have to be good with people in order to make them want to adopt the strategic beliefs of the leader. That is not enough for a manager. They have to create the actual ability and deliver the means to their people to enable them to provide the results.

Rather than explain in detail the rest of Table 15.1, I hope that readers will reflect carefully on the contrasts in the list in order to understand the key differences between leaders and managers in their specific roles when implementing strategic and tactical objectives.

Is the team more important than the individual?

An eternal question about organizations will always be whether it is teams or individuals which make the greatest contribution to success. The concept of 'organization' implies teamwork. The Industrial Revolution was founded on the concept of bringing people together to work in one place so they could be managed more efficiently. Eventually, as people came together to work, larger machines and processes were developed to get greater economies of scale. The more people worked in teams, the greater was the parallel need for managers and leaders to guide them and ensure that economies of scale were actually achieved.

Management practice since the Industrial Revolution has tended to demonstrate to managers that the role of the individual is supreme. Most organizational charts are still drawn hierarchically with the bosses at the top and the various workers below (when they get on the chart at all). The classical hierarchical organization tends to confirm to the rising manager that he makes the difference as an individual. That is why he is being rewarded by promotion and increases in salary.

The great organizations of the 21st century will be complex, multi-national and vast. They will probably be too complex for most individuals to understand or lead. The few leaders with the skills to lead such organizations will achieve premium wages and be in high demand. Those leaders will understand that the only way they can lead their enormous organizations is through the use of teams. Those teams will achieve greater creativity, more productivity and the highest quality for more customers. That will be the key to organizational life in the 21st century – the combination of rare and gifted leaders with high quality, well-trained teams to implement the vision and strategic mission of the organization.

Most managers learn too few leadership skills

Most people learn a few tools of the management trade and then apply them to all the jobs they get throughout their career. There may be a theoretical explanation to this. Herbert Simon (1957) commented on his experiments that showed that most human beings are only capable of manipulating a strictly limited number of units of data within their short-term memory when taking decisions, usually between six and eight digits of data. Only the very brightest of minds handle more. In my work on leadership I notice that many leaders use their intuition to cut through the excess data that flow their way. That is how they focus on the essential facts which guide them to their strategic vision.

If one reflects on Table 15.1, the list of differences between leaders and managers indicates that many skills needed by either are being used by the other at the same time. That is because a manager is often being a leader and a leader often still needs to carry out managerial tasks. Figure 15.1 is intended to highlight what this means over a lifetime career. What it shows is that every manager is using some leadership skills and every leader continues to use some management skills. If a manager is managing his or her career towards closing as a leader of a complex organization, then the pattern they will follow will resemble that demonstrated in Figure 15.1.

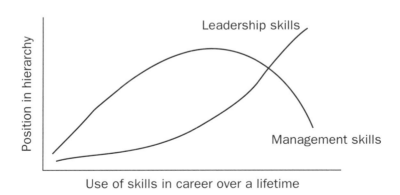

Figure 15.1 Use of leadership and management skills over a career

Judge on the future, not the past

When one reflects on whether one has the right team to make the strategy happen, it is important not to judge the team on its past achievements, but on the tasks and jobs you have in mind for the future of the organization. This is difficult but necessary. Too many people keep their jobs at senior level because the leader keeps referring back to how good they were when they ran a $40 million revenue business or a $500 million revenue business. However, if the objective in the future is for them to run their $2 billion segment of the business, then the past is not a predictor of the future. The harsh reality to be judged is whether they are showing evidence of success on the $2 billion job rather than the smaller job which they successfully pursued in the past. That was the reason they were promoted to the new job. It should not be the reason why you keep them in a new, more responsible job. That should relate only to potential future performance. This phenomenon of retaining excessive respect for past performance, rather than capacity for future achievement, explains why far too many people are kept too long in the wrong job, at levels beyond their competence, by chairmen who are making judgments based on the past, rather than the future needs of the organization.

This is not to suggest that one should not respect past achievements or neglect employees who have given sterling service but have now become worn out. I certainly believe they should be looked after. That behaviour forms part of the moral fibre and culture of the organization. But they should not be allowed to block the future because the organization owes them respect for the past. That respect can be paid in other ways which do not destroy customers' expectations, the future of the younger employees, employees' self-respect or the wealth of the business's investors.

Basic criteria of skills

There are three measures which are highly relevant to a manager's basic potential. They run in the following order of importance:

1 Loyalty
2 Intelligence
3 Enthusiasm.

The loyalty test is the absolute 'litmus test' of fitness for team member-ship. If there is any possibility of disloyalty to the leader, the organization, the strategy, the mission or the organization's values, then the executive must be counselled, allowed time to change and retested at an early date. Disloyalty cannot be contemplated from any member of a team which is asked to deliver an important strategic mission. Disloyalty is the corporate equivalent of biological cancer.

The second test is of intelligence. This does not mean that subordinates need to have a high IQ. It means they have to understand with some form of brain power what the leader is trying to do. This may be intuitive or deductive. It could be with a slow brain or a fast one. Whatever think-ing processing system they use, they have to show that they understand the strategy sufficiently well to translate it into appropriate time spans of achievement for their subordinates. I emphasize that this does not require a high IQ, but it does require some form of understanding. If they cannot show basic understanding of the key strategic messages, then they cannot possibly translate it for their people to achieve.

However, if they have at least the insight, coupled with the third ingre-dient of enthusiasm to achieve the task, then they can probably deliver the strategic objectives needed from them. The capacity to instill enthusi-asm in people around and below them with the desire to deliver and a determination to succeed is a golden quality that should be valued, trea-sured and embraced.

Audit the skills of the rest of the workforce

Core competencies were described earlier in this book (Chapter 2). The strategic implementation team must assess whether the organization has the right mix of core competencies to deliver its strategic objectives. For example, if one wanted to reduce people-based administration to an IT-led process system (as did the banks mentioned earlier), then one has to acquire compe-tencies in information technology and technology processing to deliver that part of the strategic intent. The organization will also need human resource management skills to reduce the workforce when people are supplanted by the technology. These are special skills and it is unlikely they will be sitting around in the organization waiting to be exploited. They will have to be acquired, either from competitors or by developing them in-house.

That is not a simple decision. The competencies may not be easily available in the open marketplace. The organization's need may be such an innovative use of the technology that the whole process has to be custom built from start to finish. One could buy in the service from an external supplier (e.g. EDS is a global information technology-processing organization supplying those needs to organizations around the world, usually as an insider within the organization).

When auditing the workforce one also has to understand what new skills, both technical and managerial, will be required as a result of the new or changed strategic objectives. Have your people been properly developed in the past? Does the organization need just a modification of training and development? Or do you need a new and totally organization-wide development programme? You may decide to develop special relationships with business schools or a particular consultancy organization which will invest in learning about your organization and, therefore, give you better value for money. Hopping around between suppliers can be an expensive game as you pay for each of them to go up the learning curve to understand your unique organization and the particular training needs of your people.

The structure of the organization

If you have decided to make substantial changes to the strategic purpose and objectives of the organization, you will have to re-examine the organization's structure to decide whether it fits the new needs. Will the old structure carry the new strategy or must it be changed?

The clear principle of structural change, as I have indicated in previous chapters, is to make as few modifications as possible. It has become fashionable for leaders to promise continuous change. I believe nothing can be more calculated completely to demotivate the workforce than that kind of utterly misguided statement.

The speed of industrial change is increasing. Technology and innovation have shorter life cycles than they used to have. However, even though external circumstances have changed, the nature of human beings, formed over millennia, has not changed to match. Human beings enjoy stability. They have strong hopes that tomorrow will be similar to today. People like to work in organizations where they understand what opportunities exist and where they see how they might move up the ladder of achievement to maximize the use of their skills and the limits of their ambition. Every time an organization is restructured, many of the rules of the game are changed. This leaves people ignorant about their future and fearful for their careers.

But if one has to restructure?

However, although it is our most forceful possible advice that you make as few changes to the structure of the organization as possible, how do you proceed when you have to restructure? It is a useful primary first principle to find any way you can to make the necessary changes without large-scale announcements either of redundancies or new positions and titles for your people. The basic rule is: Say as little as possible and write even less. This rule makes it much easier to move people into new positions and different responsibilities than

> **Say as little as possible and write even less.**

when you proclaim that sweeping changes are going to be necessary. That merely puts everybody into a state of fear and also induces a 'politicization' of most managers' behaviour. Equally invidious is the publication of formal organizational charts, showing definitively who appears to be a winner and, therefore, how many people are losers as a result of the changes. When you formalize the restructuring, you often generate far more demotivation than enthusiasm.

Evolution always beats revolution

Another reason for making changes as imperceptibly as possible over time, rather than instantaneously, is that the best structures are those that evolve as new needs become apparent.

It is not always easy, at the beginning of a long strategic journey, to know exactly what structures will be appropriate. Let them evolve as the need for new core competencies or different business directions emerge (whether geographical, intellectual, technological, human or capital). It is far better to wait and see than try to guess them all in advance.

Finally, another basic rule about structure is: Don't tell your competitors. Intelligent competitors will use knowledge about your organization's structure to predict your strategic intentions. If the strategic intent is worth having, it is worth keeping to yourself and your workforcee. Naturally, you cannot stop some people leaving and joining the competitors. Hopefully, you will always retain your key people. Those who understand most, at the very top of the ladder, would be wise to remain discreet in order to preserve their own reputations for integrity. Ultimately, no single person, or even group of people, can walk away from the company with all the strategic objectives and its enthusiasm to win and capacity to succeed. The potential success belongs to the organization and no single group of people should have total ownership.

Beware hubris

Your fears and doubts are also useful for another vital purpose. You can use them to help you retain your modesty and humility. These are key ingredients of great leaders. They form a protection against hubris. Hubris describes the vainglorious or excessive pride that too many leaders develop as they move up the corporate ladder. If disloyalty is a corporate cancer then hubris is a personal, managerial one. Arrogance, excessive self-belief, failure to admit doubt or fear, can have deleterious consequences for your organization. That is how hubris creeps up on you. Richard Nixon was an extreme example of hubris and its effect on moral fibre. In the end he felt invulnerable and admitted no limits to the rules he allowed himself to break because he considered himself above the law. Ultimately he was chased out of his US presidential office. No matter how high one climbs, this always only ever means that you have further to fall. At the end of the day, all human achievements are measured by standards of humanity. Organizations go on long after individuals have departed and are always bigger than even apparently brilliant individuals. Retain your humility – its loss could be damaging to your health.

I think it is fun

I have been analyzing and helping to implement strategy for over 30 years. Even now, as I move into the final part of my career teaching and passing on what I have learned, I still find every new strategic exercise exhilarating and intensely interesting. I hope I have passed on some of this sense of fun to my readers as they go through the process of strategic analysis and implementation. Whether as leader, manager or observer, enjoy your strategic analyses.

Further reading

J. Adair, *Effective Leadership*, Pan, London, 1988

I. Briggs Myers with P. B. Myers, *MBTI Gifts Differing*, Consulting Psychologists Press, Palo Alto, 1980

S. R. Covey, *The 7 Habits of Highly Successful People*, Fireside (Simon & Schuster), New York, 1990

J. Heider, *The Tao of Leadership*, Gower, Aldershot, 1993

D. Keirsey and M. Bates, *Please Understand Me* (5th edn), Prometheus Nemesis, Del Mar, 1984

C. J. Levicki, *Developing Leadership Genius*, McGraw-Hill, Maidenhead, 2002

L. D. Ryan, *Clinical Interpretation of the FIRO-B*, Consulting Psychologists Press, Oxford, 1989

H. Simon, *Models of Man*, Wiley, New York, 1957

Epilogue

Playing hard does not have to mean jogging and keeping fit in the gymnasium so that you can work longer hours for the organization. It means having a social life, going to the theatre, listening to music, having meals with friends or any of the other myriad interests which make people into more rounded human beings. Many of your subordinates are probably having high quality social lives. A distorted social life for the strategic leader or manager means he is less of a human being than the people he or she is meant to be guiding. They will know that and will judge you accordingly.

More importantly, you should judge yourself in the same light. If you find that you do not like playing or you do not enjoy a private social life, it is also possible that you are a dull being who is probably not very good at strategy, leadership or management. 'Play' is what 'earning a living' is for. Playing well enables us to be serious at work, although the luckiest people are those who find work as much fun as play.

How to be lucky

In some ways the oldest clichés are the best. All the lucky people seem to work hard. 'Working long hours' does not mean 'working long hours at the expense of a private life'. Long hours at work should be a function of total energy capacity. Some people are lucky enough to have waking hours of 18 out of 24. Others need to sleep ten hours out of 24. Your work hours should be a function of your total energy capacity. People who work hard but do not know how to play equally hard are often unbalanced leaders. Their value systems get distorted and that leads to the demonstration of wrong values within the organization. For an obvious example, people with different and lower energy levels may work long hours with no value to the organization yet do exceptional harm to themselves and their private lives.

Occasionally, one hears leaders say that they have had a lot of bad luck and that things are just not going their way or coming out right for the organization. If you ever hear yourself saying those words you should ask yourself whether the problem is luck or you. Under most circumstances, the answer is you. If it is you, do you have the courage to leave the organization? Or demote yourself to the level where you used to be competent? If ever you have a disinclination to 'do the right thing' remember, there may well be many thousands of workers below you who need those jobs much more than you need yours.

Close

I hope you have enjoyed this book and that it has shown you how to complete a strategic analysis. It should also have demonstrated some of the ways in which implementation can go well or badly. If you have used the book as a workbook and completed the audit pages as you read the chapters be aware there is a final complete workout system after this conclusion. Use it either as a check on your previous analysis or perhaps as a revision next year to see how the strategic purpose of your organization is moving along.

It is our intention continuously to improve this workout book in the light of new research and methodology as it evolves from the best business schools and organizations around the world. We continuously learn from experience and try to improve every aspect of the technique.

Good luck with your strategy. It is the most important thing you will ever do for your organization.

Dr Cyril J. Levicki
2003

Part Three

Measure your final strategy workout fitness

With any luck you have reached this part of the book and are *still* interested in defining strategy for your organization. You will have understood from Part Two that it is harder to implement strategy than to analyze it. However, you are still determined to press on. You are determined to avoid the mistakes of your peers as outlined in Chapter 11. You have learnt all the lessons of Chapter 12 and know how to avoid hubris, the dangers of ego and the need to communicate the strategy continuously to have any chance of success.

My last piece of advice before you start communicating is to have the humility to check it all out once again. On the following pages all the workout pages are set out together. Complete them again, in the light of your 'fitter' feel for the niceties and complexities of the whole subject.

If you are really fit for strategy you will almost certainly only need a few minutes now.

All the workouts are also supplied on CD in the back of the book.

THE MISSION WORKOUT

Complete the following mission audit questions.

What is the vision of the leader of the organization?

_____

Where is he or she taking the organization in the long run?

_____

What industry (industries) are you determined to participate in?

_____

What are the current core competencies of the organization?

_____

What core competencies need to be obtained?

_____

What will the organization look like in five years' time?

_____

What are the three key achievements that will be history in five years' time?

_____

THE EXTERNAL ENVIRONMENT WORKOUT

What are the most important economic factors in the organization's domestic market?

1 _____ 2 _____
3 _____ 4 _____

Where are the business' most important markets?

1 _____ 2 _____
3 _____ 4 _____

What are the most important economic factors in those markets abroad?

1 _____ 2 _____
3 _____ 4 _____

Who are your most important spheres of political law making and lobbying?

1 _____ 2 _____ 3 _____

What are the most important political factors likely to affect the organization?

1 _____ 2 _____
3 _____ 4 _____

Which legal factors affect or could affect the organization?

_____

Which laws would you want to see enacted which would most benefit your organizations' competencies?

1 _____ 2 _____
3 _____ 4 _____

Which current demographic trends may affect the organization's workforce?

1 _____ 2 _____
3 _____ 4 _____

What are the trends in demand for the organization's main services or products?

1 _____ 2 _____
3 _____ 4 _____

Is there any key political legislation which could affect your industry (industries)?

1 _____ 2 _____
3 _____ 4 _____

THE COMPETITOR ANALYSIS WORKOUT

Current industry competitors

Under each of the following categories, put in the names of companies or people where appropriate. Regard this as a simple measure of your knowledge of the industry.

Which are the top performers in your industry?

1 _____ 2 _____
3 _____ 4 _____

Are there any other important national competitors?

1 _____ 2 _____
3 _____ 4 _____

Who are strategically the most dangerous people in competing organizations?

1 _____ 2 _____
3 _____ 4 _____

Which are the important regional or local competitors?

1 _____ 2 _____
3 _____ 4 _____

Which are the current customers most likely to integrate backwards?

1 _____ 2 _____
3 _____ 4 _____

Which are the current suppliers most likely to integrate forwards?

1 _____ 2 _____
3 _____ 4 _____

Any organizations that might enter the industry?

1 _____ 2 _____
3 _____ 4 _____

THE INDIVIDUAL COMPETITOR PROFILE WORKOUT

Complete one of these for each important competitor mentioned in the previous workout.

What is the competitor's company name?

What is their annual revenue? Their annual profit?

What is the name of the competitor's leader?

What is their psychology?

_____

Is the competitor satisfied with their current position in the industry?

Yes/No

If not, what strategic moves do you think they will make?

_____

What action from your organization will provoke the fiercest retaliation?

_____

What are the competitor's most important strengths?

_____

What are the competitor's most important weaknesses?

_____

THE INDUSTRY ANALYSIS WORKOUT

Is your industry large or small scale?

_____

If small, can you see a clear route to transform it to a larger scale?

_____

What products or services command the highest profits in your industry?

_____

Are there any barriers that prevent you from entering that market area?

_____

If so, what are they?

_____

Who controls distribution channels in your industry?

_____

If it's not your business, how will you ensure you get or maintain control?

_____

Does your business have access to sufficient capital to grow into number 1 or 2 in your industry?

_____

Is cash flow positive or negative? If the latter, can this be changed?

_____

Where are the niche markets in your industry?

_____

What would it cost to leave the industry?

_____

Is your industry long or short lived (in tens of years)?

_____

Does your business have all the necessary competencies to compete successfully in this industry?

_____

If not, what skills do you have to acquire and how?

_____

How will you enhance your strongest selling products/services to increase their potential profitability?

_____

List the key political figures and senior administration bureaucrats your organization has access to

_____

What is the value of the experience curve in your industry to the best business in it?

_____

If that is not your business, how long will it take your business to achieve similar levels?

_____

What is your psychological hold over your customers?

_____

If you do not have a psychological hold, what *should* it be when you get one?

_____

STRENGTHS, NEUTRALS AND WEAKNESSES WORKOUT

Check each of the following categories in terms of its being a strength, a neutral or a weakness. Sometimes it helps to allocate a number from 1 to 5 indicating high (5), medium (3), or low (1). Thus, a neutral with a 5 on it would be very close to a strength with a 1 on the same category.

Organization function   Strength   Neutral   Weakness

Access to finance
Accounting skills (financial)
Accounting skills (management)
Business strategy
Corporate strategy
Cost structure of business
Distribution network
Divisional strategy
Entry barriers
Exit barriers
Information technology
Innovation (turning research into products)
Lateral communication
Leader's ability
Leadership in general
Loyalty of workforce
Management ability
Manufacturing skills
Marketing skills
Organization structure
Personnel administration
Products
Quality of brands
Quality of staff
Relationship with government
Relationship with regulator
Relationship with trade unions
Relationships with suppliers
Reputation as employer
Reputation in market

Organization function	Strength	Neutral	Weakness
Research and development			
Selling skills			
Services			
Technical engineering skills			
Vertical communication			
Additional categories (relevant to your particular business)			

SUMMARY OF SNW WORKOUT

Select the top four strengths, neutrals and weaknesses from your analysis on the previous workout and set them out with a brief note on how you might use, neutralize or improve the effects of each for the success of the organization's mission.

Strengths

1

2

3

4

Neutrals

1

2

3

4

Weaknesses

1

2

3

4

THE CULTURE WORKOUT

Complete each of the following categories with the most important features under each category. It is important to note the effect of each subject, e.g. for past leaders, put their name – but also what behaviours remain in the organization because of the way they did things when they were leader.

HISTORY

Event 1 _____

Effect of event 1 _____

Event 2 _____

Effect of event 2 _____

Event 3 _____

Effect of event 3 _____

What is the most important feature of the mental environment?

_____

_____

What is its cultural effect? _____

LEADERSHIP ISSUES

1 Name the most memorable past leader _____

What behaviour is still attributable to him/her? _____

2 Name the current leader _____

What particular qualities do you associate with him/her? _____

_____

What is the physical environment of head office? _____

_____

What is the physical environment of the rest of the organization? _____

_____

If your organization is 'virtual' and you work from home, do you feel you belong to a real organization?_____**How?**_____

_____

How do you understand what the business stands for and values? _____

_____

TECHNOLOGY OF THE ORGANIZATION

Which of the following technologies applies to the organization?
(Check whichever one of the following pairs applies to your organization.)

Paper based	**or**	Computer based
Batch technology	**or**	Process technology
National scale of operations	**or**	International scale
Mature industries	**or**	New industries
Product	**or**	Service

What cultural effect does each of those you have checked off have on the organization?

The way people behave in the organization is learned through the stories and anecdotes they hear when they join and while they remain. Try to think of those which have affected the way you behave.

MYTHS
(These are stories which are possibly untrue but which get told anyway.)
What is the best known myth in the organization?

LEGENDS
(These are stories which have sources long buried in the past, but which get passed on anyway, with variations.)
What is the best known legend in the organization?

STORIES

(These are probably true stories you are told to explain how to do things around here.)

What is the best known story in the organization?

ANECDOTES

(These are entertaining stories which also teach.)

What is the best known anecdote in the organization?

VALUE CHAIN ANALYSIS WORKOUT

Analyze your business' current position(s) in the value chain(s) of its main products and services.

Fill in the vertical and horizontal opportunities for products and services currently being supplied by competitors.

	Stage One	*Stage Two*	*Stage Three*	*Stage Four*	*Stage Five*
	Finding raw materials	Manufacture of components	Assembly of final product	Wholesale distribution	Retail to final user
Typical profit range					
Typical risk					
Key factors					

Consider your organization's backwards and forwards integration opportunities from the point of view of each of the following:

1 Attitude of customers

_____

_____

2 Availability of business to purchase or capability of competitors

_____

_____

3 Profit margins

_____

_____

4 Your business' competencies and alignment with the desired strategic direction.

_____

_____

THE ACCOUNTS EVALUATION WORKOUT

Are your business management accounts accurate?

_____

Does the accounting service of the business help or hinder your work?

_____

How?

_____

Do you have to deliver more figures than are used by the accounting department?

_____

Name three improvements you would make to the accounting system

1 _____

2 _____

3 _____

Are your business financial accounts accurate?

_____

Does the annual report accurately report results?

_____

If not, what does it distort and why?

_____

What is your business cash flow? _____

How does your business' financial health compare to that of the best business in your sector?

_____

What is your company ordinary share dividend rate?

_____

How well is this covered by pre-tax earnings?

What is your business PE ratio?

_____

How does this compare to that of the best business in your sector?

_____

What is your company's ROCE?

_____

How does this compare to that of the best business in your sector?

_____

Could your business borrow enough to buy it's largest competitor?

_____

LONG-TERM STRATEGY WORKOUT

Consider each of the following stakeholders and give each a mark of level of importance in your strategic thinking, with 1 for low to 10 for high influence.

Share- holders	Bond- holders	Merchant banks	Pension funds	Institutions
1 2 3 4 5 6 7 8 9 10	1 2 3 4 5 6 7 8 9 10	1 2 3 4 5 6 7 8 9 10	1 2 3 4 5 6 7 8 9 10	1 2 3 4 5 6 7 8 9 10
Staff	Pensioners	Unions	Central government	Local government
1 2 3 4 5 6 7 8 9 10	1 2 3 4 5 6 7 8 9 10	1 2 3 4 5 6 7 8 9 10	1 2 3 4 5 6 7 8 9 10	1 2 3 4 5 6 7 8 9 10
Auditors	Senior executives	Bankers	Regional bodies (EU, ASEAN, SEATO)	
1 2 3 4 5 6 7 8 9 10	1 2 3 4 5 6 7 8 9 10	1 2 3 4 5 6 7 8 9 10	1 2 3 4 5 6 7 8 9 10	

What competing products and/or services would you like in your own business' portfolio?

_____

Are there any competitors you might like to take over that are available or buyable? Name them.

_____

Are there any suppliers making superior profit margins to your own business? Could you effectively take over and successfully manage them? Name them.

_____

Are there any customers making profit margins superior to those of your own business? Could you effectively take over and successfully manage them? Name them.

_____

Should the firm grow, remain stable or diminish in size?
Which parts of the business should:

_____

Focus?   Differentiate?   Be an industry cost leader?

_____

What will be the organization's three key achievements at the end of the next five years?

_____

What will be the level of revenue in five year's time?

_____

What will be the level of profit in five years' time?

_____

What will be the main three industry areas of interest in five years' time?
1 _____
2 _____
3 _____

Will your corporation have a local, national, regional or international reputation in five years' time? For what?

How much of your budget needs to be devoted without exception to people development to achieve the strategic vision?

ORGANIZATIONAL STRUCTURE WORKOUT

What is the size of the organization?_____

People? _____ Revenue? _____ Profits? _____

What geographical area does it cover?

Local? _____ Regional? _____ Country? _____ International? _____

Does the organization provide many or a few services or products? _____

Which is better known? The company name? _____ The brand names of the products? _____

Is the organization currently centralized? _____ Or decentralized? _____

Are there lots of rules? _____ Or very few rules? _____

What is the average proportion of managers to workers? _____

How do you communicate? Verbally? _____ Written messages? _____ Electronic mail? _____

Does the organization offer the same service all the time? _____

Does almost every order require a different process? _____

How is the organization structured now?

Functional ☐ Geographical ☐ Product ☐ Matrix ☐ Mixed ☐

What is the average span of control (span of control = the number of people managed by each manager) at each level in the hierarchy of the business?

Are there rational reasons for the differences between levels in the hierarchy?   Yes   No

Why or why not?_____

How many direct supports does the leader have? _____

Does the culture encourage communications? _____

What is the total number of employees? _____

What is the total number of operators, meaning people with direct 'doing' jobs? _____

What is the total number of supervisors and managers? _____

Could you design any structure which decreases the number of managers?

(Use a spare blank sheet.)

What are the major advantages of your design? _____

What are the major disadvantages of your design? _____

SHORT-TERM TACTICS WORKOUT

Part One: The tactics

Remind yourself here of the three key long-term strategic aims.

     1   2   3

Choose three from the following areas of appropriate tactical objectives that you should focus on this year to contribute to the achievement of the long-term aims:

- product improvement
- quality improvement
- market share increase
- profit rate improvement
- distribution change
- marketing
- operations productivity improvement
- human resource development

Name precisely this year's numbers and statistics relating to the three you have chosen:

     1   2   3

Has your business ever attempted to put right or improve any of these areas before? Yes   No

If yes, what went wrong last time necessitating making them a priority again this year?

_____

What is different about this year's approach which obviates whatever went wrong last time you tried to improve each one?

1

2

3

Part Two: The accounts

To get your tactics into context

Corporation/business/department's total revenue	$/£m	———
Operating profits	$/£m	———
Profits before tax	$/£m	———
This year's profit as percentage of net revenue	%	———
Cash flow	$/m	———
Assets	$/m	———

Budget for your department

(Complete the lines that are relevant to you.)

Total expenditure	$/£ ———
Total costs	$/£ ———
Total sales	$/£ ———
Budgeted profit/loss	$/£ ———

Total number of subordinates in the department at beginning of year

Total number of subordinates in the department at end of year

Total bonus for department	$/£ ———
Targets against which the bonus is set	$/£ ———

INTERNATIONAL STRATEGY WORKOUT

If you are considering becoming international answer the following questions to assure yourself it is the right move:

Are you already exporting to any countries and should they be your first target destinations?

Which of the following seem to be the right way forward and why?

Wholly owned new startup ☐ Strategic alliance ☐ Acquisition ☐ Merger ☐

Why?

What changes will be necessitated in the domestic business and why?

Strategy?   Why?

Culture?   Why?

Complexity?   Why?

Management?   Why?

Leadership?   Why?

Accountancy?   Why?

Financing?   Why?

What aspects of the target country's (or countries') culture is most potentially dangerous to this project?

What are you doing about it?

_____

What are the key features of the culture of the target *business* from among the following?

- history
- leaders
- technology
- stories
- anecdotes
- myths
- legends

Is specific action required to deal with any potential problems this feature raises? If yes, what action?

_____

What are the key features of the culture of the target *country* from among the following?

Is specific action required to deal with any potential problems this feature raises? If yes, what action?

_____

Have you identified staff with the following qualities which are vital in executives working in foreign subsidiaries?

- tolerance of ambiguity
- interest in other cultures
- capacity for non-aggressive feedback
- open attitude
- good at communication
- skilled at constructive criticism
- know how to express feelings
- capacity for fostering trust

If you have insufficient people of this type of temperament, what search programmes are being put in place to seek them out?

_____

Further reading

J. Adair, *Effective Leadership*, Pan, London, 1988

R. Adams, J. Carruthers and S. Hamil, *Changing Corporate Values*, Kogan Page, London, 1991

M. Belbin, *Management Teams – Why They Succeed or Fail*, Butterworth-Heinemann, Oxford, 1991

M. Belbin, *Team Roles at Work*, Butterworth-Heinemann, Oxford, 1993

K. Blanchard and S. Johnson, *The One Minute Manager*, William Collins, Glasgow, 1990

I. Briggs Myers with P. B. Myers, *MBTI Gifts Differing*, Consulting Psychologists Press, California, 1980

T. Burns and G. M. Stalker, *The Management of Innovation*, Tavistock, London, 1961

A. Campbell, M. Devine and D. Young, *A Sense of Mission*, Hutchinson, London, 1990

A. P. Chandler, *Strategy and Structure*, MIT Press, Boston, 1962

S. R. Covey, *The 7 Habits of Highly Successful People*, Fireside (Simon & Schuster), New York, 1990

T. E. Deal and A. A. Kennedy, *Corporate Cultures*, Addison-Wesley, Reading, Massachusetts, 1982

J. R. Franks and J. E Broyles, *Modern Managerial Finance*, John Wiley, Chichester, 1979

A. de Geus, *The Living Company*, Nicholas Brealey, London, 1997

R. M. Grant, *Contemporary Strategy Analysis*, Blackwell, Oxford, 1995

G. Hamel and C. K. Prahalad, *Competing for the Future*, Harvard Business School Press, Boston, 1994

C. Handy, *Understanding Organizations* (4th edn), Penguin, Harmondsworth, 1993

P. C. Haspeslagh and D. B. Jemison, *Managing Acquisitions*, Free Press, New York, 1991

J. Heider, *The Tao of Leadership*, Gower, Aldershot, 1993

J. Hunt, *Managing People at Work*, Pan, London, 1981

E. Jacques, *Measurement of Responsibility*, Tavistock, London, 1956

E. Jacques, *Time Span Handbook*, Heinemann, London, 1964

J. Kay, *Foundations of Corporate Success*, Oxford University Press, Oxford, 1993

D. Keirsey and M. Bates, *Please Understand Me* (5th edn), Prometheus Nemesis, Del Mar, 1984

T. Kuhn, *The Structure of Scientific Revolutions*, University of Chicago Press, Chicago, 1962

P. Lawrence and J. Lorsch, *Managing Differentiation and Integration*, Harvard University Press, Boston, 1967

C. J. Levicki, *The Leadership Gene*, Financial Times Pitman, London, 1998

C. J. Levicki, *Developing Leadership Genius*, McGraw-Hill, Maidenhead, 2002

J. G. March, *Decisions and Organizations*, Blackwell, Oxford, 1988

J. G. March and H. A. Simon, *Organizations*, Wiley & Sons, New York, 1958

A. Maslow, *Motivation and Personality*, Harper & Row, New York, 1970

D. Parker, *The Strategic Finance Workout*, Financial Times Pitman, London, 1996

T. Peters and N. Austin, *A Passion for Excellence*, William Collins & Sons, Glasgow, 1985

T. J. Peters and R. H. Waterman, *In Search of Excellence*, Harper & Row, New York, 1982

K. Popper, *The Logic of Scientific Discovery*, Hutchinson, London, 1959

M. E. Porter, *Competitive Strategy*, Free Press, New York, 1980

M. E. Porter, *Competitive Advantage*, Free Press, New York, 1985

D. Pugh (ed.), *Organization Theory*, Penguin, Harmondsworth, 1971

D. S. Pugh and D. J. Hickson, *Organizational Structure in its Context*, Saxon House/Lexington Books, D.E. Heath, Farnborough, 1976

P. Q. Quinn, *Intelligent Enterprise*, Free Press, New York, 1992

S. P. Robbins, *Training in Interpersonal Skills*, Prentice-Hall, Englewood Cliffs, New Jersey, 1989

S. A. Ross, R. W. Westerfield and B. D. Jordan, *Fundamentals of Corporate Finance*, McGraw-Hill, New York, 2002

L. D. Ryan, *Clinical Interpretation of the FIRO-B*, Consulting Psychologists Press, Oxford, 1989

J. A. Schumpeter, *History of Economic Analysis*, Allen & Unwin, London, 1954

H. Simon, *Models of Man*, Wiley, New York, 1957

S. Slatter, *Corporate Recovery*, Penguin, Harmondsworth, 1984

F. Trompenaars, *Riding the Waves of Culture*, Economist Books, London, 1993

H. Vroom and E. L. Deci, *Management and Motivation*, Penguin, Harmondsworth, 1979

J. Welch, *Jack: What I've learned Leading a Great Company and Great People*, Warner Books, New York, 2001

O. Williamson, *Markets and Hierarchies*, Free Press, New York, 1975

J. Woodward, *Industrial Organization Theory and Practice*, Oxford University Press, Oxford, 1965

J. Woodward (ed.), *Industrial Organization, Behavior and Control*, Oxford University Press, Oxford, 1970

Index

ABZ Truck Rental 86, 91
  information technology 89
Accenture 190
accounting skills
  financial 97–8
  management 98–9
accounting and strategic numerate
    assessment 158–69
  accounting state 159
  accounts required 159
  capital raising 163–4
  cash and assets 164
  debt 165–7
  EBITDA 164–5
  financial accounts 160–1
  goodwill 168
  inflation 168–9
  PE ratios 162–3
  public company accounting 161–2
  ROCE 167
accounts
  evaluation workout 173–4
  required 159
  state 159
  for strategists 169–71
acquisitions and mergers 183–8, 248
  acquisition aftermath 187–8
  combined companies' attractive-
    ness 184
  culture 185
  due diligence 188
  earnings per share (EPS) 183

  financial rationale 186
  gearing 183
  geographical locations 187
  integration management 185
  manager competence 187
  PE ratio 183
  risk profile 183
  stakeholder backing 185–6
  synergy 184
  takeover 183
agency 248
Allen Edmonds, specialists 70
amendments to structure 5–6
Amstrad 52, 58
  service 77
analytical thinking 175
Apple 40, 51, 58
APV, profit maximization 236–7
Arthur Andersen 190
ASEAN (Association of South East
    Asian Nations) 34, 51, 77
Astra Zeneca 250
AT&T, spare capital 54
ATT 39
auditors and accountants 189–90
authority, discretion and control
    designation 210–11

Baby Bells, spare capital 54
barriers *see* entry and exit barriers
benchmarking 88
  productivity improvement 237

Berol, technology 127–8
Bethlehem Steel Corporation,
        strengths and weaknesses 94
BIC 58
Birt, John 177
BMW 39
BP Amoco 244, 250
branding 80–1
Branson, Richard 65
breakeven and exit cost
        barriers 64
British Airways (BA) 9, 52
   history 122
   mission statement 21
British Gas, relationship with gov-
        ernment/regulator 113
British Midland 52
Bryant & May 36–7
BT (British Telecom)
   accounting skills
        (management) 98–9
   creativity inhibitors 178
   integrity 78
   marketing skills 109
   mission statement 21, 24–5, 39
   myths/legends 129
budgets and tasks, tactics
        measurability 234
business 76–81
   entry barriers 80–1
   integrity 78–9
   psychological imprisonment 79–80
   relationships with political
        organizations 76–7
   service 77–8
   startup structure 212
   strategies 99

business-level strategies 194–6
   cost leadership strategies 194–5
   differentiation strategies 195–6
   focus strategies 196

Cable & Wireless (C&W) 71–2
   International Digital
        Communication 191
Cadbury-Schweppes, distribution
        channels 66
Camelot 65
Canon 65
Cap Gemini 190
capital
   raising 163–4
   requirements and cash flows 68–9
cash
   analysis 171
   and assets 164
   flow 69–70
changing minds 178–9
checklists 96–7
   strengths, neutrals and
        weaknesses 97–114
Chloride Batteries 231–2
CNN, branding 80–1
Coca-Cola
   core competencies 20
   distribution channels 66
   distribution network 101
   Japan 32
combined companies'
        attractiveness 184
communication 211, 224–5
   international markets 32
   leader 278
Compaq 51, 58, 123
   distribution network 101

competencies and deficiencies 87
competency management and
    extension 73–4
competition sources
  forwards integration 53
  integrating backwards 53
  Porter, Michael 53
  spare capital 54
competitors 5–6, 48–60
  competition sources 53–5
  competitiveness within
      industries 55–8
  competitor analysis workout 59
  individual competitor profile
      workout 60
conglomerates 182–3
continuous improvement,
    leader 276–7
control spans 222
core competencies 20–3, 176
  Coca-Cola 20
  Federal Express 20
corporate
  governance 19–20
  strategy 99–100
corporate and business
    strategies 179–81
  choice 180–1
cost leadership strategies 194–5
cost structure 100–1
creativity management 177–9
  changing minds 178–9
  creativity inhibitors 178
  creativity and people 179
creativity in organizations 175–6
  analytical thinking 175
  core competencies 176
  emotional intelligence 175

culture 185, 253–5
  business international
      qualities 254–5
  international qualities 254
  personal international
      qualities 254
  workout 133–5
  see also organizational culture
culture audit components
  history 121–2
  mental environment 123
  myths/legends 128–9
  past leaders 124
  physical environment 125–7
  present leaders 124–5
  stories/anecdotes 129–31
  technology 127–8

Dauphin Distribution 125
dead mouse syndrome 275
debt 165–7
Dell 51, 123
    distribution network 101
Dell, Michael 101
Deutsche Telecom 39
differentiation 43
  strategies 195–6
distribution
  channels 66–7
  network 101
divestment 194
Dixon's 44
domestic market saturation 246–7
downsizing 95–6, 211
due diligence 188
duties, leader 263
Dyson 50
Dyson, James 50

earnings before interest, taxation, depreciation and amortization *see* EBITDA

earnings per share (EPS) 183

EBITDA (earnings before interest, taxation, depreciation and amortization) 164–5

  gearing 165

  gearing ratio 165

economic trends 36–8

  product life cycle 37–8

EDS 292

EMI, entry and exit barriers 65

emotional intelligence 175

employee grouping 210

Enron

  Andersens 190

  monopoly 75

  strengths and weaknesses 93

entry and exit barriers 63–5, 80–1

  branding 80–1

  entry barriers 101–2

  exit barriers 102–3

  experience curve 81

  legal protection 80

Equitable Life 19, 79

Ercol, specialists 70

Ernst & Young 190

ethical considerations 17–18

  and business 17–18

EU (European Union) 34, 77

evolution 293–4

Exel Logistics, manufacturing skills 108

experience curve 81

exporting 248

external environment 5–6, 30–8

  economic trends 36–8

  industry expectations/ tendencies 31

  international markets 31–3

  legal, social and demographic factors 31

  national markets 34–6

  political events 31

  scanning 29–30

  workout 47

  see also non-controllable environment

fast moving consumer goods (FMCG) 49

fear of failure, leader 270–1

Federal Express 44

  core competencies 20

  hub and spoke system 45

Ferragamo, specialists 70

finance access 99

financial

  accounts 160–1

  objectives 238–9

  rationale 18

FIRO-B (Fundamental Interpersonal Relations, Orientations-Behaviour) test 280–1

fluffy cushion syndrome 231–2

focus strategies 196

Ford 39

  cash flow 70

foreign

  competitors 247

  subsidiaries 255–6

Forte 39

forwards integration 53

France Télécom 39
functional structures 212–14
future and past 290

Gates, Bill 7
gearing 165, 183
  ratio 165
GEC 8, 49
  cash flow 70
  competency management and
    extension 73
  Honeywell 186
  longevity 72–3
General Motors (GM) 39, 254
geographical
  locations 187
  structure 215–16
Geus, Arie de 18
GlaxoSmithKline 250
Global Crossing, strengths and
    weaknesses 94
global leader 38–46
  differentiation 43
  integrated market 44
  politics 45
  profitability 42–4
Goldmann Sachs, competencies
    and deficiencies 87
goodwill 168
  investment capital 168
Granada plc 24, 196
greatness, leader 275–6
growth
  acquisitions and mergers 183–8
  auditors and accountants 189–90
  conglomerates 182–3
  opportunities abroad 245
  public sector 191–2
  stakeholders 188–9

Hamel, Gary, competencies and
    deficiencies 87
Hanson Industries,
    conglomerates 183
Harvard 17
Hewlett-Packard 123
  distribution network 101
Hilton 39
history 121–2
Holiday Inn 39
Honeywell 186
Hoover 50
horizontal value links 137–8, 153–4
Horton, Bob 244
how the book works 3–4
HSBC 250
hubris 294
Hutchings, Greg 100, 183

IBM 23, 39, 51, 58
  competencies and deficiencies 87
  employee grouping 210
  mental environment 123
  service 77–8
implementation through leadership
    and management 259–95
  leadership 263–85
  strategic management 286–97
industries and markets 62–76
  breakeven and exit cost barriers 64
  capital requirements and cash
    flows 68–9
  competency management and
    extension 73–4
  distribution channels 66–7
  entry and exit barriers 63–5
  industries large/small 67–8
  industry profits 62–3
  longevity 72–3

monopoly 74–5
product ranges and natural
    mixes 75–6
profitability levels 69–70
specialists 70–2
industry
  analysis workout 82–3
  expectations/tendencies 31
inflation 168–9
  accounting 169
informal structures 220–2
information technology 89–90, 103
integrating backwards 53
integration and
        differentiation 197–200
  roles and time horizons 199
  time horizons and hierarchy 198
  time horizons and hierarchy
        distortions 200
integration management 185
integrity 78–9
Intel 123
internal change rate 92–3
internal strengths 95–6
  neutrals and weaknesses 5–6
  re-engineering 95
international considerations 243–58
  culture 253–5
  foreign subsidiaries 255–6
  how to trade internationally 248–9
  international evolution 251
  international strategy
        workout 257–8
  international trends 251
  leadership and management 244–7
  risks 252–3
  strategic considerations 243–4
  when to trade internationally
        249–50

International Digital
    Communication, Cable &
    Wireless (C&W) 191
International Harvester,
        differentiation strategies 197
international markets 31–3
  communication 32
  cultural differences 32–3
investment capital 168

John Lewis, differentiation
    strategies 196

Kellogg's, branding 80–1
Kennedy, John F. 12–13
King, Lord 9
Kinnock, Neil 192
Knapp, Barclay 166–7
Kodak, branding 80–1
KPMG 190
Kuhn, Thomas 14–15

Land Rover, specialists 70
lateral communications 103
Lawrence, Paul 197
leader 7–10, 286
  ability 104–5
  and leading strategic team 225
  past 124
  present 124–5
leader failure 265–9
  fear of excellence 268–9
  job growth 268
  leaders and managers 266–7
  leadership and management
        difference 265–6
  mythology 267
  weaknesses 267–8

leadership 263–85
  communications 278
  continuous improvement 276–7
  duties 263
  fear of failure 270–1
  greatness 275–6
  leader failure 265–9
  loyalty 274–5
  and management skills 289
  psychology 280–1
  roles 271–3
  stability 279–80
  stakeholder concepts 264–5
  stakeholders 277
  strategic failure 264
  strategy implementation 281–4
  subordinates 271
  team 273
leadership and management
      internationally 244–7
  domestic market saturation
      246–7
  foreign competitors 247
  growth opportunities abroad 245
  leader interest 247
  market internationalizes 245–6
legal protection 80
legal, social and demographic
      factors 31
Liberty Media 54
licensing 248
London Business School (LBS) 17
long-term strategy and creativity
      175–205
  business-level strategies 194–6
  corporate and business
      strategies 179–81
  creativity creation 176–7

  creativity management 177–9
  creativity in organizations 175–6
  integration and differentiation
      197–200
  long-term strategy definition
      181–94
  long-term strategy workout
      204–5
  strategies to avoid 201–2
  time horizons 196–7
  wisdom and cleverness 177
long-term strategy definition
      5–6, 181–94
  growth 182
  retrenchment or liquidation
      strategy 192–4
  stability strategy 192
longevity 72–3
L'Oréal 238
  strengths and weaknesses 94
Lorsch, Jay 197
loyalty 274–5, 290
  dead mouse syndrome 275
  whistleblowing 274–5
loyalty of workforce 107

McDonald's, branding 80
Major, John 16
management ability 107
manager competence 187, 286–8
manufacturing
  capacity increase/decrease 234
  skills 108
Marconi 73
market 247
  integrated 44
  internationalization 245–6

market and business analysis 61–83
  businesses 76–81
  industries and markets 62–76
  industry analysis workout 82–3
marketing 238
  skills 109
Marks & Spencer
  competitiveness within
    industries 56
  cost structure 100–1
  divestment 194
  history 122
  psychological imprisonment 79
  specialists 70–1
  stories/anecdotes 129–30
Marlboro, branding 80
Marriott 39
Marshall, Sir Colin 9
Maslow, A. 207
Matalan 56
matrix structure 216–19
Maxwell, Robert, stories/
  anecdotes 129–30
Media-One 54
mental environment 123
Meridian 39
methodology for strategic
  analysis 1–261
  competitors study 48–60
  international considerations 243–58
  long-term strategy and
    creativity 175–205
  market and business
    analysis 61–83
  mission and vision
    statements 11–28
  non-controllable
    environment 29–47
  numerical evaluation 157–75

organizational culture 120–35
organizational self-analysis 84–119
organizational structure 206–29
  short-term tactics for long-term
    strategy 229–43
  value chains and their
    analysis 136–57
  workout method introduction 3–10
Microsoft 7, 39–40, 123
  competitiveness within
    industries 56
  mission statement 20
  spare capital 54
  Windows 56–7
mission, and vision 282–4
mission statement 5–6
  definition 11–13
  versus vision statement 23–6
mission and vision statements 11–28
  core competencies 20–3
  corporate governance 19–20
  ethical considerations 17–18
  mission statement definition 11–13
  mission versus vision
    statements 23–6
  philosophy and paradigmatic
    thinking 13–17
  political mission 13
MIT, specialists 70
Mitsubishi 39
mobile telephone industry 22
monopoly 74–5
Monte, Mario 186, 192
Morita, Akio 22
motivation 211
Murdoch, Rupert 51, 64, 166
  business structure 170–1
myths/legends 128–9

NAFTA (North American Free
    Trade Alliance) 34, 77
NASA 13–14
National Cash Registers 23
national markets 34–6
  distribution costs 34
News International 51
  entry and exit barriers 64
Nissan 30
Nixon, Richard 294
non-controllable environment 29–47
  economic trends 36–8
  external environment 30–1
  external environment
      scanning 29–30
  external environment workout 47
  global leader 38–46
  international markets 31–3
  national markets 34–6
Novell 123
NTL 64–5, 166–7
  strengths and weaknesses 93
NTT 191
numerical evaluation 157–75
  accounting and strategic
      numerate assessment 158–69
  accounts evaluation workout 173–4
  accounts for strategists 169–71
  cash analysis 171

objectivity 115
opportunities analysis 84
organizational culture 5–6, 120–35
  culture audit components 121–32
  culture workout 133–5
organizational design 222–5
  communications 224–5
  control spans 222

leader and leading strategic
    team 225
  rationality 222–4
organizational self-analysis 84–119
  benchmarking 88
  checklists 96–7
  competencies and deficiencies 87
  information technology 89–90
  internal change rate 92–3
  internal strengths 95–6
  objectivity 115
  profitability 115
  strengths, neutrals and
      weaknesses 84–6
  strengths, neutrals and
      weaknesses analysis 97–114
  strengths, neutrals and
      weaknesses workout 117–19
  strengths and weaknesses 93–4
  weaknesses and neutrals 90–2
organizational structure 109–10,
    206–29, 292–3
  definition 206
  informal structures 220–2
  matrix structure 218–19
  organizational design 222–5
  purposes 209–11
  structural design bases 212–18
  structure weaknesses 220
  theory vs practice 207–8
  workout 227–8

Parker, David 183
PE ratio 162–3, 183
Peter Principle 266
philosophy and paradigmatic
    thinking 13–17
  Kuhn, Thomas 14–15
  Popper, Karl 14

physical environment 125–7
planning, definition 229
political events 31, 33, 45
political organizations,
    relationships 76–7
Popper, Karl 14
Porter, Michael 53, 62
preference shares 162
PricewaterhouseCoopers 190
Procter & Gamble, entry barriers 102
product 110
    ranges and natural mixes 75–6
    structures 214–15
product life cycle
    decline 37
    introduction 37
    maturity 37
    rapid growth 37
productivity improvement 237
    benchmarking 237
profit
    margins and value chains 152
    maximization 236–7
profitability 42–4, 115
    levels 69–70
psychological imprisonment 79–80
    sunk costs 80
psychology, leader 280–1
public company accounting 161–2
public sector 191–2

quality
    brands 110
    human resources 110–11
    improvement 235
    management 71
Quinn, James, competencies and
    deficiencies 87

Railtrack 244
    competency management and
        extension 73
    history 122
rationality 222–4
re-engineering 95, 211
Reed Elsevier 124
relationship
    with government/regulator 112–13
    with suppliers 113
reputation 111–12
restructuring 293
retrenchment or liquidation
        strategy 192–4
    divestment 194
    turnarounds 193–4
return on capital employed
        see ROCE
risk
    international trade 252–3
    profile 183
ROCE (return on capital
        employed) 167
roles 271–3
    and time horizons 199
    variations 287
Rolls-Royce, branding 80–1
Rover, focus strategies 196
Ryder, Sir Don 124

Saatchi 184
    product ranges and natural
        mixes 75–6
Sainsbury's 36, 51
    integrating backwards 53
    specialists 70–1
SAP, competencies and
    deficiencies 87

Scandinavian Airlines (SAS),
    benchmarking 88
Schlumberger 62–3
Schumpeter, Joseph, monopoly 74
Sears Roebuck, cash flow 70
SEATO (South-East Asia Treaty
    Organization) 251
Selfridges, stories/anecdotes 129–30
selling skills 114
service 77–8
shareholders 162
Shell 250, 254
short-term objectives criteria
  financial objectives 238–9
  increasing/decreasing
      manufacturing capacity 234
  marketing 238
  productivity improvement 237
  profit maximization 236–7
  quality improvement 235
  strategic business units 238
  technology improvement 234
  workforce size 235
  workforce training 239
short-term plans and tactics 5–6
short-term tactics for long-term
    strategy 229–43
  planning definition 229
  short-term objectives 234–9
  short-term tactics rule 230–3
  strategy definition 229
  tactics definition 229–30
  tactics measurability 232–4
  workout 241–2
short-term tactics rule 230–3
  fluffy cushion syndrome 231–2
Sieff, Lord 131

Silo Holdings 44
Simpson, Lord 8, 72
skills criteria 290–1
Sky Television 64–5
Sohio 244
Sony 22
  branding 80–1
spare capital 54
specialists 70–2
stability 279–80
  doubts and fears 280
  strategy 192
stakeholder 188–9, 277
  backing 185–6
  concepts 264–5
startup 248
stories/anecdotes 129–31
strategic alliance 248
strategic business units 238
strategic considerations,
      international trade 243–4
strategic failure 264
strategic fitness of organization 10
strategic management 286–97
  evolution 293–4
  future and past 290
  hubris 294
  leadership and management
      skills 289
  organization structure 292–3
  restructuring 293
  skills criteria 290–1
  team/individual 288
  translating strategy into
      tactics 286–8
  workforce skills audit 291–2
strategic process 11

strategic workout methodology 5–6
  amendments to structure 5–6
  competitors 5–6
  culture of organization 5–6
  external environment 5–6
  internal strengths, neutrals and
    weaknesses 5–6
  long-term strategy definition 5–6
  mission statement 5–6
  short-term plans and tactics 5–6
  value chains 5–6
strategy
  definition 5, 229
  to avoid 201–2
strategy concepts 5–7
  strategic workout
    methodology 5–6
strategy implementation
    209, 281–4
  mission and vision 282–4
  team examination 284
strengths, neutrals and
    weaknesses 84–6
  SWOT analysis 84–6
  workout 117–19
strengths, neutrals and weaknesses
    analysis 97–114
  accounting skills (financial) 97–8
  accounting skills
    (management) 98–9
  business strategies 99
  corporate strategy 99–100
  cost structure 100–1
  distribution network 101
  entry barriers 101–2
  exit barriers 102–3
  finance access 99
  information technology 103
  lateral communications 103

  leader's ability 104–5
  leadership skills 105–7
  management ability 107
  manufacturing skills 108
  marketing skills 109
  organizational structure 109–10
  products 110
  quality of brands 110
  quality of human resources 110–11
  relationship with government/
    regulator 112–13
  relationship with suppliers 113
  reputation 111–12
  selling skills 114
  workforce loyalty 107
strengths and weaknesses 93–4
structural design bases 212–18
  business startup structure 212
  functional structures 212–14
  geographical structure 215–16
  matrix structure 216–18
  product structures 214–15
structure, weaknesses 220
structure purposes 209–11
  authority, discretion and control
    designation 210–11
  communication 211
  employee grouping 210
  motivation 211
  reporting relationships 210
  strategy implementation 209
  tasks and responsibility
    allocation 209–10
subordinates 271
Suharto, President 33
sunk costs 80
SWOT analysis 84–6
synergy 184

tactics definition 229–30
tactics measurability 232–4
  budgets and tasks 234
takeover 183
tasks and responsibility
        allocation 209–10
team 273
  examination 284
  and individual 288
technology 127–8
  improvement 234
Tesco 36, 51
  integrating backwards 53
  specialists 71
Texaco, strengths and
        weaknesses 94
Thatcher, Margaret 16
theory vs practice 207–8
  managers 208
threats analysis 84
Tiffany's, branding 80–1
time horizons 196–7
  and hierarchy 198
  and hierarchy distortions 200
Tomkins plc
  conglomerates 183
  corporate strategy 100
  product structures 214
Toyota 39
Trompenaars, Fons 33
Trust House Forte (THF)
  focus strategies 196
  mission statement 24, 26
turnaround 193–4
  time 91–2

Ultramar Petroleum 33
Unilever 43
  structure 206

Vallance, Sir Iain 24, 186
value chain 5–6
value chain analysis 136–57
  components 143–51
  definition 136–40
  horizontal value links 153–4
  profit margins 152
  starting points 140–3
  vertical value links 152–3
  workout 155–6
value chain components 143–51
  assembly 147
  distribution 148
  manufacture 146–7
  raw materials 143–6
  retailing 148–51
ValuJet 52
vertical value links 137, 152–3
Virgin Railways 22
Vodafone 39, 250–1
  BT 186
VW 39

W. H. Smith 43
Wal-Mart
  competitiveness within
        industries 56
  differentiation strategies 196–7
  long-term strategy 230
Wallace, Graham 71–2
Walton, Sam 230
weaknesses and neutrals 90–2
  turnaround time 91–2
Weinstock, Lord 8, 72
Welch, Jack 51, 73–4, 77
  Honeywell 186
whistleblowing 274–5
who should devise strategy? 7–10

wisdom and cleverness 177
Woodward, Joan 127
workforce
  loyalty 107
  size 235
  skills audit 291–2
  training 239
workout audits 299–324
  accounts evaluation 173–4, 315–16
  competitor analysis 59, 303
  culture 133–5, 310–12
  external environment 47, 302
  individual competitor profile
    60, 304
  industry analysis 82–3, 305–6
  international strategy 257–8, 323–4
  long-term strategy 204–5, 317–18

mission workout 28, 301
organizational structure
    227–8, 319–20
short-term tactics 241–2, 321–2
strengths, neutrals and
    weaknesses 117–19, 307–9
value chain analysis 155–6, 313–14
workout method introduction 3–10
  how the book works 3–4
  strategic workout
    methodology 5–6
  strategy concepts 5–7
  strategy definition 5
  who should devise strategy? 7–10
WorldCom 39

Xerox, entry and exit barriers 65

How you can get the most from your Strategy Workout

A note from the author

I developed the techniques of the workout over many years of practical strategy analysis with leaders of organizations. It may help you to know my modus operandi.

I am usually introduced to an organization's leader by another leader who has used my services, as the result of a television or radio appearance, or as a consequence of somebody reading a book or article I have written.

When I meet the leader, I try to ascertain whether we like each other, have similar values and ethics and can tell each other the truth. If this all holds together, we usually then proceed to begin the exercise of strategy analysis shown in this book.

I usually send the workout book to all the subordinates who will be participating in the strategy appraisal or change. I ask them to complete the workout before they come to a seminar. We usually then have a three-day seminar where we work through each workout sheet, one by one, until we have complete agreement on the analysis of the essentials of the strategy.

After the seminar, the leader, usually with my help, writes up the new mission and strategy and distributes it throughout the organization, to ensure full communication and understanding. In particularly large organizations, we might involve as many as 50 or 70 senior executives in the exercise over several three-day seminars. It is a remarkably effective way of finding new strategic paths and achieving consensus on the future direction.

We appreciate that, by its very nature, this book is now probably looking a little over used. We have asked you to use it as a strategy workbook and now it is covered in your notes and ideas. Therefore, we are giving you a special offer if you wish to purchase a clean copy. This order form entitles you to a discount on your next purchase of *The Interactive Strategy Workout*. Simply fill in the details below and return it to your local bookseller or, for postal orders, please send to:

Pearson Education, FREEPOST, LON 8663, Harlow, Essex, CM20 27H Tel: 01279 623333 Fax 01279 414130

Your details

Mr/Mrs/Ms/Miss Initial ___   Surname _____

Job title_____

Department _____

Company _____

Address _____

_____

_____

Postcode _____ Tel No _____

Please send me ___ copy/ies of *The Interactive Strategy Workout* ISBN 0273 65912 X RRP £24.99; special price £21.99.

Payment details

I enclose a cheque made payable to Pearson Education for (total) £ _____

Please debit my Access/Visa/Barclaycard/Mastercard/AmEx/Switch/Diners for (total) £ _____

Card No ☐ ☐ ☐ ☐ ☐ ☐ ☐ ☐ ☐ ☐ ☐ ☐ ☐ ☐ ☐ ☐ ☐ ☐ ☐

Expiry date _____   Issue No (for Switch only) _____

Signature _____   Date _____

Please note that prices are subject to change without notification; please call to check the current price of the book.

Postage charges

UK please add £3.00 per order
Elsewhere in Europe please add £5.00 per order
Rest of the world please add £9.00 per order
(one payment per order – whether you order 1 copy or 20)

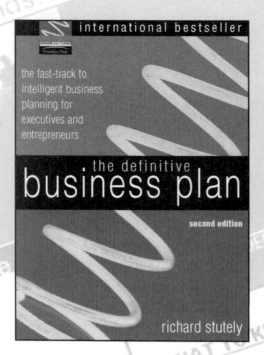